Integrating Information Literacy into the College E

Papers Presented at the Thirtieth
National LOEX Library Instruction Conference
Held in Ypsilanti, Michigan
10 to 11 May 2002

edited by
Julia K. Nims
Halle Library
Eastern Michigan University

Randal Baier
Halle Library
Eastern Michigan University

Rita Bullard
Halle Library
Eastern Michigan University

Eric Owen
Halle Library
Eastern Michigan University

Published for the University Library
Eastern Michigan University

ISBN 0-87650–368-7
Copyright ©2003, The Pierian Press
All Rights Reserved

The Pierian Press
Box 1808
Ann Arbor, Michigan 48106

LIBRARY ORIENTATION SERIES
(Emphasizing Information Literacy and Bibliographic Instruction)

*   Pierian Press's ISBN identifier is 0-87650. This identifier should precede the number given for a book (e.g., 0-87650-327-X).

Table of Contents

Keynote Speakers

Breakout Sessions

Roster of Participants 221

Preface

It is difficult to believe that LOEX just held its 30th national conference. As I look back over the themes and titles of previous conferences, I see a change not only in what we call library instruction, but also in how we define it and our roles as teachers. Thirty years ago, we taught library orientation; then it was bibliographic instruction and library instruction; now, we have evolved to teach information literacy skills, very different from library orientation.

This year's keynote speaker, Dane Ward, kicked off the conference with *"The Promised Land of Information Literacy: Making a Difference in the Lives of Our Students."* Dane inspired the audience to focus on the process of teaching and implementing information literacy programs as well as the goal of achieving an ideal information literate student population. His optimistic message and dynamic presentation style prepared the audience for the next two days of the conference.

Our featured speaker was Mary Reichel, President of the Association of College and Research Libraries. Mary's presentation, *"Information Literacy and the Learning Community: The Centrality of Teaching for Academic Librarians,"* stressed the teaching role of all librarians, not only those whose primary responsibility is library instruction. A delightful speaker, Mary encouraged the attendees to broaden their ideas of how they were involved with the academic missions of their institutions.

Dan Ream, our Friday evening speaker, challenged us to question if our students are as enthusiastic about information literacy as we librarians are. Do they understand what information literacy is? Do they believe librarians can help them become information literate? Dan shared a (hilarious) video of interviews with students answering questions about information literacy and librarians.

In addition to these three wonderful speakers, we had excellent breakout session presenters who shared their experiences and insights with the participants. Their sessions ranged from streaming video and library instruction to revising a research assignment to instructional design principles to collaborating with faculty. They deserve credit for making the conference a tremendous success.

Julia K. Nims
LOEX 2002 Conference Coordinator

KEYNOTE SPEAKERS

SEEKING THE PROMISED LAND OF INFORMATION LITERACY

Dane Ward

I have been a pilgrim on the road to information literacy for much of my life. We are all on this road, sometimes more aware of it than at other times. It is a road with no beginning or end, and the destination is more of a process than a place of final arrival. To be on the road to information literacy means to be actively engaged in our own learning, in finding, evaluating and integrating new information into our lives. Ultimately, the road to information literacy is about creating relationships between ourselves and the world, and as instructors, about facilitating those connections between students and their worlds.

However, there remains some confusion about the nature of information literacy within our profession, and perhaps about our true responsibility as teachers. I sense a frequent desire for simple solutions, such as tutorials that satisfy the basic information literacy needs of our students. Or a course on "information literacy" skills that continues to focus on teaching tools. Without exploring the deeper reality of information literacy, we risk falling into the trap of thinking that developing instructional programs is merely a matter of working out the details.

Unfortunately, it's not that easy. Integrating information literacy into the college curriculum is not business as usual. Information literacy is part of a larger reform movement, sweeping across all levels of education that focuses on student learning and instructional accountability. The information skills that students need for success in college and throughout their lives are far too complex to be taught in a limited fashion, and therefore cannot be provided merely as a variation of traditional library instruction.

To succeed in teaching the information skills and competencies required, we must seek the Promised Land of Information Literacy, stretching ourselves to teach more than the basics, more than what's prescribed. I use "Promised Land" as a metaphor to explore our ultimate goals in teaching information literacy. When we talk about information literacy programs, what is it we are trying to achieve? Even more, what are the possibilities, and how will we know it when we get there? Such discussions must begin with an attempt to define exactly what we mean by information literacy. What do we include in our definitions and what do we exclude? What is relevant and what is not?

At the same time, the Promised Land includes a personal element. Personal meaning rests at the center of this inquiry, since it provides the power behind our role as teachers and facilitators. To reach the Promised Land, we must continue to enhance the personal and professional meaning of information literacy. This is an important distinction. Information literacy is not something we teach only in the library; it is a way of being, a way of life. To reach the Promised Land, we must hold fast to a conception of information literacy that will sustain us on the long road towards program development.

In order to take this journey to the Promised Land, we will travel through the lands of *definition* and *metaphor*, two ways of knowing information literacy. Definitions permit common understanding of a thing

---

Ward is the Associate Dean for Public Services at Milner Library, Illinois State University.

by identifying its specific characteristics. Definitions provide us a foundation upon which to build further discussion. Without agreed-upon definitions, we experience difficulty sustaining meaningful conversations because we may not be talking about the same thing. In contrast, metaphors expand our meanings by establishing a connection between seemingly dissimilar things. Metaphors allow us to think creatively about something in order to understand it in another manner, and perhaps work with it differently. Definitions and metaphors are both important in our pursuit of the Promised Land, though they possess different purposes and powers.

A Definitional Way of Knowing Information Literacy

To begin talking about the goals of information literacy, we must come to some agreement about what it is we are talking about. During the last ten years, we have witnessed numerous discussions about the definition of information literacy. While most librarians seem to have agreed on a general concept or definition, we have been much less united in our understanding of the details and the process of implementing programs.

There is good reason to believe that we are not all on the same page when we talk about information literacy. Librarians have expressed their concern about this possibility for a number of years. In 1997, Snavely and Cooper asked whether "all those in academe who use the phrase 'information literacy' have the same understanding (p. 53)?" Since many librarians are beginning with different definitions, the answer is "probably not." Consider a few of our "favorite" definitions. In 1989, the American Library Association Presidential Committee on Information Literacy gave us one of the best known of these. The information literate person, according to that document, is "able to recognize when information is needed and have the ability to locate, evaluate, and use effectively the needed information (online)."

Some librarians prefer to think of information literacy more aphoristically as the ability to think critically in an information environment. Many others agree with Shapiro and Hughes that information literacy should be defined "more broadly as a new liberal art" that involves understanding the social, economic and political aspects of information (1996: 33). One also finds definitions that incorporate a wide range of related competencies such as resource-based learning, computer literacy, and lifelong learning.

Related to this discussion, we should consider the implications of a definition that includes lifelong learning. Certainly, we talk a great deal about the congruity between, even the identity of, information literacy and lifelong learning. If the information literate person is one who is also a lifelong learner, then we must be committed to teaching students how to learn, how to be curious, and how to be engaged. It's a challenging conceptualization of information literacy, though one that I would certainly advocate.

Our difficulties with definitions seem to be threefold. First, there is the problem of ambiguity—the lack of clear correspondence between our words and the thing to which we refer. Information literacy is an abstract concept that possesses numerous and diverse exemplars. As users of information, everyone has an opinion and definition. Second, different definitions lead to different ideas about implementation. Where information literacy is considered synonymous with bibliographic instruction, one finds less of an emphasis on critical thinking outside of a library context. This is very different from those interpretations of information literacy that incorporate notions of lifelong learning.

Third, definitions can lead to an over-simplification of sophisticated concepts. Taken to the extreme, definitions reduce collective understanding to the least common denominator; this is certainly the case with definitions that suggest that bibliographic instruction is the same as information literacy.

Fortunately, the continuing analysis of information literacy has led to greater clarification about the specific characteristics associated with it. ACRL's *Information Literacy Competency Standards for Higher Education* (online) have elaborated on the 1989 definition by identifying numerous performance indicators and learning outcomes. At the same time, our definitions have become more sophisticated. For instance, Christine Bruce's work—especially *The Seven Faces of Information Literacy*—has helped us to recognize the importance of defining information literacy within specific contexts.

Definitions represent one way of knowing information literacy. This "convergent" approach to knowledge focuses on dividing something up into its basic components as a way to create a workable definition. Through analysis, we are able to limit the multiple meanings that may be attached to an idea. Meanings "converge." With this methodology, we attempt to grasp the whole by managing the details. Most of the discussion about information literacy has focused on this approach. This convergent strategy is important because it provides a map of the territory that can more readily lead us to implementation.

Unfortunately, analysis may fail to inspire us.

A Metaphorical Way of Knowing Information Literacy

An alternative way of knowing is through "divergent" or metaphorical thinking. Rather than giving us a map *of* the territory, it gives us a map *to* the territory by permitting us to establish creative connections and personal meanings. It serves a different purpose than that of definitions. The power of the metaphor is that instead of limiting the meanings of words, it expands them. It is holistic and relational. It fills us with the possibility of meaning and personal value.

It is the latter approach to information literacy that can inspire us. If we intend to reach the Promised Land of Information Literacy, we must keep our eye on the prize. Notice how the use of "promised land" in the context of information literacy links those words, and simultaneously engages our minds in finding the connections between those ideas. It conjures powerful images and impressions, perhaps requiring some reflection to make sense of them.

"Metaphor" is defined by Merriam *Webster's Collegiate Dictionary* as "a figure of speech in which a word or phrase literally denoting one kind of object or idea is used in place of another to suggest a likeness or analogy between them." Instead of asking about the ultimate goal of information literacy instruction, we are seeking the "promised land."

Promised Land is a good metaphor for talking about the future and ultimate goals of information literacy. It is a metaphor that carries a tremendous number of meanings that may have significance for us as we connect it to information literacy.

The idea of "promised land" originates in the Old Testament. God promised Abraham that his children would be given the land of Canaan. The covenant was kept when Moses led his people "out of bondage" in Egypt to the Promised Land, a "land flowing with milk and honey." It required a long, difficult, and circuitous journey of forty years, but their effort was well-rewarded. The Promised Land depicted here is a final destination, a place of fulfillment and security. There were requirements of course. God insisted that His people fulfill a covenant. As part of this divine contract, these travelers were destined to attain their Promised Land.

When we apply some of the symbols of this journey to information literacy, we begin to uncover some of our own meanings. For me, the application of this metaphor produces a sense of our destiny as librarians to help "our" people. In this era of information overload, we can help students escape from the bondage of not acting in the world because of an inability to make good use of information. For me,

the Promised Land is a place where we and our students are able to achieve our greatest aspirations because we continue to cultivate the critical information skills that permit us to navigate our way through the rapids of a continually changing social and economic environment.

I picture this Promised Land as having some similarity to Shapiro and Hughes' vision. "We are talking about a new curricular framework," they wrote, "one that equips people not only with...technical skills but with a broad, integrated and critical perspective on the contemporary world of knowledge and information, including...its potential for human emancipation and...domination, and for growth and destruction (p. 34)." In my Promised Land, we are striving together to achieve the greatest good.

However, the important point here is that we each seek our own Promised Land, a personal vision of information literacy that will motivate and inspire us even during the darkest of nights. Without it, we may lack the commitment and capacity to persevere with the struggles of teaching and implementing our programs. It is all part of our journey. As we continue to seek our own meanings and become revitalized, we bring life to the information literacy that we bring to class.

Conclusion

While definitions provide a map *of* the territory, metaphors provide the energy, the sustenance, and the map *to* the territory. Neither one is better than the other. They both play a role. We must be able to define what it is we are talking about so that we can come to a common understanding. At the same time, to sustain our commitment to information literacy, we need to find the ability to persevere against opposition on the long road that each of us travels. Metaphor provides staying power.

Metaphor is also a catalyst for action. It mobilizes our energies and those of the people we work with. Why? Because it helps us to create relationships with those things in our world that matter most to us. There's a clear relationship between librarians finding meaning in our pursuit of information literacy and that of our students. By connecting to the Promised Land of Information Literacy, we permit ourselves to think and feel more expansively about our teaching responsibilities. As we find our own meanings, we can become the mentors that we had, or wished we had.

The Promised Land is all about relationships. It is about discovering and connecting to our meanings about information literacy, and it is about helping students discover their own meanings. In my

Promised Land, librarians are the advocates, the freedom fighters for the teaching of information skills that will improve the lives of students and citizens. I wish you well on the journey in seeking your Promised Land.

References

American Library Association Presidential Committee on Information Literacy. (1989). Report. Accessed 4 March 2002 at http://www.ala.org/acrl/nili/ilit1st.html

Association of College and Research Libraries. (2000). *Information Literacy Competency Standards for Higher Education.* Accessed 4 March 2002 at http://www.csusm.edu/acrl/il/toolkit/standards.html

Bruce, C. (1997). *Seven Faces of Information Literacy.* Adelaide, Australia: Auslib.

Shapiro, J. and Hughes, S. (March/April 1996) Information literacy as a liberal art. *EDUCOM Review,* pp. 31-35.

Snaveley, L. and Cooper, T. (Fall 1997) Competing agendas in higher education: finding a place for information literacy. *Reference & User Services Quarterly 37* (1): 53-62.

—DANE WARD—

INFORMATION LITERACY MEETS THE REAL WORLD: AND THE WINNER IS...

Dan Ream

Greetings from "The Dark Side" of the Information Literacy Movement. I am your host, Darth Vader. Well, perhaps that's overstating my position a little, but I have a feeling that the "Information Literacy" movement isn't going to work.

After many years of enthusiastically teaching college students how to find information, it has gradually dawned on me that doing research in a library is not regarded as "fun" or even "interesting" by the vast majority of my students. Oh sure, maybe four or five students in every class would respond with a "wow" when shown the tricks of the library research process. And if you're like me, you may focus on those interested few and think you're really reaching this class. But the majority of students usually react in ways that vary from a polite smile to blatant boredom—unless I get them at their teachable moment, which we'll talk about later.

Is it me? Am I a boring instructor? Well, I don't think so, and judging by the thousands of students, faculty, and librarian-written evaluations of my teaching over the years, I would have to conclude that I am pretty good at making this material interesting for most people. So why aren't more Virginia students giving me a "wow"? And more importantly—why won't more students attend the variety of useful open-enrollment workshops my library—or yours—might

---

Ream is the Head of Education and Outreach Services at the Virginia Commonwealth University in Richmond, VA.

offer on searching *Lexis/Nexis* or using other excellent research tools? How many here tonight have ever prepared for a workshop and had no one show up? Or just one or two?

☞ Welcome to the ranks of the stood-up librarians! We could form our own association; but, no, you probably wouldn't show up for the meetings.

My answer comes back to the simple idea that, for most people, information literacy isn't fun. By this, I mean what ALA defines as "information literacy" at their *Information Power* website http://www.ala.org/aasl/ip_nine.html, which can be paraphrased as "accessing, evaluating, and using information". Librarians, and even professors or teachers, hearing this statement might be quick to disagree—of course, this is fun! Ah, but it is fun for people who grow up to be librarians or teachers or professors; we're the seekers and have chosen lives that assure that we can indulge in our passion for finding information. However, the majority of college students are not like us; they don't have any interest in finding information beyond that which will help them succeed in their immediate situation. As a student, library skills are great if they help you get an "A" on that immediate research paper and in the work world, fact-finding skills are great if it helps you put across a proposal or report successfully. But on a Friday night, these folks would rather be watching TV; and it won't be the Library Instruction Channel they're tuning in to. Will this majority become our "information literate" population of tomorrow?

An analogy comes to mind. Though I love doing library research, there is a similar information-processing task that I really dislike, and that's filling out my income tax forms each year. How many of you here tonight really enjoy doing your tax returns? I usually put it off until late March, despite having all the necessary data and forms by February 1st or so. Why do I wait? Probably because it isn't fun and because I feel uncertain about my ability to perform this task as well as I should. Kind of like doing what library research feels for the mass of college students. As every reference librarian knows, last minute work is one of the identifying marks of the undergraduate, though I have increasingly noticed that this is a graduate student tendency too. Why, given an assignment weeks in advance, will students wait until just a day or two before the assignment is due, to come to the library? Because it isn't fun and they are unsure if they can do it well!

So, how can I do my taxes better and be more successful at it? Getting a refund as large as possible is certainly as motivating to me as getting an "A" is for most students. An extra hundred dollars or two could mean an extra night at the beach this summer! I could take a tax preparation class, right? How about taking one this weekend (May 11-12)—or in August or September? Of course not. I'd rather take it in February or March, when I'm ready to do my tax forms. Hmmmm. Kind of like point-of-need, curriculum-tied library instruction.

But college libraries all do big tours and orientation events in August or September when school begins. If the students all roll in the door at the last minute to do their library research in late October, is it any wonder they don't remember a thing we showed them in late August? Would you like a tax accountant to sit down at your kitchen table to show you the ropes of tax filing in September? Or would you rather have him or her—in fact, love to have him or her there on that night in March when you try to do your tax forms? Hey, we might even pay him money to be there at the point of need! But why is doing taxes a dreaded event? I usually get a refund each year, shouldn't that make this fun? The refund helps motivate me to do it well, but somehow it isn't really fun.

Does everybody hate doing their taxes? I doubt it. Just as there are seekers out there (like librarians and professors), there are also puzzle lovers and problem solvers among us who must think that doing tax forms is fun; let's hope they've grown up to be tax accountants and financial officers.

Why do most people hate doing their annual income tax forms? Probably because we don't do them often enough to develop a sense of competency and confidence about the process. Just like the student who may do one library research assignment each semester, the infrequency of practice is not building confidence and skill levels. And this may partly explain why college freshmen show up at our reference desks seemingly as blank slates—without any previous library experiences. If their high school librarians could see them as we do, they'd die, or at least want to. Yet, I have found that many high school students have received excellent library instruction in their high schools. It just hasn't been retained for lack of practice.

Tax forms always have changes in them from year-to-year, so that even if you did masterfully on last year's form and somehow miraculously remembered how, the steps have now changed. Hmmmm. Kind of like the way that printed index became a locally mounted CD-ROM and then a web-based database, then changed vendor and then added full-text and then….. The changes in our searching tools, which have largely been for the better, have been so fast and furious in the past five years that even our fellow seekers, the professors, are sometimes heard to groan that they can't keep up with the changes (if they're not so embarrassed they remain silent or send their grad assistants in to use these tools instead). After all, how many years did we teach *Reader's Guide* or *Psychological Abstracts* without substantial changes in the process?

Many, many years, it now seems. On the other hand, my library's "Welcome to the Internet" workshops featured the wonderful world of "gophers" as recently as 1994. What year was it that I last saw a gopher site on the web? Remember *Searchbank*? Oh, that's called *InfoTrac* now, or is it *Expanded Academic Index*? Oh, it's both? And do we still have *PsycInfo*? Or is it *PsycLit*? And how about *Science Citation Index*? That's called *Web of Science*, now? Oh never mind! And what was that you said was a truncation symbol? A "?" in the online library catalog? A "*" in *Infotrac*? A "!" in *Lexis/Nexis*? A "$" in the *Dow Jones* database? Gee, could you make this any harder to remember? Sounds remarkably like the kind of details that a tax accountant might be needed for, doesn't it?

Ahh, but I hear you say, information literacy will teach them concepts, not the mechanical details. Perhaps, but this returns me to my earlier point about interest levels. Only those of us who will probably grow up to be librarians or professors really want to know concepts. For the masses, it's the mechanical skills that light their fires at the moment of need.

So, let's look at the information literacy movement and how this ties in. Will the majority of college students ever become information literate? I doubt it, just as the majority of them will never really be "seekers" beyond any immediate need to find an answer. Most people want answers, not information or instruction, just as when I call a plumber, I don't want him to teach me how to fix my pipes—I want him to fix them.

As a colleague of mine has commented several times, librarians talk out of both sides of their mouths—they tell their users, "we're the experts, so, ask us for help" and then they say "now, let me show you how to do this yourself!" I'm glad my plumber doesn't want me to be "water flow literate" and my mechanic doesn't want me to be "internal combustion literate" though I know there is a cadre of people out there who would love to be both.

Do I think library instruction is a waste of time? Absolutely not! Not only do I enjoy teaching these skills, I think they are tremendously appreciated when delivered at precisely the right time. Just like that tax accountant who offers to come join me at the kitchen table on tax preparation night, a library instruction session at the teachable moment, when students feel the need, can seem like the cavalry coming over the hill to the rescue. Yet, neither the tax accountant nor the cavalry would seem especially useful when neither taxes nor a rescue was needed. (Oh darn Martha, here comes that cavalry again, now all the good campsites will be taken and there goes our peace and quiet. Or—gee Henry, it's nice of you to drop by to talk taxes, but we had an outing to the symphony planned for tonight.)

Can the majority of students, who aren't particularly interested in the subject matter, be made information literate? Perhaps a lesson lies in the "Let's Go Metric" movement of the 1970s. Those old enough to remember this movement (just who did organize that effort, anyway?) might recall that all schools were going to teach the metric system of measurement to their students and within a few years such terms as "inches", "miles", "quarts" and "acres" would be used only by old-timers. So what happened? If someone ran up to you right this second and said, "Quick, give me a kilogram of flour" or "help, I need a gram of salt" would you know how much they need? Is 85 cents a liter a good price for gasoline? (Canadians, would know, but few from the US, I suspect.) The point is that other than perhaps a two-liter bottle of Coke or a fifty-meter race in swimming, metric units have not become common knowledge among those in the US, despite over twenty years for the metric movement to catch on. Why? Perhaps because people didn't feel a need to know. Information literacy may face a similar fate from an indifferent majority. Why do I need to be information literate if a librarian is available to help me when I need to find an answer?

Added to this mix must be the growing phenomenon of "a-literacy." An "a-literate" is someone who has all the necessary skills to read but chooses not to. We can thank "a-literates" for the decline in newspaper readership and the prosperity of Cliff's Notes. In a 14 May 2001 article in the *Washington Post*, author Linton Weeks cites a drop in newspaper readership and a 1999 Gallup Poll that reports only 7 percent of Americans were voracious readers (more than one book per week) while 59 percent said they read fewer than 10 books in the past year. Last but not least, the Gallup Poll notes that the number of people who don't read at all has been rising for the past 20 years. This is an interesting article that cites many examples of the impact of "a-literacy" on everything from road signs to package design.

Even this past Sunday in our *Richmond Times-Dispatch*, columnist Dave Barry's column was entitled "This Gadget Could Hike Readership" in which he notes the decline in newspaper readership, which was all started, Barry claims, by his incompetence as a delivery boy in 1960. It's been downhill ever since. The gadget Barry reports on is a newspaper vending machine that clamped shut on a woman's clothes when she bought a paper outside of a Walmart. When she called for Walmart staff to free her, they cited their policy not to offer refunds on newspaper vending machines.

Do I, Dan Ream, want to be information literate? Absolutely, because I really enjoy both searching for and finding information. Like you, I am a seeker. Among our college students, there is a small group of budding seekers also. They're the ones who choose to come to those library tours and workshops without being required to. Let's nurture them, for both their sake and ours. But let's not ever expect that every student in our university will want to become information literate, even if forced to acquire a baseline of knowledge or concepts. If they don't use that knowledge regularly through curriculum-based assignments, that baseline will erode as quickly as the Spanish we learned in high school, where our tiny amount of retained vocabulary is probably because they never changed the words the way "gophers" changed to the "web" and *Searchbank* changed to *InfoTrac*.

What of the Information Literacy movement? Let's be realistic about what the vast majority of students want to know and feel the need to know. Let's be that cavalry to the rescue and that tax accountant on the night of need with curriculum-tied, point-of-need library and Internet research skills instruction. Teaching twenty students who are ready to learn at once certainly beats twenty one-to-one dialogues at the reference desk. By sticking to time-of-need library and Internet skills instruction, our efficiency will be much greater and our students will love us more.

Before coming to speak here at LOEX, I thought it might be interesting to test my own thinking on information literacy and what the real world (the non-librarian world) thinks of it. I decided I would interview college students and a few non-students about information literacy and share with you the highlights of those talks. I was extremely tempted to do "man on the street" interviews, but quickly realized that many technical obstacles present themselves, particularly the overwhelming background noise of our campus, which seems perpetually under renovation.

So I decided I would interview students in my office. To do so I asked a few teachers if they would offer some amount of extra credit to their students for coming to the library and interviewing with me for 5 minutes. Between April 8th and 22nd, I interviewed 21 such students who volunteered and contacted me and you'll see the highlights of those talks in just a moment. Are these typical college students? Well, you'll see they're a tremendously diverse lot in age, race, and interests. They do share a certain ambition to get "extra credit" by doing these interviews and in that they are not typical. At least 200 students could have responded—these are the only 21 who did within my time limit, so in that sense they are a-typical. Another wrinkle—about half of these students came from an "Introduction to Internet Researching" class taught by our School of Business and students in this elective course may not be a representative cross-section of our university student body. But nonetheless, these folks were an interesting sample of college students today. I asked them four questions, which will be restated in the videotape.

1. What do you think information literacy is?
2. Are you information literate?
3. How did you learn the information literacy skills you now have?

With my fourth question, I wanted to go right to the heart of the matter and figure out how important information literacy was to them. I could have asked, "Would you attend an information literacy workshop?" but suspected they'd say the polite thing, "yes," and then never show up.

So, I made the question more interesting:

4. Would you rather have this coupon for one hour of information literacy training—or a dollar?

If they asked me, "when is the training"? I answered, "Whenever you want, it'll be a personal training session." That killed off their chance of saying, "Awww, I'm busy that day."

Before we watch the video, I want to see what YOU think they'll do. Of twenty-one college students offered this choice, I want you to predict how many will take the dollar.

On the slips of paper at your table, write down your name and a single number that represents how many of our 21 college students will take the dollar bill. I have a prize for those who guess it correctly. And here it is. A CD I have entitled "Information Literacy's Greatest Hits." It's made up of information literacy songs acquired using information literate methods of song searching and acquisition. Some of the titles include "You Can't Judge a Book By Looking At The Cover" "Lazin in the Shade of the Information Superhighway", "Sweet Librarian" "I Read It In The Tabloids", "First Redneck on the Internet", and 'I'll Never Forget The Day I Read a Book". You can't buy this in stores!

Now, please fill out your slips—include your name and guess your number. Julia Nims will collect these from each table.

Last of all, before rolling the video, I should also say that I expanded my interviews past the twenty-one college students by taking my video camera to a Wednesday night church supper at Bon Air Presbyterian Church on April 17th and talking to 11 folks of various ages and backgrounds about these same questions. They will be shown in the video and you'll even see their choices between coupon and the dollar—but they are not part of the 21 students you're guessing about.

< Part one of video shown >

First, we'll see how our non-college students at the church supper decided about the information literacy-training certificate—or the dollar.

Okay here is where the rubber meets the road—will they take the information literacy training coupon or the dollar. I'll keep score on this chart.

< Part two of video shown >

Okay, it's a tie at ten for coupon and ten for dollars, so those who guessed either ten or eleven will be the winners. But a bigger question looms—which will be the majority. We'll leave it up to Ashua and here she is.

< Part three of video shown >

—DAN REAM—

You may have noticed that at dollar choosing time, a few of our students were missing—here they are now.

< Part four of video shown >

I hope you enjoyed my video adventure. My thanks go to my co-editor of the video, Jimmy Ghaphery, also of the Virginia Commonwealth University Library. It may not be scientifically valid, but for me at least it was fun. While it partly confirmed my expectations that most students would take the dollar, it also affirmed for me that a good number of students really do love to learn and as a teacher, that feels good. I still expect that a TRUE cross-section of our students would show a greater majority of dollar takers than coupon takers compared to what we saw here tonight, but until someone gives me more time and more dollars, I'll just have to guess. And meanwhile we can dream of a day when Information Literacy will mean more than a dollar to every college student.

I hope you found my program thought provoking and worthwhile. Thank you.

BREAKOUT
SESSIONS

FOLDING INFORMATION LITERACY INTO THE GENERAL EDUCATION MIX: RECIPES FOR GETTING STARTED

Susan E. Beck and Kate Manuel

Introduction

In the United States, general education is commonly described as developing "the knowledge, skills, and attitudes that most of us use and live by during most of our lives."[1] General education programs typically describe their benefits, and justify their existence, in terms that closely correspond to the goals of information literacy instruction. General education claims to build character, promote personal and spiritual development,[2] and "foster the desire and capacity to keep on learning continuously."[3] Similarly, information literacy is frequently cited as an essential attribute for life-long learners, those who know how to "re-educate" themselves throughout their lives independent of formal schooling.[4] General education seeks to develop capacities "for active and effective participation in society"[5] and for good citizenship.[6] Likewise, the *Information Literacy Competency Standards for Higher Education* note information literacy's place in preparing students for "roles as informed citizens and members of communities."[7] General education aims to serve as the "foundation of the curriculum," the "center of the college's mission."[8] Information literacy, too, has been described as the key liberal art.[9] General education is said to develop "the ability to communicate with precision and style,[10]" while the *Information Literacy Competency Standards* explicitly note that the

information literate person chooses effective communication media and communicates "clearly and with style."[11] Both general education and information literacy claim to develop the "capacity to think clearly and critically."[2] Both seek to foster problem-solving abilities and a capacity for teamwork.[13] Each emphasizes students' involvement in active learning.[14] In short, general education and information literacy programs are natural allies in terms of their goals.[15]

Beyond shared goals, general education programs also have advantages, as potential partners, in their pervasiveness and in their positioning as chief loci of institutional assessment efforts. Over ninety percent of colleges and universities in the United States have general education requirements in some form.[16] A few have a core curriculum, with common courses mandated for all students; most have a distributional requirements system, with students selecting specified numbers and types of courses from a pre-set menu of options. A few have a competencies model, where students must demonstrate that they have attained specified skill levels from elective courses.[17] In addition to being common, in some fashion, to most colleges and universities, general education programs are often the focus of institutional accountability efforts. Of the eighty-two percent of colleges and universities that have implemented or are now implementing outcomes assessment, sixty-seven percent concentrate their assessment programs on general education as a "core ingredient of the college experience."[18] This focus on assessment of general education is significant because information literacy programs, given their own focus on assessable outcomes, should collaborate with programs having similar emphases.

Beck is the Head of the Humanities and Social Sciences Services Department at New Mexico State University. *Manuel* is currently Instruction Coordinator at NMSU, Las Cruces, NM.

Integrating information literacy into general education programs offers all the commonly recognized benefits of curriculum-integration: it allows for the incorporation of information literacy "skills and knowledge...into the...curriculum content;" it provides for the development of information literacy throughout the baccalaureate degree program; and it ensures that information literacy is not "thought of as an accessory or a bolt-on extra" to the "real" content of higher education.[19] Indeed, this particular partnership is far from a new idea. A number of library instruction programs have used the creation of new general education programs,[20] or the revision of existing ones,[21] to accomplish integration. Most libraries reporting such efforts, however, seem to have concentrated their efforts either upon creation of a credit-bearing information literacy course required of all students as part of general education,[22] or upon inclusion of information literacy segments within required composition,[23] computing,[24] or introduction-to-the-university courses.[25] While these strategies are certainly an advance over course-related one-shot library instruction sessions, they can still leave information literacy marginalized or, worse yet, viewed as an inorganic add-on. Stand-alone courses can be subject to claims that "after that one-credit course, students should not need any further library instruction," while course-integrated initiatives at the lower levels are often trivialized, with the library serving as one stop in a "tour" of campus services.[26] Few libraries have yet attempted to infuse information literacy broadly throughout their institutions' general education curricula,[27] or have sought to mandate non-library faculty's involvement in the assessment of information literacy outcomes or the accomplishment of information literacy instruction within general education programs.[28] Fewer still have made recommendations that other libraries could consult in integrating information literacy into general education programs on their own campuses.

General Education at New Mexico State University

During an overhaul of the existing general education program at New Mexico State University (NMSU) in 1986-1987, the Library made a proposal that (1) a "library skills component involving bibliographic instruction" be incorporated into the required English composition courses; that (2) courses in each of the core subject areas within the general education curriculum "should contain instruction in subject related information sources;" and that (3) a "member of the Library faculty should be appointed to the permanent standing committee" on general education at NMSU. In Fall 1987, the Library began

teaching instruction sessions for English 111, an introductory course required of all students as part of the general education program. Over the years, library instruction in English 111 came to be course-integrated and to highlight basic information literacy skills: three of the four writing assignments in the course revolve around information literacy competencies, and information literacy is included in the locally produced textbook for the course, *Paideia*. Information literacy competencies were also written into Part I (Developing Critical Thinking and Modes of Expression) and Part III (Viewing a Wider World) of the NMSU general education requirements enacted in 1989.[29] Part I specifies basic capabilities in information retrieval and familiarity with the University Library, while all courses giving Part III/Viewing a Wider World credit must demonstrate, as part of the course certification process, the presence of a substantial research component. All NMSU Colleges (Agriculture & Home Economics; Arts & Sciences; Business Administration & Economics; Education; Engineering; and Health & Social Services) teach Viewing a Wider World general education courses, as does the Library, which offers Library Science 311: Information Literacy. This history of integration of information literacy into the general education program at NMSU enables the authors to make some recommendations about how to get started, with whom to work, and what data to gather when attempting to integrate information literacy competencies and instruction into general education programs.

Getting Started

Whether your institution is developing a new general education program or is overhauling an existing one, you will be lobbying for library involvement and need to consider the following issues. If your institution is planning to adopt a new general education program, it is important to position yourself within the campus information loop. Find out when and where open governance meetings occur and attend them. Find out who the key general education players on campus are and schedule meetings with them to discuss the role of information literacy within the general education framework. Meet and offer to work with other interested faculty. Volunteering one's services can be exhausting but ultimately beneficial. In this day and age when everyone has more than enough to do, your willingness to work on committees will be welcomed. Nevertheless, be prepared to encounter competing visions of general education that may not include information literacy. Also, realize that you may end up devoting several years to this project and that, in the end; you may not totally achieve your goals. Much will depend upon the type and values of the general education program that is implemented. A general education program devoted to teaching students core content, for example, may not be hospitable terrain for a required information literacy skills course, while a general education program focused on fostering oral communication skills or service learning may not be overly receptive to course integration of information competencies.

If working to overhaul an existing program, many of the same points noted above apply. Be ready to position both yourself and the library as key participants in the program's analysis and its overhaul. Terrain is often more contested in revisions of existing general education programs than in creation of new ones: with existing programs, many people have experience with the current program, have ideas about what is "wrong" with it, and have agendas to promote. With new programs, fewer people may have visions to share. Gather your data, package it, and present it to committees, department heads, deans, administrators and other key players. Use your well-developed skills as an information professional to assist others in gathering and presenting their data. Your assistance will convince others of your sincere interest in general education, dispelling any possible misconceptions that you are just using general education to further your own agenda. Because you are working to overhaul an already established program, you should seek to build strong partnerships between the library, the faculty and the administration. Plan on devoting both your time and your energy to the project for an extended period. Overhauling an existing program may even take longer than creating a new one! Be visible and be vocal throughout the program's restructuring.

Building Partnerships

In seeking to establish good working relations with campus-wide programs and with individuals, consider the different types of possible partnerships. Specifically, you will need to build both programmatic partnerships, formal long-term working relations with units, groups, or departments, and pragmatic partnerships, informal activity-based relations with the purpose of accomplishing specific tasks. No matter what structure your institution's general education program has, you need to work through official channels to set up programmatic partnerships with the key-decision makers. First, look closely at how the general education program is structured within your institution. Is there a coordinator? Is there a committee? What are their roles? What is the overall governing body? The university or the college administration?

The faculty senate? A specific college? Who are the decision makers? How do initiatives get communicated, discussed and approved? How is the library involved with campus governance? Is the library a member of the general education committee? Is it advisory? Ex-officio? Any combination of these options is possible at particular institutions, but each has different ramifications for setting up programmatic partnerships. Where librarians are full members of the faculty and general education is managed solely through the faculty senate, librarians need to concentrate on maximizing their presence on the faculty senate. In contrast, where librarians are not full members of the faculty, or where general education is managed by a specific college or a particular committee, librarians must persuade the university administration to appoint them—in advisory or, better yet, ex officio capacities—to the relevant governing bodies.

In positioning oneself to work with a general education committee, its coordinator, or its governing body in a programmatic partnership, you also need to think pragmatically. You do need to be connected formally to those nominally in positions of power over the general education program, but you also need to "be in with" those who really can and do make the decisions about the program. Begin by analyzing the roles and power bases of the players. How do decisions *really* get made and who makes them? Is the coordinator merely a figurehead (and for whom?), or does that individual have decision-making authority? Also consider who initiates course proposals within the general education program. At many institutions, the library does not have a primary role in proposing general education courses; typically, faculty work through their departments or colleges to propose courses. If this is the case, the library may need to work with faculty within departments to propose, revise, or possibly withdraw courses. When working with teaching faculty on courses, you will also need to work with those within the library who have already established relationships with departments–the library's subject bibliographers, departmental liaisons, or subject fund managers. They may not be particularly well-informed about general education or information literacy, and they may not be accustomed to working with faculty on these issues. Failure to work with them, however, leaves you vulnerable to charges of impinging on their "turf," while working with them informs their knowledge-base and can enhance their work with academic departments and teaching faculty. On a final and very pragmatic note, get to know the administrative assistants and the staff who actually do the work of supporting and maintaining the general education program. These are the people who have that day-to-day view of operations and can actually get something done for you.

Gathering Data

Become the expert on your institution's general education program. Research its history and evolution. Talk with the early adopters (if they are still around) and document the activities and individuals that shaped its course. By doing a little homework on the origins of the general education program, you will not only initiate relations with the program's pioneers but you might also find out problems and pitfalls of the past that can be easily avoided today or in the future. Learn about and document with all the procedures and policies that the general education program mandates. Opportunities for integrating information literacy may arise at any moment, and you do not want to begin the process of educating yourself about the program then. Have on hand a list of requirements of your accrediting body, or bodies if you have professional schools (nursing, engineering, business), and keep current of their changes. These documents may help you persuade local faculty about the merits of integrating information literacy into the general education program.

Also, consider your student population base. Find a demographic snapshot of this group and study it. Consider race, income level, and geographic background. Do the students come from rural or urban areas? On the average, how many students were in their high school graduating class? Who is the group you are serving and how will they benefit, or not, from both general education and information literacy initiatives? Pay particular attention to how your institution awards advanced placement credit and what the transfer requirements are. For example, tying information literacy programming to a first-year English course that ten percent of your student body place out of may not be a wise choice, nor is tying your programming to courses that transfer students do not take. Above all else, pay strict attention to your collective student knowledge base and their learning needs in relation the requirements of the general education curriculum. Do they match? Or are you proposing a program that these students either don't need or can't handle at this stage of the learning program? Also look closely at the syllabi of courses proposed for the general education program—being alert for places where information literacy competencies match with the skills outcomes of these courses and opportunities for curriculum integration exist.

NOTES

1. Task Group on General Education, *A New Vitality in General Education: Planning, Teaching. and Supporting Effective Liberal Learning* (Washington, DC: Association of American Colleges, 1988), 3. In reality, each college or university defines for itself what constitutes these "knowledge, skills, and attitudes," and how they are best to be promoted. Thus, the "term, 'general education' has no generic meaning and can only be made sensible in the context of looking at what a particular school requires as core coursework for its students." Steven J. Osterlind, "A National Review of Scholastic Achievement in General Education," *ASHE-ERIC Higher Education Reports* 25, no. 8 (1997): 1-194.

2. Ibid.

3. Task Group on General Education, 3. Cf. Mark A. Schlesinger, *Reconstructing General Education: An Examination of Assumptions, Practices, and Prospects* (Bowling Green, OH: Bowling Green State University, 1977) and Gary A. Woditsch, *Developing Generic Skills: A Model for Competency-Based General Education* (Bowling Green, OH: Bowling Green State University, 1977).

4. Association of College and Research Libraries, *Information Literacy Competency Standards for Higher Education, 2002*, http://www.ala.org/acrl/ilintro.html (3 April 2002).

5. Joyce Baldwin, "Why We Still Need Liberal Arts Learning in the New Millenium," *The Education Digest* 66, no. 4 (Dec. 2000): 4-9.

6. Harry S. Broudy, *General Education* (Bloomington, IN: Phi Delta Kappa Educational Foundation, 1974).

7. Association of College and Research Libraries.

8. Robert H. Arnold, "Educators' Perceptions of Curriculum Integration Activities and Their Importance," *Journal of Vocational Education Research* 24, no. 2 (1999): 87-101 and Florence B. Brawer, "The Liberal Arts," *New Directions for Community Colleges* no. 108 (Winter 1999): 17-29.

9. Jeremy J. Shapiro and Shelley K. Hughes, "Information Literacy as a Liberal Art," *EDUCOM Review* 31, no. 2 (March/April 1996) <http://www.educause.edu/pub/er/review/reviewarticles/31231.html> (3 April 2002).

—SUSAN E. BECK AND KATE MANUEL—

10. Arnold; Peggy L. Maki, "From Standardized Tests to Alternative Methods," *Change* 33, no. 2 (March/April 2001): 28-31, and Paula Zeszotarski, "Dimensions of General Education Requirements," *New Directions for Community Colleges* no. 108 (Winter 1999): 39-48.

11. Association of College and Research Libraries, Information Literacy Competency Standards for Higher Education: Standards, Performance Indicators, and *Outcomes 2000* http://www.ala.org/acrl/ilintro.html (3 April 2002).

12. Maki; Zeszotarski. Lori Arp, "In Search of a Definition of Critical Thinking," in *Russian-American Seminar on Critical Thinking and the Library*, ed. Cerise Oberman and Dennis Kimmage (Urbana-Champaign, IL: University of Illinois, Graduate School of Library and Information Science, 1995), 57-67, and Steven J. Herro, "Bibliographic Instruction and Critical Thinking," *Journal of Adolescent & Adult Literacy* 43, no. 6 (March 2000): 554-558.

13. Arnold; Association of College and Research Libraries; Maki.

14. Jeanetta Drueke, "Active Learning in the Library Instruction Classroom," *Research Strategies* 10 (1992): 77-83; Task Group on General Education.

15. General education programs themselves seem likely to value the library—and information literacy instruction—as a partner in their mission. A survey in the late 1980s, not repeated since, found that forty-eight percent of administrators and faculty responding felt that the library contributed "very much" or "quite a lot" to furthering general education. Another forty-one percent said the library contributed "somewhat." Jerry G. Gaff, *New Life for the College Curriculum: Assessing Achievements and Furthering Progress in the Reform of General Education* (San Francisco: Jossey-Bass, 1991), 128.

16. James L. Ratcliff, "Quality and Coherence in General Education," in *Handbook of the Undergraduate Curriculum: A Comprehensive guide to Purposes, Structures, Practices, and Change*, ed. Jerry G. Gaff and James L. Ratcliff (San Francisco: Jossey-Bass, 1997), 141-169.

17. Zeszotarski.

18. Osterlind.

19. Lynne Wright and Catriona McGurk, "Integrating Information Literacy," in *Information Literacy around the World: Advances in Programs and Research*, ed. Christine Bruce and Philip C. Candy (Wagga Wagga, New South Wales: Centre for Information Studies, 2000), 83-97.

20. Rachel F. Fenske, "Computer Literacy and the Library: A New Connection," *Reference Services Review* 26, no. 2 (Summer 1998): 67-78; Judy Reynolds, "University Approval of Library Research Skills as Part of the General Education Curriculum Requirements," in *Integrating Library Use Skills into the General Education Curriculum*, ed. Maureen Pastine and Bill Katz (New York: Haworth Press, 1989), 75-86; and Gabriela Sonntag and Donna M. Ohr, "The Development of a Lower-Division, General Education, Course-Integrated Information Literacy Program," *College and Research Libraries* 57 (July 1996): 331-338.

21. Sarah Blakeslee, "Librarian in a Strange Land: Teaching a Freshman Orientation Course," *Reference Services Review* 26, no. 2 (Summer 1998): 73-78; Susan Griswold Blandy, "Building Alliances," in *Integrating Library Use Skills into the General Education Curriculum*, ed. Maureen Pastine and Bill Katz (New York: Haworth Press, 1989), 57-73; Rachel F. Fenske and Susan E. Clark, "Incorporating Library Instruction in a General Education Program for College Freshmen," *Reference Services Review* 23, no. 3 (1995): 69-74; Carla Higgins and Mary Jane Cedar Face, "Integrating Information Literacy Skills into the University Colloquium," *Reference Services Review* 26, no. 3-4 (Fall/Winter 1998): 17-31; Dennis Kimmage, "Library Instruction and General Education: The Plattsburgh Experience," *The Bookmark* 46 (Fall 1987): 9-13; Ben Lents and Carl Pracht, "The New General Education and Bibliographic Instruction at Southeast Missouri State University," *Show-Me Libraries* 41 (1990): 20-22; Carroll H. Varner, Vanette M. Schwartz, and Jessica George, "Library Instruction and Technology in a General Education 'Gateway' Course: The Students' View," *Journal of Academic Librarianship* 22 (Sept. 1996): 355-359.

22. Kimmage.

23. Reynolds; Alice M. Spitzer, "Bringing an Interdisciplinary World View to English 101," in *Integrating Library Use Skills into the General Education Curriculum*, ed. Maureen Pastine and Bill Katz (New York: Haworth Press, 1989), 113-121.

24. Fenske.

25. Blakeslee; Fenske and Clark; Lents and Pracht; Varner, Schwart and George.

26. A further problem in implementing information literacy instruction via a required general education course is noted by Kimmage (1987), who says that "general education requirements are resented by many students because of the time they take from electives and courses needed in areas of major concentration."

27. Among the exceptions are Hudson Valley Community College, which built "library component[s]" into all credit courses and California State University, San Marcos, which established information literacy goals and competencies for courses in the mathematics and sciences; humanities and arts; and social sciences sections of general education. See Blandy and Sonntag and Ohr.

28. Only California State University, San Marcos reports integrating information literacy into the general education curriculum in such a way that non-library faculty are required to "demonstrate how information literacy and use of the library will be represented in their courses." See Sonntag and Ohr.

29. Part II of NMSU's General Education requirements is Establishing a Common Background.

—SUSAN E. BECK AND KATE MANUEL—

Appendix

Getting started

- Position yourself within the campus information loop
- Attend open meetings about the general education program
- Introduce yourself to the key general education players on campus and meet with them
- Meet and offer to work with other interested faculty
- Volunteer to serve on general education committees or working groups
- Get a sense of others' visions of general education
- Gather your data, package and present it
- Realize these projects are long-term, be willing to dedicate your time

Building partnerships

- Find out how the general education program is structured and who has responsibility (A coordinator? A committee? A college? The faculty senate? The university or college administration? A combination of these?)
- Figure out where the library fits within the general education framework (Advisory? Ex-officio? As regular faculty?)
- Learn how decisions are made and who makes them; become involved in the decision-making process
- Understand the course proposal process (Who proposes courses? Departments? Colleges? The library?)
- Develop partnerships within the library to achieve buy-in for information literacy courses proposed through other departments
- Get to know the administrative assistants and staff who actually do the day-to-day work of the general education program

Gathering data

- Become the expert on your institution's general education program (Research its history and evolution; interview early adopters and document their activities)
- Document all policies and procedures related to the general education program
- Keep up-to-date on the requirements of your accrediting body/bodies
- Research your student demographics (Race, Income level, Geographic background, Urban, Rural, Average size of high school graduating class, Their needs and knowledge base)
- Determine how your institution awards advanced placements and what the requirements are for transfer students
- Obtain copies of the syllabi for all general education courses and review how they relate to information literacy

THE INTEGRATION OF INFORMATION LITERACY SKILLS IN A YEAR-LONG LEARNING COMMUNITY PROGRAM: A FACULTY AND LIBRARIAN COLLABORATION

James B. Young and Ashley Taliaferro Williams

Background

This paper outlines a faculty-librarian relationship in the context of integrating information literacy into a first-year learning community program at George Mason University. Integration is achieved, in part, by a collaboration characterized by mutual respect, co-mentorship, librarian involvement in curriculum design and revision, and by closely tailoring library instruction to the learning community's mission and philosophy. Integration is described by Ernest Boyer as "making connections across the disciplines," "placing specialties in a larger context," and "serious disciplined work that seeks to interpret, draw together, and bring new insight to bear on original research."[1] Information literacy is defined by the American Library Association as the ability to "...recognize when information is needed and have the ability to locate, evaluate, and use effectively the needed information."[2] Information literacy programs are increasingly common at major universities such as George Mason University. However, closely integrated information literacy programs driven by strong faculty-librarian collaborations are less common.

Young is a Reference/Instructional Services Librarian at New Century College, George Mason University; *Williams* is a Visiting Assistant Professor at New Century College, George Mason University, Fairfax, VA.

With a few exceptions, the George Mason University Libraries follow the traditional liaison model of library service. Each public services librarian is a subject specialist and is, therefore, responsible for serving the research, instructional, and collection needs of their respective academic department(s). The New Century College liaison librarian is a variation on this model. In addition to the aforementioned duties, the librarian is fully integrated into the college as a faculty member. Responsibilities as a librarian-faculty member include curriculum development, assistance in student orientation, co-management of the year-long integrative project, portfolio assessment, and strong presence in a mature technology across the curriculum program. In addition, the librarian attends faculty meetings, faculty development sessions, and social events sponsored by the college. There are several reasons why the librarian has such broad departmental access. This access is primarily motivated by an open-minded college administration and the faculty's willingness to accept librarians as full partners in the teaching and learning mission. Perhaps the central reason, however, is the learning community context of New Century College that provides for rich, integrative, cross-departmental partnerships.

What is New Century College?

New Century College is home to George Mason University's learning community programs. A learning community is "a curricular structure that links together several existing courses so that students have opportunities for deeper understanding and integration of the material they are learning, and more interaction with one another and their teachers as fellow participants in the learning enterprise."[3] According to Lenning and Ebbers, a learning community is an intentionally developed community that attempts to promote and maximize learning. "For learning communities to be effective, they must emphasize active, focused involvement in learning and collaboration that stimulates and promotes the group's and group members' learning."[4] Learning communities come in many shapes and sizes: learning organizations, curricular models, faculty learning communities, or student learning communities. New Century College is a combination of all of these.

New Century College awards a Bachelor of Arts or Science in Integrative Studies. Within Integrative Studies, students choose a concentration or design an individualized course of study. In each option, the program of study includes a mixture of interdisciplinary learning communities, traditional university courses, plus 12-24 experiential learning credits. Students fulfill their general education requirements during an intensive first-year curriculum consisting of four highly collaborative, team-taught, interdisciplinary courses known as *units*, each lasting seven weeks. These courses introduce students to the college competencies of communication, critical thinking, problem solving, valuing, group interaction, global perspective, effective citizenship, aesthetic response, and information technology. They also serve as vehicles to thread important habits of mind such as information literacy or writing (see Appendix A). As part of their curriculum, students also engage in regular self-evaluation and self-reflection via extensive course portfolios. In New Century College, learning is interactive and social. The stress is on interplay among ideas and among students and faculty, the *less knowing* and the *more knowing*. New Century College is what Boyer refers to as a "purposeful community" or a "place where faculty and students share academic goals and work together to strengthen teaching and learning on campus."[5]

Each unit of New Century College's Integrative Studies first-year program is taught by a team of approximately five or six faculty from various disciplines, supplanted by a number of resource faculty. Course instructors are drawn from a variety of ranks ranging from tenure to non-tenure line faculty to graduate teaching assistants. The New Century College liaison librarian has served on three teaching teams and continues to play a highly visible role throughout the first-year program. One way that New Century College is rare is in how faculty and librarians mirror,

albeit on a different level, the student experience. In doing so, they stress community, make connections across disciplinary boundaries, collaborate, interact, and share expertise in groups. Senge refers to these cross-disciplinary groups as "multi functional project teams" using a "collocation of project members" with plenty of "face to face meetings of networks of committed people."[6] Damrosch sees this kind of collaboration, *i.e.* seeking out and working with persons less like you, as vital. He advances the notion that true collaboration across disciplinary perspectives promotes a unique, multi-layered, and rich dialogue.[7] These sustained interactions are a central feature of faculty and librarian peer contact in New Century College.

Faculty-Librarian Contact: A General Overview

Perhaps the best way to achieve the integration of information literacy skills into an academic unit is for faculty and librarians to work closely together. Offering relevant course-integrated instruction is the most meaningful way of accomplishing this. Regardless of instructional approach, the success of library instruction often depends heavily on faculty support. "No matter how hard librarians work, without the cooperation and support of teaching faculty, the library instruction program will be unsuccessful or severely limited. This happens because the attitude of the faculty is a major determinant in the response of the students to the program."[8] Without strong faculty support and participation, library instruction is often disconnected, isolated, and unrelated to particular student needs.

"Faculty see students more often than librarians. They initiate their students' library assignments. To the extent that faculty are misinformed or uninformed about the library, their students will be misinformed or uninformed; and conversely, the better the faculty's understanding of the library, its resources and services for themselves, the more likely their students will have that better understanding."[9] In turn, some faculty sometimes see librarians as specialists who provide important skill training rather than educators whose work is central to the teaching mission of the university. A supportive faculty culture in the context of relevant, closely integrated library instruction helps to change the way students looks at information: how to find it, how it is organized, communicated, and particularly evaluated. There are many levels of integration involved in an information literacy initiative. Integration cannot happen unless faculty and librarians seek each other out, break down stereotypes, and begin to see how they can mutually facilitate student learning. In New Century College, librarian and faculty have been collaborating closely on curricular issues, writing grants, and co-managing New Century College's year-long integrative research project known as *Transformation*.

Information Literacy: An Integrated Curriculum

New Century College students are introduced to a comprehensive integrated information literacy program throughout their first year. They are exposed to information literacy in each first-year New Century College Unit via a combination of presentations, hands-on labs, and out-of-class assignments. Use of the library is expected in order to gain an appreciation for finding and using information resources of many different perspectives and formats. This process involves formulating research questions and search strategies, developing an understanding of how databases work, recognizing the range of information resources available, and identifying and evaluating specific resources. In doing so, students are asked to think about information in many contexts and from multiple perspectives. They are required to demonstrate their learning and apply their knowledge of information literacy via ongoing, formative, and summative assessments throughout the first-year program. In the process of integrating these skills, the librarian co-designs and co-teaches information literacy sessions with many NCC faculty, but mostly those closely associated with *Technology Across the Curriculum* or *Writing Across the Curriculum* initiatives. The information literacy program is very visible in New Century College and fosters sustained contact with students in many configurations and locales: in the library instruction room, in the New Century College classroom, via the student listserv, and by distribution of course-specific print or web-based publications. Students are also offered out-of-class opportunities for assistance with their research. They are especially encouraged to visit the reference desk or make appointments with librarians for in-depth research consultations.

In New Century College, information literacy skills are not introduced to students in isolation. Students apply what they learn to various assignments, especially to New Century College's year-long integrative project, *A Transformation Story: One of Many*. The *Transformation Project*, as it is commonly known, depends heavily on the information literacy integration and librarian-faculty collaboration. For this assignment, students create a cultural biography designed to link the first-year units and serve as a vehicle for acquiring a progression of research, writing, and technology skills. Each student chooses an individual (for example, a political figure, a spiritual

leader, or even a family member) to study for the year. In each successive unit, students research and write about their person in the context of course themes and issues. This assignment calls for four chapters, one researched and written in each unit and a self-evaluation, and reflection completed for a year-end portfolio. In *Unit I*, *Community of Learners*, students are responsible for the first chapter of *Transformation*. This chapter is designed as a research proposal describing: (a) why the individual has been selected as a subject, (b) why this subject is interesting to the student, (c) how this person has undergone one or more "transformations," (d) how the subject has been affected by social, cultural, historical, or political influences and (e) a population of which the person is or was a part. In *Unit II*, the *Natural World*, students write about this population, and find and analyze quantitative information about the subject. In *Unit III*, the *Social World*, focus shifts to the study of a social context and how the person is influenced by this context. In *Unit IV*, *Self as Citizen*, the project comes full circle. Students re-visit their person and reflect upon their personal values in the context of citizenship and community. Finally, in the self-evaluation completed at the end of the year, students are asked to review and assess their learning: about their person *and* the writing, technology, and research skills they gained by viewing a subject through many lenses and from many contexts for an entire year. Throughout the year-long process, students are regularly immersed in information literacy concepts that are pervasive and serve as glue for integrating skill and content, thinking and learning.

The co-authors work closely throughout the academic year, playing strong roles in the design, implementation, and teaching of the project. They find the connection between writing and information literacy to be a natural one. After five years of collaboration, neither claims complete ownership over their initial domain of expertise. That is, both are comfortable sharing what they know, learning from each other, and collaborating in both the writing classroom *and* the library instruction room. As a diverse group of faculty teaches in the first-year program, it is (perhaps ironically) the librarian who is the central faculty member who has year-long sustained access to students throughout the year. In this way, the librarian facilitates learning in a way that other faculty cannot by providing unit-by-unit context and connections for both students *and* faculty. In addition, the librarian develops unique knowledge about how the project functions as a whole and how the project might be revised from year to year. Additionally, the librarian participates with other members of the faculty team in evaluating year-end portfolios that include all chapters of The Transformation Project.

Information literacy skills are further reinforced through interactions with faculty and students in workshop sessions linked to Transformation called *Read-Arounds*. The purpose of the *Read-Around*s is to afford students the opportunity to read and learn from each other while gaining feedback from faculty and librarians. Some sessions take place in rooms with Internet connections so the librarian can provide on-the-spot assistance. Feedback—from peers, faculty, and librarians—in these workshops can be focused on all aspects of the paper, from content to research to writing technique to rhetorical issues. When students receive this kind of feedback from librarians and faculty, they better understand the role both can play in their learning and gain a greater understanding of the complexity of good research writing.

Benefits of Faculty and Librarian Collaboration in a Learning Community

Measuring success is not always easy with an integrated curriculum. This is due, in part, to the richness and complexity of integration itself. There are, however, many ways in which success is achieved. The most distinctive benefit of integrating a librarian into a learning community is the opportunity for sustained, year-long contact with students. Since all freshmen experience a common first-year curriculum, the librarian has the opportunity to work with a relatively finite, unchanging student community. This allows opportunities, a-typical of most information literacy programs, to build strong working relationships with students, and to measure year-long growth. Due to this year-long presence *and* assistance in providing important out-of-class connections, the librarian is arguably the most visible member of New Century College teaching team. The front-line access to students is essential to establishing trust and helping to change the traditional image of librarians. In doing so, the library begins to move from the periphery of undergraduate education to a more central, integrated role in student learning.

Another benefit to librarians from working in learning communities is the potential for building and sustaining collaborative relationships with a diverse group of faculty. Integration in the college serves two overarching purposes. As part of a diverse team, the librarian is afforded the opportunity to be a part of the curriculum on a very personal level. This helps not only to change the way librarians view both faculty *and* integrated curricula, but also helps to change faculty stereotypes of librarians. Another benefit of close collaboration in a learning community is the change in

world view that takes place over time. Both the librarian and the writing instructor noticed changes in their teaching due to long-term interaction with colleagues outside their domain of expertise. This allows space for co-mentor ship and gives both the opportunity to expand their ways of knowing. Given the integrated nature of New Century College's first-year program, no one faculty member can be the *de facto* expert in all parts of the curriculum. Therefore, instructors collaborate in order to bridge expertise and create rich learning environments for students. In this context, librarians *and* faculty combine their practiced (and expected) role of *expert/teacher* with the newer role of *facilitator/learner*. This creates a unique dynamic of shared authority reinforced by a culture of day-to-day social contact in which librarians and faculty find collaborations to be a natural progression of their teaching duties.

Conclusion

"Traditional library orientation and bibliographic instruction programs have failed to command the interest of students and to satisfy the expectations of faculty. Effective information literacy programs must be embedded in specific courses and progress throughout an entire curriculum. The importance of information literacy for today's graduates argues against such instruction being pedantic or random."[10] True collaboration entails gaining a way to best communicate one's area of expertise to others who are novices or learners and, in turn, gaining an appreciation for how *others* do things. By close collaboration in New Century College, librarians and faculty expand their ways of knowing and often traverse areas in which they are not entirely comfortable. To accomplish this, both librarians and faculty need to move beyond traditional roles and work together to provide students with meaningful and integrative learning experiences.

NOTES

1. Ernest L. Boyer, *Scholarship Reconsidered: Priorities of the Professoriate* (Princeton, NJ: Carnegie Foundation for the Advancement of Teaching, 1990).

2. American Library Association, Presidential Committee on Information Literacy. Final Report, 2002 http://www.ala.org/acrl/nili/ilit1st.html (4 April 2002)

3. Faith G. Gabelnick, Jean MacGregor, Roberta S. Matthews, and Barbara Leigh Smith, *Learning*

—JAMES B. YOUNG AND ASHLEY TALIAFERRO WILLIAMS—

Communities: Creating Connections Among Students, Faculty, and Disciplines, New Directions for Teaching and Learning, no. 41 (San Francisco, CA: Jossey-Bass, 1990).

4. Oscar T. Lenning and Larry H. Ebbers, *The Powerful Potential of Learning Communities: improving Education for the Future* (Washington, DC: Graduate School of Education and Human Development, George Washington University).

5. Boyer.

6. Peter M. Senge, *The Dance of Change: The Challenges to Sustaining Momentum in Learning Organizations* (New York, NY: Currency/Doubleday, 1999).

7. David Damrosch, *We Scholars: Changing the Culture of the University* (Cambridge, MA: Harvard University Press, 1995).

8. David Carlson and Ruth H. Miller, "Librarians and Teaching Faculty: Partners in Bibliographic Instruction," *College and Research Libraries* 45, no. 6 (1994): 483-491.

9. Anne G. Lipow, "Outreach to Faculty: Why and How," in *Working with Faculty in the New Electronic Library: Papers and Session Materials Presented at the Nineteenth National LOEX Library Instruction Conference held at Eastern Michigan University 10 to 11 May 1991*, edited by Linda Shirato (Ann Arbor, MI: Pierian Press, 1992).

10. D. W. Farmer and Terrence Mech, *Information Literacy: Developing Students as Independent Learners* (San Francisco, CA: Jossey-Bass, 1992)

Appendix A: New Century College Freshmen First Year Program

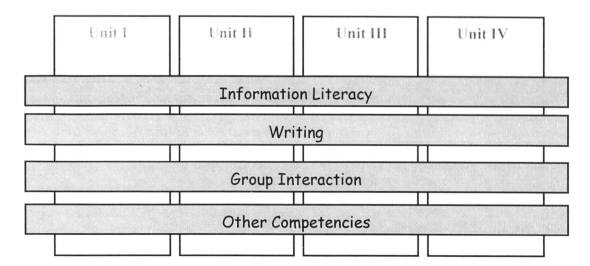

Unit I – NCLC 110: *Community of Learners* (**8 credits**)
- **English 101**: Introduction to Composition (3 credits)
- **Communications 100**: *Introduction to Oral Communication* (2 credits)
- **Math 106**: Concepts of Mathematics: Analytical Reasoning (1 credit)
- **Information Technology 100**: *Information Technology Basics* (2 credits)

Unit II – NCLC 120: *The Natural World* (**8 credits**)
- **Math 106:** Concepts of Mathematics: Analytical Reasoning (2 credits)
- **Biology 104:** *Introductory Biology* (4 credits)
- **Communication 100:** Introduction to Oral Communication (2 credits)

} Fall Term

Unit III: NCLC 130: *The Social World* (**8 credits**)
- **History 100:** History of Western Civilization (3 credits)
- **Arts** (1 credit)
- Global Understanding (3 credits)
- **English 201:** Reading and Writing about Text (1 credit)

Unit IV: NCLC 140: *Self as Citizen* (**8 credits**)
- Social Science (3 credits)
- **Arts** (2 credits)
- **English 201:** Reading and Writing about Text (2 credits)
- **Information Technology 100:** Information Technology Basics (1 credit)

} Spring Term

MEETING MILLENNIALS IN THEIR MEDIUM: FUSING STREAMED VIDEO AND LIBRARY INSTRUCTION

Colleen Boff and Catherine Cardwell

According to the *Statistical Abstracts of the United States (2000)*, watching television and listening to the radio ranked highest among multimedia activities for the total 18-24 year old population. Slightly more than 92 percent of persons in this age group had watched television during the prior week while nearly 91 percent said they had listened to the radio during the same period.[1] These numbers support our assumptions that our current college students engage in multiple media, specifically audio and visual mediums. Furthermore, as educators we realize that students have different learning styles and a wide range of learning preferences. Given both the tangible numbers and our hunches based on anecdotal evidence, we decided to approach students in a medium that is more familiar to them, one they naturally gravitate towards in their everyday lives. In an effort to complement our existing tried-and-true instructional materials, we decided to stretch our comfort levels as instructors and develop materials in a way that would have a greater appeal to our students.

Background Information about Bowling Green State University

Bowling Green State University (BGSU) is a doctoral-granting, four-year institution with nearly 21,000 students on its main and branch campuses. Of these students, nearly 5,500 are first-year students.

Boff is the First-Year Experience Librarian and *Cardwell* the Coordinator of Library User Education at Bowling Green State University, Bowling Green, OH.

Most entering first-year students begin their studies with a General Studies Writing (GSW) program's composition courses, one of which is required for graduation and is taken for general education credit. Most students begin their first semester with either English 110 or 111. Neither of these are required to graduate, but depending on skill level, must be taken as pre-requisites if students do not place directly into English 112, a graduation requirement. This is the only point in an undergraduate student's education at BGSU where the library may provide instruction in a formal way. Beyond the composition courses, our contact with students is hit or miss.

BGSU's Library User Education (LUE) Department consists of eight instruction librarians. All are subject liaisons other than one who works specifically with unique first-year programs on campus. With a campus BGSU's size, it has not been possible to provide in-person instruction to the hundreds of composition courses each semester. Instead, librarians have developed and continually revise a self-guided library tour that is a required paper exercise in most of the English 110 or 111 courses. Librarians also offer Research Project Clinics (RPC's) year round and intensively during the peak four-week period when research papers are assigned each semester. These are one-on-one appointments where students can work with a librarian for individual help on their research papers. The self-guided library tour and the RPC's are both very successful, but the librarians are always looking for ways to provide more personalized contact with students.

To further set the stage for this project, BGSU's Information Technology Services (ITS) had recently completed an enhancement to the campus network. Nearly nine miles of cable were installed campus-wide providing faculty, staff and students with a state-of-the art campus network capable of handling broadband Internet projects, such as streamed digital video productions.

Growing the Idea for Our Video Project

During Spring 2001, librarians were working on an orientation packet for new student employees and were investigating what other institutions were doing with virtual library tours. Most of what we found was done with Macromedia Flash software. A few institutions had created library tours using streamed digital videos. We began to think of this technology as something that could go beyond an orientation to a physical space and started to consider that if there weren't instructional possibilities for this technology as well.

Given BGSU's new multi-million dollar technology infrastructure, our hunch had potential to become a reality. Due to an existing collaboration with BGSU's Center for Teaching, Learning, and Technology (CTLT), the Libraries were offered an opportunity to participate in the development of a pilot to explore and create *DataLine BG*, a digital video project. After much discussion with the digital video project manager, we decided to pursue a collaboration with GSW because of our long-standing relationship with that particular program and because almost all of our first-year students were registered in composition courses. In essence, we had the opportunity to develop an instructional tool that would have a broad impact on the student population and would introduce new students to the e-learning environment at BGSU early in their academic careers.

Overview of *DataLine BG*

Dataline BG http://www.bgsu.edu/colleges/library/infosrv/lue/dataline.html started as a collaboration among three different units on campus: ITS' Bowling Green Digital Video Project (BGDV), the Libraries, and GSW. *DataLine BG* consists of seven instructional streaming video modules that are mounted on a Web site with links to additional sources. The modules are set in the context of a mock news show that explores a common theme with humor imbedded throughout each piece.

Collaborators

Initially, librarians and GSW instructors met on several occasions to discuss problems that students and instructors face as well as the kinds of student skills and knowledge that needed improvement. An earlier assessment survey also revealed two critical problem areas in student learning: 1) students didn't understand the differences between the Libraries' catalog and research databases, and 2) they did not understand how to structure an effective search, specifically the use of Boolean operators. Because of these discussions, the group was able to come to a common understanding of the project's desired outcomes. While the librarians and instructors provided content and a solid understanding of the teaching and learning environment, two students from BGDV provided expertise in the creation of digital video. The students were responsible for taping, lighting, editing, compressing, and putting the videos on the Web.

Content Development

We started developing the content for *DataLine BG* by thinking of outcomes first. We originally wanted our users to be aware of the following after viewing the videos: 1) where to go for help, 2) how to find books, 3) how to find articles, 4) when to use research databases or the Web, 5) how to know the difference between a topic and an issue, 6) how to talk to a database, 7) how to search the Web, 8) how to find reserve materials, and 9) how to view online circulation records.

We began writing a script and thinking of characters, settings and screen shots for each module. Our original scripting and photo shoots were staged much the same way we tend to teach students in the classroom or at the reference desk. Frankly, our first attempts were boring and too scripted. Fortunately, the BGDV students who provided the production expertise were also a good litmus test for the content. They wanted to see more humor, and we wanted to see more of a theme throughout the modules. Several BGDV students were friends with a newscaster at a local news station who happened to be enrolled in the telecommunications program at BGSU. We were able to offer him credit towards his degree in exchange for his real-life talent as a newscaster. Thus, the *DataLine BG* theme was invented which involves a newscaster following viewer leads on "Research Stress Syndrome," an affliction recently seen on the BGSU college campus.

Our content was further modified when we realized that the strictly process-oriented types of instruction didn't work well in this medium or with our attempts to be humorous. In an effort to use this medium to teach conceptual content, we decided to eliminate the originally suggested modules of "view your circulation record" and "finding reserves." However, we did provide links to other print materials on both of these topics from the *DataLine BG* Web page.

Success of *DataLine BG*

Is this project a success? Yes, we believe it is for several reasons. First, the Web site is being used in the GSW classes. It has been accessed more than 16,000 times since January 2002. We have had considerable outside interest in the project, ranging from institutions asking if they could link to the page or specific modules to asking if they could purchase a CD-ROM of the project.

One of the more rewarding measures of success is hearing responses from instructors who have used the modules with students. In addition to students and instructors finding them humorous, instructors are pleased with the content. One instructor mentioned that a non-traditional student had a breakthrough in thinking about subject heading vs. keyword searching because of the videos. Even though the instructor explained the differences several times to her, it wasn't until she watched the videos that the concept clicked. All of the instructors with whom we've talked have stated that the video modules reinforce what they regularly tell their students.

We had hoped to implement a formal large-scale assessment survey to measure student learning and to find out if watching the modules resulted in a better understanding of the concepts and skills we hoped to improve. This is still one of our priorities, but due to recent budget cuts we were not able to administer the same tool we used for a different project earlier. However, we have a brief online assessment tool on the *DataLine BG* Web site and are urging GSW instructors to have students complete it.

Reasons for Success

We have presented this project to several departments on campus as well as at a statewide conference. The project was also shared on BI-L, the Bibliographic Instruction Discussion List. We are frequently asked the question, "How did you do it?" Specifically, people want to know why we were asked to participate in such a pilot and how we collaborated so broadly and successfully. They also want to know more about the necessary technical expertise and essential hardware and software. The collaboration

was successful because all three parties communicated frequently, were flexible, and contributed ideas and support throughout the entire life of the project. The manager of the digital video project started talking to us about possibilities in March 2001; we then met with GSW in April to continue exploring ideas. Our group met and e-mailed throughout the month of May. After three months of extensive talking and exploring, the group set to work and continued meeting and talking throughout the life of the project. Once early versions of the modules were ready to share, we previewed them, gathered valuable feedback, and revised our plans as a result.

Another important reason the project was effective was that all parties were flexible. Because the Libraries were working in such a new medium, we didn't always understand how complicated it was to create an effective video project. We had to cut back the number of modules, mostly because we were running out of time and resources. We also had to be very open to the advice the BGDV students were offering us, especially since they had expertise we sorely lacked.

All three parties contributed time, money, and most importantly, ideas throughout the project and all were invested in the outcome. The Libraries' administration invested librarian and student time; they also contributed money to hire two GSW instructors on overload pay to contribute content and work on the project. GSW also contributed money to hire the GSW instructors to contribute content. The GSW instructors who were hired were also expected to conduct workshops for other instructors so that the project was more likely to be used in classes.

In addition to students with video expertise, ITS provided equipment, such as cameras and lights, as well as digital videotape and server space to house the final videos. Although these financial contributions were important, what proved even more important were the ideas and specific expertise actively contributed by all three parties. We learned enough about digital video to be able to talk about our project with the BGDV team as well as with the administrators who supported the project. However, we didn't learn enough to create such a polished product on our own.

Tips for Developing a Digital Video Project

Consider these tips if you're thinking about creating your own digital video:

- Make sure your project fits a real need in the curriculum and be sure to invite the group that "owns" this curriculum to be a part of your project. Otherwise, you may spend a lot of time working on a project that doesn't get used.

- Start small. It takes a long time to create and edit video.

- Take a workshop in capturing an editing digital video. You don't need to become an expert, but you do need to be able to articulate your concerns and understand the concerns of people providing technical expertise. In addition, having a better understanding of the medium will help you to conceptualize a realistic, manageable project. Hire students or find an intern to be the person who shoots, edits, and compresses the video. Unless you already have advanced skills in this area, you will be more successful if you can contribute your own content expertise and rely on someone else's video expertise.

- Understand video project management. Someone has to manage the assets of the project. That is, someone has to keep track of scenes, actors, scripts, and locations and make sure all the details are taken care of. In many ways, it's similar to coordinating any other project. You will keep a time line and long-term and short-term to-do lists, which are always changing as your project evolves. However, if you are new to video, you will have additional factors to consider, including getting permission to shoot on location and completing release forms for all participants, even those individuals who appear in background shots.

- Consider local "talent" to act in the video. We didn't start setting our video in the context of a mock news show. Rather, we had an experienced student newscaster willing to act in our video, so we were able to re-write our script based on his participation. It would have been much harder to

get an actor to play the role of a newscaster, especially since we had no directing skills. We also relied on a student library employee to play herself in the video. We had a much easier time getting a library student to feel comfortable in front of a camera than getting actors to feel comfortable talking about the library even though they were not camera shy.

- Offer the videos at various compression rates on the Web to accommodate the ways users may be accessing the materials. Cal-State Fullerton's video is an excellent example http://www.library. fullerton.edu/tour/. Since our project was intended for use on a campus with a powerful, high-speed network, we offered only a high-speed Web version. (Almost all of our first-year students live on campus.)

- Deliver the video on VHS and CD-ROM in addition to on the Web. If instructors want to use the product in the classroom, they may not be able to if the room isn't wired or doesn't have a fast enough computer or a projector. Some instructors may feel more comfortable showing the video on a TV.

- Offer workshops to show people how the content can be used. That will make them aware of the resource and get them thinking about how to use it.

NOTE

1. U.S. Census Bureau, *Statistical Abstract of the United States: 2000* (120 edition) Washington, DC, 2000, Table No. 911.

–COLLEEN BOFF AND CATHERINE CARDWELL–

A System-Wide Multi-Campus Approach to Integrating Information Competence Into the Learning Outcomes of Academic Departments in the California State University System

Ilene F. Rockman, Ph.D., Delores Nasom McBroome, Ph.D.,
Marlowe Berg, Ph.D., and Maria Grant

Introduction

Since 1995, a strategic direction of the California State University (CSU) system, serving 388,700 students and 42,000 faculty members on 23 campuses (the largest system of higher education in the country), has been information competence to ensure that all students graduate with exposure to, and an understanding of, this important lifelong learning skill.

Information Competence within the CSU is defined as the fusion or integration of library literacy, computer literacy, media literacy, technological literacy, ethics, critical thinking, and communication skills with the goal of helping students to develop a conceptual framework for successfully addressing any information need.

A broadly constituted committee has functioned as a "work group" to guide the activities of the Information Competence Initiative http://www.calstate.edu/LS/infocomp.shtml. Members are appointed by the Vice Chancellor of Academic

Rockman is the Manager, Information Competence Initiative for The California State University; *McBroome* is Professor and Chair, Department of History at Humboldt State University; *Berg* is Director, College of Education, San Diego State University; and *Grant* is a Graduate Student in the College of Education, San Diego State University.

Affairs, and represent such constituencies as library administrators, discipline faculty members (including statewide academic senators), library faculty members, senior level university administrators (such as provosts), assessment coordinators, faculty development directors, and Chancellor's Office administrators and staff.

The work group has guided the implementation of various projects through an active program of competitive grant proposals. These have resulted in the development of web-based instructional tutorials, summer faculty professional development workshops to reshape assignments and curricular offerings, outreach effort to high schools and community colleges through teacher-librarian collaboration, support for a campus online information competence graduation requirement, quantitative and qualitative assessment activities, and the creation of various information competence courses and programs at the undergraduate and graduate levels.

In addition, the system has supported faculty fellowships and system-wide conferences to further advance the information competence agenda. Successes have been achieved within local environments, between campuses, and across the system. These have been shared with the broader library community and documented in the library literature.[1]

During the 2001-2002 academic year a concerted decision was made to encourage the integration of information competence into the learning outcomes of academic departments and graduate programs using the Association of College and Research Libraries' *Standards, Performance Indicators, and Outcomes* as a guide.[2]

A unique aspect of the latest Call For Proposals grant process in 2001 was the deliberate targeting of discipline-based faculty members (rather than library faculty members). The CSU Vice Chancellor for Academic Affairs, indicating the importance of the topic, sent the "Call" to campus presidents, in addition to library directors/deans.

Deliverables included:

(1) A list of the department's student learning outcomes that includes the skills of information competence.

(2) Syllabi for required courses in the department that specifically identify assignments that promote information competence.

(3) Representative assignments indicating that students are being asked to demonstrate the various skills of information competence.

(4) Web pages that provide the proposal, the activities and the deliverables.

Requirements specified that:

(1) Activities must result in a statement of information competence as a learning outcome for the degree program.

(2) Activities must result in assessments that certify that a student has met the information competence requirement.

(3) An appropriate member of the library faculty must play an integral role in the project activities.

(4) Specified learning outcomes must be consistent with the ACRL standards on information literacy for higher education.

Of the 25 awards distributed across the system this year, two serve as excellent models. They represent small (Humboldt) and large (San Diego) campuses, and undergraduate (history) and doctoral (education) levels. The exemplar projects are:

(1) "Integrating and Assessing Historical Skills and Information Competencies Throughout the Undergraduate History Major," submitted by the department chair, Dr. Delores-Nasome McBroome, Humboldt State University.

(2) "Information Literacy Standards in a Doctoral Program: Forming an Integrated Definition of Competence," submitted by graduate program director, Dr. Marlowe Berg, San Diego State University.

Information Competency for History Majors

In Spring 2001, the History Department of Humboldt State University was awarded an information competence grant to create a fully integrated History major with clearly defined information competency standards throughout the major that culminated in the Senior Seminar and Portfolio Assessment.

A faculty retreat was held in the Fall of 2001 to bring members of the department together to review and endorse the ACRL standards, and to begin to identify information competence assignments.

Fortunately, the grant also provided funding for a consultant to (1) identify upper-division course objectives, especially in relation to information competency standards and goals and to (2) develop a Website about information competence for history majors.[3] This information was designed to provide up-to-date information for the history majors about the objectives and skills they should be developing while taking various history courses in the major.

Since evaluating information and critically analyzing data is central to the historian's task, the History Department faculty members believe that students will benefit from identifying various skills and information competency abilities when they register for courses.

Three history courses are designed to introduce information competency skills:

- History 210 (Introduction to History)—this course introduces students to what it means to be a practicing historian. Students are exposed to the bulk of the skills listed in the ACRL Standards, and begin to understand the relationship between those skills and the discipline of history. The basic skills introduced are research skills/gathering information, facility with primary and secondary sources, critical thinking, history methodologies, historiography, facility in oral presentation, and production of coherent and analytical historical writing.

- History 226 (Computing Research in History)—this course is intended to introduce history majors to the uses of the Internet for historical research. The first half of the class focuses on the various ways in which the Internet can assist researchers in accumulating sources, evaluating information,

—ILENE F. ROCKMAN, DELORES NASOM MCBROOME, MARLOWE BERG AND MARIA GRANT—

identifying relevant issues and engaging in dialogues with others. During the second half of the course, student groups design well-researched historically-based Web pages. This portion helps students learn about different ways of presenting research, as well as master the mechanics of creating web pages with Microsoft Front Page.

- History 492 (Senior Seminar in History)—History 492, the history research seminar, is the culmination of a history major's progress through the program. It is designed to be taken during the senior year. Ideally, all of the skills emphasized in lower and upper division courses (and identified in the ACRL standards) will be used in this course. The goal of this class is the production of a seminar paper, a piece of original research and analysis drawing on a wide variety of secondary, and ideally, primary courses. By this time, students should have learned to ask interesting and fruitful questions, find and accumulate sources, evaluate those sources, and produce a well-written and well-argued seminar paper. Students may also have initial drafts of that paper evaluated by their peers, who share their evaluations in oral and written form. This experience serves as a capstone to a student's progression through the major, and allows him/her to function as a historian by producing original research.

In addition to the three courses mentioned, there is another class, a one-unit exit course, which supports information competence in history as part of its assessment model:

- History 493 (Portfolio Assessment for History Majors)—this course is designed to ascertain how well the basic skills of the historical discipline and information competency have been integrated into student work throughout the major. A portfolio of work gauging improvement (or lack thereof) of disciplinary skills throughout the major is required of all students. It also serves as a model for emphasizing competency skills and analytical abilities that students may use after graduation when engaging in resume writing.

The next few years will allow this model to be tested among the Humboldt State University students.

Information Competence in a Doctoral Program

Information literacy is a foundational pillar of research and scholarship. In this age of information proliferation, it becomes an even more critical skill as scholars work to access and evaluate the myriad of information sources available. And, while critical in academic settings, information literacy extends into all aspects of 21st Century life where information and its productive and ethical use lie at the heart of global interactions.

A significant aspect of information literacy is found where information and technology intersect. Schlechty (1996) has long asserted we labor in an information age serviced by technologies, and the product of this work is knowledge. He goes on to say that an individual's most critical skill in developing knowledge is the ability to work critically with data drawn from a variety of sources through a mixture of mediated forms.[4]

Reinking, et al. (1998) argues that "we are heading toward a post-typographic world; that is, one in which printed texts are no longer dominant."[5] The editors comment that while it might seem ironic that their message is carried in the form of a conventional textbook, they note that the technological underpinnings of the text, including frequent e-mail messages among the editors and authors, extensive research conducted in multiple media formats and making decisions about which portions of the text would be made available on the World Wide Web, are woven throughout the thinking, writing, and final production.

The role of universities in preparing leaders in education to participate in this changing, knowledge-rich scenario for the future is pivotal. Strong programs will be instrumental in developing leaders who can transform information into knowledge, basing their work on new definitions of information literacy and information technology, particularly with a focus on the overarching concept of competence. This leadership will directly influence work in K-12 schools and in communities and the business world beyond the classroom. In fact, notions of school-as-building and classrooms as places with walls and blackboards are currently being challenged as educators become increasingly cognizant of how newer views of harnessing information literacy and forms of technology create new avenues for information access, communication, problem solving and critical thinking.

The new San Diego State University-University of San Diego (SDSU-USD) Joint Doctoral Program in Education was created in response to the need for a program that could prepare leaders in the areas of literacy and educational technology. As the new program began in Fall 2000, it became evident that not only was it a merger of two universities in the delivery of a doctorate, but the merger of faculty delivering a program that had very clear points of intersection. It has become even clearer that to maximize the full potential of this program for all, the joint faculty must identify these intersections and their significance for course development and revision, for student work and for the future contributions of today's doctoral students. The activity involved with the formation of an integrated definition of information literacy competence proved to be a powerful starting point for this discourse.

At the center of the Information Literacy Competence project undertaken by the faculty and students in the Joint Doctoral Program were a series of questions:

(1) What are the information literacy standards and competencies that are integrated throughout the program and in what ways?

(2) Which competencies are emphasized strongly across courses; which competencies are covered, and where are there identified areas of need that should be dealt with in order to produce a leader in education who is a highly literate user of information sources and processing skills?

Using the ACRL standards as a focus, actions were taken to develop clear understandings among both faculty and students about information literacy competencies. These conversations have led to an examination of and extended understanding of literacy and educational technology interactions at a doctoral level. This collective effort will culminate in a definition of competence and a program commitment to the continued development of the most important elements of information literacy needed for life long learning.

Conclusion

Since 1995, the California State University's Information Competence Initiative (http://www.calstate.edu/LS/infocomp.shtml) has made great strides in its commitment to advancing, promoting, and integrating information competence principles into academic course work on the campuses. With strong collaboration, cooperation, and partnering between discipline faculty, library faculty, and academic administrators, the initiative has focused on assisting both undergraduate and graduate students so that they will achieve a greater understanding and knowledge of information competence leading to

success in the university, the workplace, and in society at large.

NOTES

1. Lorie Roth, "Educating the Cut and Paste Generation," *Library Journal* 124, no.8 (1 November, 1999): 42-44; Sariay Talip Clay, Sallie Harlan, and Judy Swanson, "Mystery to Mastery: The CSU Information Competence Project." *Research Strategies* 17, no. 2/3 (2000): 157-166; Susan Curzon, "Developing a Program of Information Literacy: How California State University Did It," *College and Research Libraries News* 61, no. 6 (June 2000): 483-6, 491; Ilene F. Rockman, "More than Faculty Training: Integrating Information Competence into the Disciplines," *College and Research Libraries News* 6, no.3 (March 2002): 192-194; Kathlen Dunn, "Assessing Information Literacy Skills in the California State University: A Progress Report," *Journal of Academic Librarianship* 28, no. 1 (January/March 2002): 26-35.

2. Association of College and Research Libraries (2000). *Information Literacy Competency Standards for Higher Education: Standards, Performance Indicators, and Outcomes* http://www.ala.org/acrl/ilstandardlo.html.

3. *Information Competency for History Majors at Humboldt State University* (2002). http://sorrelfp.humboldt.edu/ap23/infocomp/index.htm

4. Phillip Schlechty, *Schools for the Twenty-First Century* (San Francisco, CA: Jossey-Bass, 1996).

5. David Reinking, et al. *Handbook of Literacy and Technology: Transformations in a Post-Typographic World*. Mahwah, NJ: Lawrence Erlbaum Associates, 1998.

BEYOND THE RESEARCH PAPER: WORKING WITH FACULTY TO MAXIMIZE LIBRARY-RELATED ASSIGNMENTS

Glenn Ellen Starr Stilling

Since 1993, I have presented, for various audiences, a two-hour workshop on how college faculty can make their assignments that require outside resources more effective. Three times (most recently March, 2002) the workshop was sponsored by Appalachian State University's Hubbard Center for Faculty Development. I also presented it for graduate teaching assistants and for my library's reference and instruction team. The workshop's advice and materials are drawn from the literature of a variety of subject areas (composition, critical thinking, psychology, college teaching, and bibliographic instruction) as well as my own twenty years' experience in reference work and bibliographic instruction. In-text references are two items listed on the workshop bibliography (Appendix 1). All other facts and ideas that were presented (very informally) in the workshop are from sources listed in the bibliography or from my own observations and experiences.

What follows is an abbreviated version of that workshop, with brief concluding remarks on how librarians can use these ideas and materials in working with college faculty. The appendices reproduce some of the materials faculty received at the workshop. Please note that after this paragraph, my assumed audience in this paper is college faculty.

Introduction

I first gave this workshop in 1993. I have continued to develop it because, as a librarian, assignments that require outside resources are very

Stilling is a librarian at Appalachian State University, Boone, NC.

important to me. They are the primary way that our students learn information literacy skills. Information literacy is a central focus of the library's mission. I worry, however, that faculty may be dropping such assignments—because students don't do good work on them (relying too heavily on Internet sources or using sources that aren't relevant enough or are at an inappropriate scholarly level); because syllabi are overcrowded with other goals to meet and material to cover; or because grading such assignments is too time-consuming.

My idea, in designing this assignment, was to present suggestions for revising such assignments so that students' work on them is more effective and so that they do "double duty" by developing multiple competencies. I will introduce ways to incorporate both information literacy and critical thinking skills. In addition, there will be ideas for "staging" the assignments to help students avoid procrastination and learn the skills involved in small steps; examples of short assignments that require less grading time; and ways the library can help prepare students to be successful at finding the information your assignments require.

[At this point, workshop participants look at and discuss the definitions of information literacy and critical thinking on the workshop outline. They then complete a short writing exercise and briefly share their responses.]

Aligning Assignments Closely with Course Goals

Two writers—Carole E. Barrowman and Barbara E. Walvoord—emphasize the importance of tying every assignment closely to course goals. They recommend developing course goals that focus more on what students will be able to **do** upon completion of the course than on what they will **know**. To achieve this focus, begin your course plan with a list of assignments, spacing them evenly throughout the course. Then, fill in the in-class activities, mini-lectures, and readings that will support the assignments. Telling students up front how each assignment relates to course goals might motivate them and reduce their objections to the assignment.

[At this point, workshop participants complete a second short writing exercise. They briefly share their responses.]

Factors to Consider in Designing Effective Library-Use Assignments

1. Break large assignments into steps or stages—or consider using several short assignments. Composition and writing-across-the-curriculum specialist, John C. Bean, notes that the papers most students submit for grades are first drafts (29). If the assignment required outside resources, it is possible that students' less-than-satisfactory work stemmed from the fact that the research—as well as the writing—was done only a day or two before the assignment was due. I believe that one of the primary factors in poor performance on research-based assignments is procrastination. Both college faculty and librarians tend to joke or show cynicism about student procrastination—but it is, in fact, a serious problem. Janssen's literature review estimates the prevalence of procrastination among college students at 46-95%. In addition, Janssen's sources note that students procrastinate more the longer they are in college and that procrastination can cause low self-esteem, test and social anxiety, depression, and poor course grades. Thus, a key strategy for helping students avoid procrastination is setting up mandatory deadlines (that can't be circumvented) for submission of parts of the assignment. Coupled with procrastination might be writer's block and its associated problems of perfectionism, bingeing, and hypomania. Faculty can help students immeasurably by teaching them some of Robert Boice's techniques for managing the work routines and psychological aspects of writing.

Another benefit of breaking a large assignment into stages is that it reduces the cognitive load of the assignment. Students' thinking and writing is not as clear and focused as it should be if—due to procrastination and writer's block—they are gathering sources for a paper, reading the sources (many of which might contain difficult academic language and concepts), figuring out what their reactions are to all this information, and writing and editing a paper—all in a few short days or hours. Forcibly spacing these tasks over a longer period of time will also help students retain longer the information they learn from the research and writing process, just as spaced learning and review are superior to cramming for tests. Here are some additional suggestions:

* Have students turn in an annotated bibliography of outside sources at an early stage. To ensure that they actually start reading the sources early—and to determine if the sources really are relevant for their topics—require that the annotations explain which information they will use from each source and how it is relevant to the paper.

*Have students turn in printouts from database searches as an early step. Ask a librarian to look over them and help you evaluate the effectiveness of students' research strategies.

* Rather than one large assignment divided into steps, consider having students do three or four short assignments, spaced throughout the semester. Micro themes (Bean, 74), summaries of articles (Bean, 128-129 and Meyers, 75-767), or Infomercials (Appendix 2A) are examples. Students' skills should improve each time they do the assignment and get feedback from you.

2. Give clear, unambiguous instructions. Both John C. Bean (83-85) and Chet Meyers (73-73) recommend this practice. Bean advocates developing a separate instructions sheet for each assignment, rather than incorporating the assignment instructions in the syllabus or giving them orally. He suggests including these sections in the assignment instructions: task, role or audience the writer should assume, format (parts or sections to include), process to follow in completing the assignment (particularly scheduled steps or stages), and evaluation criteria. Here are some additional suggestions:

*Have a colleague **and** a librarian review the assignment instruction sheet before giving it to students.

*Make available to students (perhaps on reserve in the library) a model or example of an excellent completed assignment.

*To be certain that students have read (in advance) and understood the assignment, take class time to have them read it silently, then pair up and discuss it with each other. Follow this by having students explain the assignment to the entire class and mention questions they have.

3. Have the assignment make use of real-life problems and situations or everyday examples of a theory or principle. This strategy has (at least) two advantages. First, it requires students to relate new information to information they already know—thus effecting deeper processing. An example is a sociology assignment in which the professor decides not to have students simply "write about" a topic. Instead, she asks them to read outside sources about role strain and role conflict. Then, they think about situations in which they experienced each one and write about how their experiences illustrate these phenomena.

Secondly, for novices, creating learning situations that are, as much as possible, as if the environment in which they will actually use the information in real life will help trigger the retrieval of the information in the future. The situation in which we learn information is encoded along with the information. An example is a Recreation Management course at Appalachian State University. Students work in pairs to develop a grant proposal related to recreation or leisure. They are encouraged to work with a leisure provider in the area of the university or in their own hometown and write the proposal as if that agency were the author. They research all aspects of the grant proposal (the agency, the funding source to whom they are writing, the leisure activity involved, and the city or town which the grant will serve). They present the grant proposal to a mock funding board composed of their classmates.

The "Responsible Patienthood" assignment (Appendix 2B) is another excellent example from Earlham College which has been used at Appalachian. Others from Appalachian are:

*A counseling theories course in which, after studying several major theories, students write their own theory (which can include elements of the others) and explain why they believe it will work well for them.

*A Holocaust course in which the professor gives each student a dollar bill at the beginning of the course. At the end, they must give the dollar bill to the organization, or person they believe can do the most to prevent a future Holocaust. They submit a researched paper justifying their choice.

4. *If the assignment will require critical thinking,*

provide direct support for students to learn the critical thinking skills you expect. Student papers may disappoint you because you asked students to "compare," "synthesize," "evaluate," or "argue"—and they did something else. The reason might be that if students don't know what you mean, or have never been taught how to do it, they'll resort to some other writing strategy. Many writers about critical thinking emphasize that these skills must be taught explicitly and made a priority in the course. Linda Flower (48) conducted research on the influence of task representation on student writing. She asked students to talk aloud as they worked on a writing assignment. When one student read the assignment's requirement to "interpret and synthesize," he said, "What the hell does that mean? Synthesize means to pull together, no, to make something up. Why would I want to make something up? Synthesize sounds like I'm making a chemical compound. Hm. Put together 'all of the relevant findings in the text.' How can I do this?" The student resumed writing, but his method was to summarize.

As a means of teaching critical thinking skills, Marilla Svinicki gave a useful and stimulating overview of the cognitive apprenticeship method in her workshop for an IDEA Active Learning Seminar.

Faculty who are creating assignments and want them to stimulate critical thinking might find Wolcott and Lynch's "Task Prompts for Different Levels in 'Steps for Better Thinking,'" (available at www.wolcottlynch.com) helpful. For each of the four steps in critical thinking, Wolcott and Lynch give several phrases that lead students to think and write in that manner.

5. Consider specifying an audience for the paper that's someone other than you, the professor. Several guides to teaching critical thinking recommend having students write for another, lower-level student or for a reasonably informed layperson—someone who know less about the topic than the student does. The rationale is that students will feel freer to write naturally and will emphasize understanding of the topic rather than presenting facts. A. J. Cohen and J Spencer, two economics professors, asked students why their term papers didn't contain any arguments. Students replied, "How can you expect an undergraduate to say anything original?" and "How can I (the novice student) tell you (the expert instructor) anything you don't already know?" (quoted in Bean, 199).

6. *Require students to use "highly relevant" or "excellent" information sources, and enforce this expectation.* If your assignment instructions simply

state the number of sources and/or types of sources for students to use, they'll focus on that requirement (and other mechanics). They'll feel they've "met their end of the bargain" and should get a good grade simply for complying with your format requirements. Barbara Valentine's 2001 article in *Journal of Academic Librarianship* provides useful insight, based on two research studies, into student expectations regarding grades versus amount of effort on research papers.

Librarians observe that many students have the tendency to choose the first few sources that are full text, or that the library owns, or that have words from their topic in the title—from the first one or two screens of a database search. They may not know database search techniques beyond the most basic, and they may also not know the many tips and clues that can be used to judge the relevance or validity of a source based on information in the citation, abstract, and other parts of the database record.

Insisting that students meet the criteria of using "excellent" or "highly relevant" sources, and providing instruction for them to learn how to do so, will help them become information literate.

7. *Consider having students respond to a thesis, especially if one goal of the assignment is developing critical thinking skills.* If an assignment includes no specifications for structure of the writing (for instance, if it simply says, "write a 3-5 page paper on [topic]"), or if there is no guidance on how students should process the information they gather (they aren't asked to compare and contrast, analyze, or choose the best option), students will resort to a writing structure to which they're accustomed. John Bean lists three of these: "all about," or encyclopedic order (22-23), "and then" or chronological order (20-22), and "data dumping"—a random string of paraphrases and quotations (23-24). "Data dumping" is understandable in assignments that require outside sources but provide no focus. If students haven't successfully narrowed the topic, or if the topic has been heavily written about, database searches may retrieve hundreds of results. Without a thesis to respond to or an aspect of the topic to focus on, students have no mechanism for selecting a few sources from among these long lists. Similarly, they have no way of deciding which facts and ideas to cull from their outside sources.

Thus, rather than having students write a paper on "something that interests them" concerning mental disorders, have them write about a topic such as "the effectiveness of electroconvulsive therapy for depression or chemical treatments for schizophrenia."

Some assignments may not easily lend themselves to responding to a thesis. Here are some alternatives used by faculty at Appalachian State:

*A Recreation Management professor was getting poor results on 10-12 page research papers outlining the characteristics of a particular industry in commercial recreation. The professor wanted to retain several sections of the research paper that required gathering of factual data but still get students to select and integrate information to determine what issues and trends the industry is facing. We shortened the assignment considerably and provided more structure for students by making it into an article for a commercial recreation encyclopedia, borrowing from the article layout and author's instructions of Salem Press encyclopedias.

*A history professor requires freshmen to prepare a 30-50 item annotated bibliography on one of the *Time* "Top 100 Personalities of the 20th Century." He is able to focus students' choices of sources by giving them types of sources that must be used and telling them to choose 30-50 "excellent" sources from among many more that are available. He also requires that the sources chosen justify the person's inclusion in the *Time* 100 list. Thus, students know that each annotation must mention some recognition or achievement that justifies this status.

8. *Consider giving students a controlled list of topics.* All too often, librarians witness students struggling with choice of a topic—spending far more of their time and energy at this stage than is warranted and, consequently, probably spending less on choosing good sources, developing their ideas, and revising their writing than is needed. For many students, the freedom to choose a topic that interests them is in actuality a burden. They may not know enough about the subject area to choose a workable or suitably focused topic. They may worry excessively about "what the professor wants," whether there are enough sources (preferably full text) available, whether the topic is easy enough, or whether they can adapt a paper they have written about in the past. They may end up submitting to the professor a topic that is not workable for them and, due to procrastination, may not make that discovery until it's so close to the due date that they are ashamed to ask for help choosing a new topic.

Providing students with a list of topics lets you give them additional exposure to important course concepts; cuts down on wasted student effort and needless procrastination at this stage of the project; and allows you, with the help of librarians, to check on whether the library's holdings are adequate and at a suitable level to support the topics. All these advantages lead to students having a positive experience with the library research aspects of the

—GLENN ELLEN STARR STILLING—

assignment. To pique students' interest in the topics, you could provide a brief annotation with each one and even list a key source they could read to help them decide whether to commit to the topic. Students could also elect to choose their own topic, subject to your approval.

9. *To increase student mastery of the subject matter and transformation or integration of ideas from outside sources, design the assignment to require use of several different sources.* Jennifer Wiley reports on two experiments with undergraduate students that required them to write, using documents they read first, about why Ireland's population changed between 1846 and 1850. Half wrote from documents presented in a Web-like format (looking like separate books on a bookshelf); the other half received the exact same information but presented as one textbook chapter. Students were also instructed to write a narrative, a summary, an explanation, or an argument. Students writing from the Web-like sources had a greater proportion of **transformed** (rather than borrowed or added) sentences than those writing from the textbook chapter. Students who wrote an argument wrote more transformed, integrated, and causal essays when using Web-like sources than those using the textbook chapter. Students writing arguments performed better on exercises requiring the verification of inferences and the identification of principles related to the topic of the source materials.

Wiley concluded that if we want students to gain a deeper understanding of subject matter, the writing assignment must require knowledge-transforming rather than knowledge-telling. To bring about knowledge-transforming, (1) require students to use a variety of sources, rather than just one and (2) structure the task so that students must present their own "take" on the information they read. There also seems to be something special about asking for an "argument," rather than a summary, narrative, or explanation.

10. *Provide a way for students to learn the library skills needed to complete the assignment.* Even if you think the skills required are simple, students may not know how to find the information they need and may not be willing to ask you or librarians for help.

Librarians can offer assistance in a variety of ways, and we can match the assistance we provide with the time constraints of your course. If you don't have time for us to instruct the students in the library during a class period, we could develop a handout or Web page to support your assignment. You could also refer students to our reference desk, email reference, or RAP session (one-on-one assistance by appointment) services.

When we work with your students during a class period in our computer classroom, we're careful to teach research skills in a way that is generalizable and transferable to other classes and other assignments.

[If enough time remains, participants look over and discuss the model assignments provided as handouts (Appendices 2A-D). The workshop concludes with a third short writing exercise.]

Using the Concepts and Materials with Faculty

Besides presenting these ideas in faculty development workshops open to faculty across campus, librarians might shorten or adapt them for specific faculty audiences. Appalachian State has used the ideas in the library's segment of the annual campus workshop for distance learning faculty and plans to use them in the annual training sessions for faculty who teach freshman seminar. Librarians can also use these ideas in working one-on-one with faculty—especially if they indicate dissatisfaction with their current assignment or interest in trying something new.

For my first workshop, held in 1993, I prepared an extensive annotated bibliography of published writings on creative assignments, with a subject index, so that faculty could see what assignments in their own disciplines had been written about. I found, however, that some of the assignments faculty tried and liked best were adapted from other disciplines.

Appendix 1

A selective bibliography of sources consulted
for the "Beyond the Research Paper" workshop

• Barrowman, Carole E. "Improving teaching and learning effectiveness by defining expectations." In: *Preparing competent college graduates: setting new and higher expectations for student learning*. Ed. Elizabeth A. Jones. (New directions for higher education, no. 96) San Francisco: Jossey-Bass, 1996. Pages 103-114. Belk Library LB 2331.72 .N48 no. 96 [Explains how Alverno College has defined its expectations of students, beginning institution-wide with eight abilities, then going to department-level student outcomes. Gives examples of assignments which ". . . bring the student as close as possible to a situation in which she will be using her learning in life beyond the classroom" (p 108). The two stimulating case study assignments (one in English, one in history) ask students to assume a persona. Student evaluation criteria are also touched on.]

• Bean, John C. *Engaging ideas: the professor's guide to integrating writing, critical thinking, and active learning in the classroom*. San Francisco: Jossey Bass, 1996. ASU Main Stacks PE 1404 .B36 1996

• Bean, John C.; Dean Drenk; and F. D. Lee. "Microtheme strategies for developing cognitive skills." In: *Teaching writing in all disciplines*. Ed. C. W. Griffin. (New directions for teaching and learning, 12) San Francisco: Jossey-Bass, 1982. pp. 27-38. [A more general elaboration of micro themes. Discusses two types: summary (useful for summarizing journal articles on the same topic but showing divergent points of view) and thesis-support (more details on Drenk's micro themes for finance).]

• Blakey, George T. "Breathing new life into research papers." *College Teaching* 45.1 (Winter 1997): 3 (4 pages). Full text available in the Academic Search Elite database. [Describes an assignment in which students select the 10 most important events from 1945.]

• Boice, Robert. "Adam Smith's rules for writers." In: *The politics and processes of scholarship*. Ed. Joseph M. Moxley and Lagretta T. Lenker. Westport, CT: Greenwood, 1995. [This chapter provides a concise introduction to Boice's methods. Those who want more detail can consult some of his other works, including *How writers journey to comfort and fluency* (Praeger, 1994) and *Advice for new faculty members: nihil nimus* (Allyn and Bacon, 2000).]

• Browne, M. Neil, and Stuart M. Keeley. *Asking the right questions: a guide to critical thinking*. 4th ed. Englewood Cliffs, NJ: Prentice-Hall, 1994. [A 5th edition is now available.]

• Drenk, Dean. "Teaching finance through teaching writing." In: *Teaching writing in all disciplines*. Ed. C. W. Griffin. (New directions for teaching and learning, 12) San Francisco: Jossey-Bass, 1982. Pp. 53-58. [On the thesis-support micro theme.]

• Flower, Linda. "The role of task representation in reading-to-write." In: *Reading-to-write: exploring a cognitive and social process*. Ed. Linda Flower. New York: Oxford UP, 1990. Pages 35-75. Belk Library PE 1404 .R375 1990

• Halpern, Diane F. "The war of the worlds: when students' conceptual understanding clashes with their professors'." *Chronicle of Higher Education* 14 March 1997, pp. 84-85.

• Hardesty, Larry, ed. *Bibliographic instruction in practice: a tribute to the legacy of Evan Ira Farber*. Ann Arbor: Pierian Press, 1993. [Farber, longtime director of the library at Earlham College, developed a nationally recognized model for integration of library skills into the college curriculum. These essays describe Farber's philosophy and how it has been realized at Earlham. They also explain various Earlham and Eckerd College departments' approaches and assignments (biology, English, foreign policy, sociology, and psychology). In addition, Farber's chapter, "Alternatives to the term paper," summarizes 27 different assignments dealing with psychology of women, psychological processes, children's literature, Japanese culture, Renaissance and Baroque Europe, Shakespeare, U. S. history, animal behavior, the plant kingdom, human biology, American government, American foreign policy, terrorism, philosophy, art history, international relations, economics, history of theater, and 20th-century art.]

● Janssen, Tracy, and John S. Carton. "The effects of locus of control and task difficulty on procrastination." *Journal of Genetic Psychology* 160.4 (Dec. 1999): 436-442.

● Kantz, Margaret. "Shirley and the Battle of Agincourt: Why it is so hard for students to write persuasive researched analyses." (Center for the Study of Writing. Occasional Paper no. 14) University of California at Berkeley and Carnegie Mellon University. November, 1989. ERIC ED 312 669. 20 pages. Belk Library—Microforms. [This useful analysis of student writing strategies, based on rhetoric and composition theory, has much to offer concerning student assumptions about and difficulties with the researched writing assignment. The main example is Shirley, a hypothetical student who is a composite of many students, and student difficulties, the author has come across as a composition teacher. In writing her paper on the Battle of Agincourt, Shirley reads her source texts as narratives and as "the truth" and writes her paper as a narrative, rather than (as the assignment required) a researched argument. Kantz makes clear the difficulties students have in reading, or thinking about, their sources in a rhetorical context; indeed, they may never have been taught to do so. Other difficulties students have with research papers—cognitive overload, the demands of multiple tasks the papers require, and their own expectations that they can produce the paper in a single draft—are discussed. Kantz uses and adapts Kinneavy's triangular diagram of the rhetorical situation, and ideas from Haas and Flower (1988), to create heuristics that can help students think rhetorically.]

● Keeley, Stuart M. "Coping with student resistance to critical thinking: what the psychotherapy literature can tell us." *College Teaching* 43.4 (Fall 1995): 140 (6 pages). Full-text available in the Academic Search Elite database. [Gives very perceptive advice, comparing student resistance to challenging critical thinking class discussions and assignments to client resistance to a counselor's "homework assignments." Includes useful steps for managing critical thinking assignments.]

● Keeley, Stuart, and M. Neil Browne. "Assignments that encourage critical thinking." *Journal of Professional Studies* 12 (Winter 1998): 2-11. [Advocates using writing assignments to enable students to practice critical thinking skills, since in-class time is limited and all course objectives cannot be met there. To be effective, however, such assignments must explicitly address the attitudes and skills that comprise critical thinking. If the assignment simply asks students to "critically evaluate" a work or idea, they won't be able to comply unless they know what the phrase means and have been shown how to do so. The article explains eight general assignment strategies that can help develop students' critical thinking, then describes the authors' taxonomy of nine questions for critical thinking, giving assignment ideas that utilize each question. Several of the ideas can be adapted or expanded to include library skills.]

● Longrie, Michael. "Billy Joel's history lesson." *College Teaching* 45.4 (Fall 1997): 147 (3 pages). Full text available in the Academic Search Elite database. [Describes the assignment in which students research historical and cultural allusions prior to 1965 in Billy Joel's song, "We didn't start the fire," then argue for people and events he should include if he rewrites the song to include their generation.]

● Lowman, Joseph. "Assignments that promote and integrate learning." In *Teaching on solid ground: using scholarship to improve practice*. Ed. Robert J. Menges, Maryellen Weimer, and associates. San Francisco: Jossey-Bass, 1996. Pages 203-231. Belk Library LB 2331 .T418 1996 [This useful chapter begins by making distinctions between what is best accomplished during class time (given the importance of addressing higher-order educational objectives rather than transferring information) and what can be done through assignments and homework. Lowman also discusses valuable ways to motivate students to devote their best efforts to assignments; he then offers suggestions on effective reading, writing, problem-solving, and observational or hands-on assignments. He gives succinct advice on evaluating written assignments.]

● Lutzker, Marilyn. *Research projects for college students: what to write across the curriculum*. New York: Greenwood, 1998.

● Lynch, Cindy L., and Susan K. Walcott. "Helping your students develop critical thinking skills." IDEA Paper no. 37. Manhattan, Kansas: The IDEA Center, October 2001. 6 pages.

http://www.idea.ksu.edu/pdf/Idea_Paper_37.pdf [Like all the IDEA Papers (many available as PDF files at http://www.idea.ksu.edu/products/Papers.html), this one is an extremely useful, concise but detailed, research-based introduction to its topic. Lynch and Walcott summarize their developmentally grounded Steps for Better Thinking, which faculty can use to help students learn to think about open-ended problems. Figure 3, "Task prompts for the four different levels in Steps for Better Thinking,'" shows a number of phrases and sentence starters that faculty can use as they design writing assignments that will teach critical thinking. It is included with the workshop handouts.]

• Meyers, Chet. *Teaching students to think critically: a guide for faculty in all disciplines.* San Francisco: Jossey Bass, 1986. Main Stacks LB 1590.3 .M49 [Argues that developing critical thinking skills, more than transmitting facts, should be our primary goal as educators. Critical thinking skills must be taught and exercised in all courses and must be taught "stepwise." Explains how to integrate critical thinking skills into courses by balancing lecture with interaction and by using analogy, metaphor, and discussion. Chapter 6, "Developing Effective Writing Assignments," is especially helpful. Meyers presents three characteristics of effective written assignments and discusses five types which develop critical thinking skills.]

• Parker-Gibson, Necia. "Library assignments: challenges that students face and how to help." *College Teaching* 49.2 (Spring 2001): p. 65 (6 pages). Full text in EBSCOhost Academic Search Elite database. [This article provides a helpful overview of factors that motivate students to perform on library-related assignments; students' natural inclinations regarding library research—including the Principle of Least Effort—and suggestions for creating effective assignments. The author also discusses assignment criteria <u>not</u> to use; she explains the problems these criteria cause for students as well as librarians.]

• Svinicki, Marilla. "The cognitive apprenticeship model." Presented at IDEA Active Learning Seminar, San Antonio, TX, 24 February 1999. Svinicki's outline of the model was adapted from: Collins, A., et al. "Cognitive apprenticeship: teaching the crafts of reading, writing, and mathematics." In: Resnick, L., ed. *Knowing, learning, and instruction: essays in honor of Robert Glaser.* Hillsdale, NJ: Lawrence Erlbaum Associates, 1989.

• Tigner, Robert B. "Putting memory research to good use: hints from cognitive psychology." *College Teaching* 47.4 (Fall 1999): 149 (4 pages). Full text available in the Academic Search Elite database.

• Valentine, Barbara. "The legitimate effort in research papers: student commitment versus faculty expectations." *Journal of academic librarianship* 27.2 (March 2001): page 107 (9 pages). Full text Full text available in the Academic Search Elite database. [This article is based on two research studies involving interviews with students working on research papers. Many useful observations are presented. They include the findings that students are motivated primarily by grades, so they devote much of their energy to trying to discern what the professor wants (WTPW); they tend to use the most familiar and (for them) the easiest information sources (the Web, full text articles, or databases they've searched before); generally, they'll use new library research techniques only if the professor requires it; and they are reluctant to ask the professor or librarians for help, turning instead to friends, relatives, or their own ideas. Thus, they often don't find the best information for their projects—but most of them feel that their grades are acceptable for the amount of effort they expend on a paper.]

• Walvoord, Barbara E., and Virginia Johnson Anderson. "Making assignments worth grading." In: *Effective grading: a tool for learning and assessment.* San Francisco: Jossey-Bass, 1998. Pages 17-42. Belk Library LB 2368 .W35 [Because the focus of the book is on grading, Walvoord begins this useful chapter with the recommendation that faculty " . . . plan your grading from the first moment you begin planning the course" (p. 17). The recommended steps in planning the course so that assignments will be effective are: "(1) Begin by considering what you want your students to learn; (2) Select tests and assignments that both teach and test the learning you value most; (3) Construct a course outline that shows the nature and sequence of major tests and assignments; (4) Check that the tests and assignments fit your learning goals and are feasible in terms of workload; (5) Collaborate with your students to set and achieve goals; (6) give students explicit directions for their assignments" (pp. 17-18). Each of these suggestions is discussed in detail, with examples and with lists of sources for further reading. In Suggestion 4, "Check tests and assignments for fit and feasibility," Walvoord gives stimulating examples of how a sociology professor, a biology professor, and a business management professor adapted assignments to better fit course goals. Appendix B is a comprehensive list of "Types of assignments and tests" (pages 193-195). Although I dislike some of the modifications to library-related assignments that de-emphasize or eliminate the research components, I find the other suggestions in this chapter extremely helpful.]

- Wiley, Jennifer. "Constructing arguments from multiple sources: tasks that promote understanding and not just memory for text" *Journal of educational psychology* 91.2 (1999): 301-311. [Reports results of two experiments in which undergraduate students wrote about Ireland between 1800 and 1850. Half of the students used eight separate source documents in a Web-like environment (each document was presented as a book on a bookshelf). The other half received the exact same information, but it was presented as one textbook chapter, adding only an introductory paragraph and some transitional phrases. Students were told to write a narrative, a summary, an explanation, or an argument about what caused significant changes in Ireland's population between 1846 and 1850. The results of these experiments have valuable implications for the construction of research-based writing assignments.]

Other ways to find examples of writing / library research assignments:

- Glenn Ellen's 1993 annotated bibliography, which lists 71 sources (some discussing one assignment, some several)--with a subject index for locating assignments by content area or discipline.
- *The Teaching Professor*, a newsletter which can be read in Belk Library or at the Hubbard Center.
- A search of the ERIC database. Search strategy (substitute your discipline for biology):
  biology and (assignment* or research papers student or library)
- *College Teaching*. Can be read in print on the Periodicals floor of Belk Library, or can be browsed or searched, full text, in the EBSCOhost Academic Search Elite database
- Library / information science journals, such as *Research Strategies*

Glenn Ellen Starr Stilling
Belk Library
Appalachian State University
Boone, NC 28608
Last updated: 1 March 2002

Appendix 2: Infomercials

You will present a minimum of four two-minute oral reports (that's the equivalent of one page, typed, double-spaced—and you can get a great deal of information into that space!) either as an independent researcher or as part of a research team of two persons. Each report will enlighten the class on some aspect of your "area of specialization" as it illuminates the play currently under discussion—in other words, your report will be in the nature of a detailed annotation in a critical edition of a play.

A.   At the beginning of the term, you will sign up for an area of expertise which will be your bailiwick for the entire semester—all of your reports will focus in some   way on the broad subject of your area.

B.   Each report must be accompanied by a bibliography (copy for each class   member) of sources from which your information comes.

C.   Each report must explain the significance of some reference in the play currently under discussion. Reports must get right to the point and stay focused.

D.   To ensure that you stay within the time limit, here are some suggestions:
   1)   Write what you have to say, practice reading it ten times, and more or less read it to the class.
   2)   Resist the urge to compare your findings to life today (sure, Charles II and Bill Clinton probably have some similarities, but that's not really relevant to understanding period drama!)
   3)   Use handouts for material that you can't cover within the time limit, and don't read your handouts to the class—they can read!

E.   The grade for each report will come for two sources:
   1)   Content: How well do you describe the importance of your information to an understanding of a specific play? How well have you selected the focus of your report (let's face it, some facts really are more significant than others)? How well have you organized your information?
   2)   Delivery: You will be rated on intelligibility, pace, eye contact, volume and vocal emphasis, and adherence to time constraints (the delivery grade will be dropped with each half minute over the limit). You will get a written evaluation after each report so that you can build on what you do well and improve your weak points.

F.   Your grade for this assignment will come for two evaluations: qualitative and quantitative

   1)   Quantitative: the minimum number of oral reports is four (4)—that number is worth a grade of D. You don't have to do a report for every play on the reading list. The upper limit for reports is nine (9). Grade assignments are as follows:
   9 reports: A   6 reports: B
   8 reports: A-   5 reports: C
   7 reports: B+   4 reports: D

   2)   Qualitative: The qualitative grade will be the average of the individual grades for your reports (see E above). Qualitative and quantitative grades will be averaged to produce a single grade which accounts for 20% of your final course grade.

From the syllabus of Dr. Edelma Huntley (Appalachian State University, Boone, NC) for English 4710, Advanced Studies in Women and Literature, focusing on female dramatists from the Restoration through the Eighteenth Century

Appendix 2A: Infomercials

You will present a minimum of four two-minute oral reports (that's the equivalent of one page, typed, double-spaced—and you can get a great deal of information into that space!) either as an independent researcher or as part of a research team of two persons. Each report will enlighten the class on some aspect of your "area of specialization" as it illuminates the play currently under discussion—in other words, your report will be in the nature of a detailed annotation in a critical edition of a play.

A.   At the beginning of the term, you will sign up for an area of expertise which will be your bailiwick for the entire semester—all of your reports will focus in some way on the broad subject of your area.
B.   Each report must be accompanied by a bibliography (copy for each class member) of sources from which your information comes.
C.   Each report must explain the significance of some reference in the play currently under discussion. Reports must get right to the point and stay focused.
D.   To ensure that you stay within the time limit, here are some suggestions:
1) Write what you have to say, practice reading it ten times, and more or less read it to the class.
2) Resist the urge to compare your findings to life today (sure, Charles II and Bill Clinton probably have some similarities, but that's not really relevant to understanding period drama!)
3) Use handouts for material that you can't cover within the time limit, and don't read your handouts to the class—they can read!

E.   The grade for each report will come for two sources:
1) Content: How well do you describe the importance of your information to an understanding of a specific play? How well have you selected the focus of your report (let's face it, some facts really are more significant than others)? How well have you organized your information?
2) Delivery: You will be rated on intelligibility, pace, eye contact, volume and vocal emphasis, and adherence to time constraints (the delivery grade will be dropped with each half minute over the limit). You will get a written evaluation after each report so that you can build on what you do well and improve your weak points.

F.   Your grade for this assignment will come for two evaluations: qualitative and quantitative.
1) Quantitative: the minimum number of oral reports is four (4)—that number is worth a grade of D. You don't have to do a report for every play on the reading list. The upper limit for reports is nine (9). Grade assignments are as follows:
      9 reports: A
      8 reports: A-
      7 reports: B+
      6 reports: B
      5 reports: C
      4 reports: D
2) Qualitative: The qualitative grade will be the average of the individual grades for your reports (see E above). Qualitative and quantitative grades will be averaged to produce a single grade which accounts for 20% of your final course grade.

From the syllabus of Dr. Edelma Huntley (Appalachian State University, Boone, NC) for English 4710, Advanced Studies in Women and Literature, focusing on female dramatists from the Restoration through the Eighteenth Century. Used with permission.

Appendix 2B: Responsible Patienthcod

RESPONSIBLE PATIENTHOOD PAPER

Sara Penhale

Responsible Patienthood Paper

Imagine that you or a friend or family member has been diagnosed with one of the following conditions, and that the accompanying treatment has been prescribed or at least suggested (see "Diagnosed Conditions and Prescribed Treatments" list). As a responsible patient, you seek to investigate the nature of the condition and the effectiveness of the treatment. A thorough search in the Science Library should provide you with this information.

Consult "Library Resources on Medical Topics," which follows in this manual.

Prepare a three- to four-page word-processed, double-spaced essay which covers:

1. a description of the condition and its symptoms,

2. the etiology (cause) of the condition,

3. the prognosis (outcome) of the condition,

4. evidence of the effectiveness of the prescribed or suggested treatment, its side effects, and contra-indications (conditions under which it should be not used), and

5. if you do not recommend the prescribed or suggested treatment, a comparison of the relative effectiveness of an alternate treatment that you do recommend.

Suggestion: The paper need not go into the physiological mechanism of action of the treatment. Otherwise mode of action could take a considerable portion of the essay and preempt space that should be used for iteration of the evidence of effectiveness, contra-indication, and the justification of your recommendation, which are central to the assignment. Moreover, mode of action is likely to involve subject matter beyond the scope of this course.

Organize your paper for clarity of expression directed at a lay audience with no prior knowledge of the disease or of human biology. Emphasize numerical evidence and statistical significance. Deduce conclusions from the evidence indicating the specific lines of reasoning you employed. For example:

Three hundred patients who had been diagnosed with the disease by a team of physicians having nothing to do with this study were divided into two groups matched for people with the same severity of symptoms. A double blind study of the treatment was conducted as follows: One group was given pink pills and the other group was given blue pills. Only after evaluation and analysis of results was it disclosed that the pink pills contained drug xxx and the blue pills contained a placebo. After the treatment the pink group had significantly fewer symptoms of the disease ($p < .01$); however they experienced a marked loss of memory when compared to the blue group on a conventional memory management scale ($p < .001$) (Jones, 1989). Considering the statistically significant effect of the drug on the disease and because of the seriousness of the disease I would (or would not) recommend the pink treatment despite (or because of) its consequences of loss of memory. Furthermore... [go on with your personal justification and recommendation].

Cite at least six sources, three of which must be primary sources. In the text of your paper, cite the sources of your information and list the sources you cited in a "Literature Cited" section at the end of the paper. Refer to "Format for Citing References" for specific directions.

Appendix 2C: Encyclopedia of Commercial Recreation

Article specifications

Length: 2000 words. This comes out to around 5 1/2 pages, double-spaced, in 10 point font. You may go 5% over or under.

Sections of the article are listed below. Use bold type for the section headings.

- **Title:** Name of the industry (example: Cruise lines)

- **SIC and NAICS codes**

- **Definition** (200 words)
What is done in the industry? Are there major areas of the country in which it is focused? What are some of the products and equipment connected with it? Name two to five major companies in the industry.

- **Historical overview** (500 words)
If you are unable to find this information for the industry as a whole, use historical information on the major companies.

- **Discussion** (1,000 words)
Mention annual sales (for the industry as a whole or, if this is not available, for the major companies) for the last three years.
Discuss issues and trends connected with the industry. Include any of the following which seem important: demographics of consumers; new products and services; legislation; competition from other countries; and predictions that are being made regarding the industry.

- **Resources** (75 words)
List any important associations, publications (such as trade journals), or Web sites.

- **Bibliography** (225 words)
Provide citations, with brief annotations, for five to seven sources that you used to compile this article and recommend that readers consult for additional information.

Glenn Ellen Starr Stilling
Belk Library
Appalachian State University
Boone, NC 28608
September 1, 1998

Appendix 2D: Annotated Bibliography

continued from previous page

Soulé: Since Family Science comprises a wide range of topics, students are free to choose what truly interests them. The topics can be personal in nature, and many students have clarified their own life experiences through reading the current research. For instance, a student with attention deficit hyperactivity disorder annotated articles on gender differences in reading and behavior among ADHD children. Students of all ages have appreciated using the assignment to explore life stages.

T&LA: Why use this assignment instead of the research paper?

Soulé: Besides the library skills, critical thinking, and writing concisely, I think the strength of this assignment lies in the fact that feedback can be provided quickly and efficiently. The closer the feedback occurs to the time the assignment was completed, the better. There is the opportunity to make changes, to learn one more step in the critical thinking process.

Starr: I believe that, like writing and critical thinking, library skills need to be practiced and built upon in nearly every course. I'm also aware of the time and effort required to write and grade research papers. The efficiency of this assignment is an excellent alternative for both teacher and student. It gives first- and second-year students much more guidance in choosing suitable library materials on their topic. Students don't experience the frustration of "drowning in a sea of information" that I often see when they're trying to select materials for a research paper on a topic that has been heavily written about or that they don't understand very well.

T&LA: What are the advantages of your collaboration?

Starr: I appreciate the prominence Carol gives to the assignment itself and to the library session. Carol gives the assignment a weight of 25% in her grading for the course, which motivates students to do good work. The library session is also supported in that students receive points for attending it and more points for completing the library worksheet.

Soulé: Meeting with Glenn Ellen is important for the students because she introduces them to library resources that they might not know about. It also implies that there is some kind of agreement about how to "do the library thing." Students see that the librarian and instructor get along with each other—the atmosphere is one of cooperation in learning. And we minimize the frustration students would feel if they were not equipped with the proper language and skills to complete an assignment. Seeing how the assignment has developed and evolved over the past four years has been satisfying, and it continues to improve as Glenn Ellen and I share our thoughts about teaching and learning.

T&LA: How could the assignment be adapted for other courses?

Soulé: For Freshman Seminar I emphasize the differences between magazine articles and journal articles. The topics students choose in that course focus on the college experience—ranging from roommate relationships to alcohol use to study skills. I spend more time with this class in the library, helping students learn to use the databases and locate periodicals.

Starr: The assignment could work with journals in most any discipline—especially where the articles are research-based. The "Points to Consider" handout could be expanded to include other questions specific to the topic or discipline. For third- and fourth-year students, the number of articles annotated could be increased. The assignment would meet even more learning objectives if students made oral reports on the articles they read. It would expand coverage of important course topics if each student were assigned a different topic and then students got copies of each others' bibliographies.

WORKS CITED

[1] Engeldinger, Eugene. "Bibliographic Instruction and Critical Thinking: The Contribution of the Annotated Bibliography." RQ 28 (Winter 1988): 195-202.

[2] Meyers, Chet. Teaching Students to Think Critically. San Francisco: Jossey-Bass, 1986.

[3] Browne, M. Neil, and Stuart M. Keeley. Asking the Right Questions: A Guide to Critical Thinking. 4th ed. Englewood Cliffs, NJ: Prentice-Hall, 1994.

APPENDIX 1
PREPARING AN ANNOTATION: POINTS TO CONSIDER

In an annotated bibliography, the annotation follows the reference (or citation) for the article. An annotated bibliography could include books, journal articles, magazine articles, newspaper articles, essays, book chapters, films, etc. This handout refers to journal articles, since your assignment is to use journal articles only. The annotation's purpose is to describe the article in enough detail so that the reader can decide whether or not to read the article. Any of the following points could be addressed in an annotation; there will not be room to address all of them. As you read an article, you can decide which points are most important, or most useful, for that particular article.

AUTHOR
What do you know, or what can you find out, about the author(s)? What is the author's occupation, position, academic background, prior publishing experience, etc? Is the author qualified to write on the topic addressed in this article?

PURPOSE
What was the purpose for writing the article, or doing the research described in the article? Is the purpose specifically explained? Is a certain message conveyed in the article?

INTENDED AUDIENCE
To whom is the author speaking? Is the article intended for the general public, scholars in the same

discipline as the author, students, teachers, professionals, or a variety of audiences? Does the author's writing style, vocabulary, or arrangement of the article reflect a particular audience?

AUTHOR BIAS

Can you tell if the author has a bias, or perhaps makes assumptions in the article's arguments or research? What are these assumptions?

INFORMATION SOURCE

How was the information or data in the article obtained? Is the information based on a laboratory experiment, a questionnaire, personal interviews, observation, standardized tests, library research, or a combination of several of these methods?

AUTHOR CONCLUSION

What conclusions does the author make? Are they specifically stated, or are they implied?

CONCLUSION JUSTIFICATION

Are the author's conclusions justified by the research conducted or by the other information presented in the article? Does the author have any biases that skew the conclusions?

RELATIONSHIP TO OTHER WORKS

How does this article compare to other articles on the same topic? Do the conclusions agree with, or differ from, established scholarship, government policy, or conventional wisdom on the topic? Does the author mention other studies or published sources that agree or disagree with his/her point

of view? Is the information presented primarily <u>for</u> or <u>against</u> the author's point of view?

SIGNIFICANT ATTACHMENTS

Does the article include graphs, tables, photographs, bibliographies, questionnaires, tests, or other documents? If so, do the attachments enhance the article? If not, do you feel the article <u>should have</u> included such attachments?

■ *This handout is based on a handout called "Critical Evaluation Exercise," prepared by Eugene Engeldinger, Library Director; Ruthrauff Library, Carthage College, Kenosha, WI 53140-1930*

APPENDIX 2
EVALUATION SHEET FOR ARTICLE ANNOTATIONS

For this assignment you will select a topic related to Family Science and prepare three article annotations on that topic. You should choose three professional, research-based articles to review. The articles may come from different journals or the same journal. The annotations must be typed and proofread.

Following the list below, your annotation should include information for items 1, 2, 3, 4, and 5. Then select **one** additional criterion—either 6, 7, 8, or 9—to address.

CRITERIA:

1. Selection (article research-based, citation complete) .... 10 pts.
2. Abstract .... 10 pts.
   (Note: Students turn in an abstract obtained from a database search, from the article itself, or that they have written themselves.)
3. Author .... 10 pts.
4. Purpose .... 10 pts.
5. Intended audience .... 10 pts.
   And **one** of the following (worth 50 pts.):
6. Author bias .... (50 pts.)
7. Justification of conclusion .... (50 pts.)
8. Relationship to other works .... (50 pts.)
9. Theory and/or perspective .... (50 pts.)
   (identify; examples: family systems, family development, multicultural, feminist)

_____

Total = 100 pts.

EVALUATION CHART FOR ANNOTATIONS:

1. Selection .... _____/10
2. Abstract .... _____/10
3. Author .... _____/10
4. Purpose .... _____/10
5. Intended audience .... _____/10
6. Author bias, **or** justification of conclusion, or relationship to other works, **or** theory and/or perspective .... _____/50

Total: _____/100 ■

From: Soule, Carol, and Glenn Ellen Starr. "The annotated bibliography assignment: improving students' skills in library use, critical thinking, and course content." <u>Teaching and learning at Appalachian</u> **2 (1997/1998): 12-15. Reproduced with permission.**

Bringing "Law and Order" into the Library: Evidence-Based Inquiry in Information Literacy Instruction at the Wheelock College Library

Esme DeVault, Amanda Gluibizzi, and **Ann Glannon**

Introduction

Over the course of the past five years, the Wheelock College Library has developed an Information Literacy program that is grounded in constructivist learning principles, literacy theory and strategy development, and elements of the backward design model as described by Grant Wiggins and Jay McTighe in their work *Understanding by Design*. The end-goals of the program as it has evolved are to improve students' critical thinking skills, to align the library's instruction with the ACRL *Information Literacy Competency Standards for Higher Education (2000)*, and to incorporate assessment tools and measurements throughout the curriculum.

To this end, Information Literacy components have been placed throughout the four-year undergraduate curriculum at Wheelock, across subject areas and majors, as well as in the graduate school programs. Undergraduates pass through a highly structured program in which they receive uniform instruction in two required first-year courses, one required second-year course, a variety of subject-specific third-year courses, and finally, in the seminar or "capstone" final year courses. This variety of

DeVault is a Reference and Information Services Librarian; *Gluibizzi* is the Electronic/Access services Librarian, and *Glannon* is the Curriculum Resources Librarian at Wheelock College, Boston, MA.

interactions is intended to be student-centered in its presentation and involve active learning to the greatest degree possible. This string of interactions also includes graded assignments, individual research appointments, hands-on "laboratory" sessions, as well as a series of workshops equal to 10 percent of the students' final English grade in their first year.

This framework was designed utilizing the notion that identifying critical concepts and guiding questions first, before creating lesson plans and activities, was crucial to developing a meaningful learning experience for the students and for reaching the higher levels of critical inquiry to which the ACRL Information Literacy Competency Standards aspire. In creating this curriculum, we constantly asked ourselves, "What are the one or two things that we really want the students to have learned from this experience?" and "Do these activities really address the core concepts we are trying to teach?" Battling the desire to fall back on traditional activities and prior experiences that seemed to have worked (to one degree or another) is not always easy; backwards curriculum design is at best painful, even as the resulting outcomes are much richer and more meaningful than the typical "how do I fill this hour time slot" library instruction of the past. The interesting thing is that this type of design often forces the students to experience a similar phenomenon (pain with eventual understanding) that has much greater staying power than the point and click learning of recent years.

The entire process is founded on inquiry-based instruction models that utilize a guiding question or focus question as the center of the learner's experience. Students are first asked to identify prior knowledge that will aid them in navigating new waters of discovery. The intent is not to make the student merely feel comfortable with what is about to happen, but rather to create a space in which the student will be actively engaged in constructing a new sphere of knowledge by using both what they know and new ideas (and inputs) that they will uncover. The instructor presents the student with a series of "crises" or opportunities for which the students will use their own prior knowledge, peer knowledge, and the instructor's assistance as scaffolds for reaching new levels of understanding. All interactions place an emphasis on evaluation, reflection and revision; students are not simply asked to carry out tasks, but rather are forced to think about each step of the process, assess what they find, and describe what they might have done differently. In this way, students are also providing much useful assessment information for the instructors as well as for themselves, as these reflections are collected for additional analysis so that we can reflect upon and revise our instruction. In the following section, we will outline one unit of the information literacy program at the Wheelock College Library that serves as a sample of this type of learning and instruction.

Bringing *Law and Order* into the Classroom:

In this session, we will describe the information literacy workshops, activities and assignments that students experience as part of their first year required English course, English 111, that account for 10 percent of their final course grade. It is important to understand that these particular activities compose only one piece of the first-year experience with information literacy instruction. Another required course provides an additional arena in which exposure to other basic opportunities (to search the library catalog, for example) is presented. The sequence of instruction for this component has evolved dramatically over time as a result of continuous assessment. Some change has come due to trial and error, some from formal faculty feedback, some from student feedback and examination of samples of student work, and much has come from our own reflection and revision. This is the first year (2001-2002) in which all activities and their sequence have remained constant for two semesters in a row; we feel that this is quite an accomplishment! It also helps, in terms of assessment, to be able to examine the same student outputs more than once in order to be able to recognize patterns (both good and bad) as well as inconsistencies.

The sessions rely on the metaphor of researchers as investigators looking for clues that will help them formulate questions that drive their search for evidence to build a case. As an introduction to this notion, students are shown a five-minute clip of the television series *Law and Order*. The show opens with a brief snippet of a crime (in this case a murder) and proceeds to follow the shows' two top detectives as they search for evidence, develop questions, gather information, and interview witnesses, experts and professionals. The clip serves many functions: it frames the work that the students will be doing during the session and establishes the metaphor (under which they will be operating), and it also provides a hook with which to engage the students, surprises them ("TV murder in a boring Library session? Huh?"), and immediately catches their attention. Putting the students off balance right away is a way to wipe the slate clean of all the past negative associations that Library instruction might hold for them. Simply put, they have no idea where things are going and actually wake up in order to find out. They are told before the clip runs to pay careful attention to the detail of what clues and questions might arise, as each student will be required to contribute his or her observations orally after the clip.

Once the clip has run, the whole class participates in an exercise to answer the following three questions: 1) What information do the detectives already have in terms of evidence or clues? 2) What questions will they be trying to answer? and 3) What resources (books, witnesses, experts, etc.) will they use to answer their questions? The purpose of the first question is to have the students acknowledge and understand the importance of prior knowledge in approaching any research question and specifically to detail what information the detectives have immediately at hand. This is generally a fun question for the students as they are easily able to detail the clues (the body, the weapon, the footprints) and can see that even before they start investigating, they have a considerable amount of readily available information.

The second question pushes the students to think about what the purpose of the entire assignment really is by creating focus questions that will serve to guide the investigation. Students have no problem identifying questions regarding suspects, motive, alibis, time of incident, and so forth, and again seem to enjoy doing so. The hardest question for students to address (which validates the purpose of the session altogether) is question three, which speaks to the resources they will need to consult in order to find their answers. Students are usually able to offer up witnesses, law books, and ballistics quite easily, but struggle with the notion of asking experts for advice.

—ESME DEVAULT, AMANDA GLUIBIZZI, AND ANN GLANNON—

This is what makes the use of the show *Law and Order* so appropriate. Most students are familiar with the format of the series in which the first half of the show is spent investigating the crime and the second half is spent in courtroom drama, where typically many expert witnesses are called to testify. The translation from crime to research (in which librarians and faculty are the experts) is one that most students are able to understand. It is the students who provide all of the information required in this first exercise and the students who set the stage for themselves for what is about to unfold.

The larger purpose of this opening exercise is to establish an atmosphere of active inquiry rather than relying on traditional passive methods (e.g. "I show, now you do"). We try to put the students in a situation where they are propelled to act as a means of cultivating learning. The students are immediately required to identify prior knowledge, to construct the scene of the crime (as they will construct their own learning) to create guiding questions and to plan what course of action they will take and what resources they will look to for assistance. The students are propelled into an immediate crisis (i.e. solve the murder) and they themselves must determine how to resolve the crisis with our guidance. The emphasis here is on larger understandings about the research process in general ("Ought I start with what I already know?" "What am I really looking for?" "What do I identify first?") rather than specific skills (such as learning a particular database), which tend to have great limitations. Students are asked to evaluate what they have seen and reflect on how they think they should proceed, instead of being told how they will proceed.

Examining the Clues: Citations as Evidence

After this initial opening exercise, students are presented with a list of citations that are written in MLA format and asked to address what the purpose of citations are. Most students respond to the fact that citations are necessary to avoid plagiarism and to prove to your instructor that you have indeed used outside resources in writing your paper. With some prompting, most students are also able to offer that citations provide you with the information needed to locate the resource being cited. This is the moment at which the idea of citations as "clues" that create a trail of evidence for the students to follow emerges. Students are capable of understanding that the citations they find in scholarly resources can lead them to additional resources; what they are less easily able to grasp is that they are contributing to this trail of evidence when they provide references in the papers they write. This idea of a scholarly discourse, an

exchange in which the students are now going to participate as scholars, is entirely alien to most students at this level, which is precisely why we address the notion in this session. We want the students to know that they will now be active participants in this process as college students, rather than passive receivers of information. Thus, the transformation begins!

Next, the students are given printouts of records from the library catalog and from a database to restructure, first individually and then as a group, into MLA formatted citations. We purposefully have chosen to have the students grapple with the pieces of information in the format in which they will encounter them online. This presents another crisis to them that will soon occur without our being there to advise them. Databases and online catalogs often present the students with superfluous pieces of information (subject headings, accession numbers, etc.) that they must learn to sift through, rather than copying and pasting whole entries, including these unneeded pieces of information, as we have seen they are apt to do.

After having corrected the citations, students are presented with mini-bibliographies (see Appendix A) that include a focus question (such as, "Is Alice Walker a feminist author?") and a list of four citations to resources that they will then locate and retrieve from within the library. The list includes one reference resource, one scholarly article, one general readership article and one circulating book. The students work in pairs to retrieve these resources from the Library collections and return to the classroom to examine the items more closely. Many students struggle with locating the journal articles; sometimes pages are missing, issues are misshelved, citations difficult to decipher, and most often frustration ensues. It is by design that students experience these problems with us there to help them solve the problem. This is another instance of forcing the crisis to happen while there is help available, rather than at 10 P.M., when the student would no doubt leave muttering about how "the library doesn't have anything." We want them to experience real life with a safety net (us) before it actually happens without one; we are trying to scaffold their learning experience. In this way, students are able to work through the problems of locating materials and move ahead, rather than being altogether halted by them. They are the detectives using the clues they have been given to locate the evidence they will need to answer their focus questions. In some cases, clues lead to dead ends, but that doesn't mean that the investigation should be cast aside entirely.

Evaluation, Analysis and Reflection: The Trinity of Critical Thinking Skills

Once students have retrieved their resources, the real work begins. The students are given an assignment sheet (see Appendix B) that prompts them to examine each item carefully to determine which one will best answer the question at hand. It is not that the students themselves are expected to know the answer to the question; indeed, most of the questions would require a fair amount of research to address adequately. Rather, the expectation is that they must quickly figure out which resource will best respond to the question and be able to articulate how they came to their conclusion. The assignment prompts the students to examine the resources for a variety of factors including organization, depth of information, understandability, relevance, scholarly content, etc. The students record their observations and are asked at the end of the session to share their conclusions and explain how they came to them. The interesting and beautiful thing is that each group will choose a different type of resource as being the best. The sharing helps the students to understand that sometimes an article will be the most appropriate resource, sometimes a reference book is best and sometimes an ordinary circulating book provides the required information.

The students are also asked to make note of which resources include references to other resources that might be useful. This helps to extend the metaphor of following clues down a trail of evidence as part of the scholarly discourse. All of this work is collected and evaluated by the library instructors as one small piece of the assessment process. The students leave this session having actively created their own metaphor of understanding, created MLA citations, located a variety of resources throughout the Library, evaluated those resources and reviewed the process as a whole—all in one hour and 20 minutes! At this time, the students sign-up for a lab session that will occur outside of their scheduled time for English class that will use the concepts just learned to build new realms of knowledge.

Planning Your Research: *Inspiration*™ as Preparation

The second session begins with a group exercise in brainstorming and research planning that utilizes the *Inspiration*™ software program. *Inspiration*™ is concept-mapping software that allows students to identify and graphically organize ideas, topics, concepts, and terms before attempting to search for actual resources. We supply the term "Shakespeare" and then go around the room and have each student identify at least one thing (a play, a movie, a historical or biographical fact, etc.) that they know about Shakespeare. The purpose here is, once again, to have the students identify prior knowledge that they have on a given topic before endeavoring to formulate a focus question to research. We are reinforcing these concepts from the past session and having the students move forward with them in an entirely new way. Students generally have no problem creating a list of terms as a group; some examples of terms students typically provide include; "Macbeth," "West Side Story," "Queen Elizabeth," "The Globe Theatre," "sonnets," "male actors in female roles," "the plague," etc. (for a complete *Inspiration* diagram, see Appendix C). As a group, we organize these terms into different disciplines (a term that is unfamiliar to many students, who think more in terms of subjects) such as history, literature, film studies, sociology, etc. This allows the students to see that they may go to many different types of resources in many different disciplines to write a paper on a topic for a specific course.

This helps them to see beyond the notion of always returning to the same resource for every project (our students often use the ERIC database to search for everything!). From all of this, we ask the students to formulate one question that they might be interested in doing research on, such as, "How were gender roles different in Shakespeare's time from what they are now?" From a seemingly amorphous and gigantic topic (Shakespeare) the students have determined what they already know, which disciplines might provide information, and have generated a research question. We then have the students do individual *Inspiration* diagrams on the topics they are researching for their final paper in English 111. The students love using *Inspiration*! *Inspiration* provides many different pictures, fonts, colors, and diagramming possibilities and the students get very excited about creating their own concept maps in this way. The broader purpose of this exercise is to emphasize to the students the importance of brainstorming, thinking, organizing and planning before they even begin to really search for actual books, articles, etc. We want them to know that this intermediate step is very important (even if done less formally) and if they choose to skip it, they will likely end up frustrated and lost as they try to navigate the never-ending selection of online resources.

Next, we guide the students to the Library's subject area database list and ask them to select a database to search based on the focus question they have chosen to research and the terms they have identified on their concept maps. We do not tell them a particular database to search, but rather ask them to examine the database descriptions and make the best

—ESME DEVAULT, AMANDA GLUIBIZZI, AND ANN GLANNON—

decision they can. Typically, mayhem ensues. Students have no idea what to select and may choose the first database on the list, one that has a familiar name (*e.g.* *Encyclopedia Britannica*), or one that is utterly inappropriate (*Grove's Dictionary of Art* for a paper on cloning) for the topic they are researching.

Again, we are purposefully forcing the students into a crisis that they would otherwise experience alone (no doubt at midnight in their dorm rooms) and most likely would lead to great frustration and anxiety. What a learning experience! We ask the students to talk to us, to talk to one another, to try different databases and to try a variety of terms. The students are given a guidance sheet that asks them to try to identify and record three potentially relevant citations and to reflect upon and describe the process they went through to find those citations. These "reflection sheets" (see Appendix D) become an invaluable form of assessment for us that help us to identify problems that the students are having, areas we need to cover in future instruction sessions, and things we did that confused the students, etc. The sheets are also beneficial to the students, as they press them to recognize that they do go through a process, that research is not just haphazard, and that there is much reflection, revision and reorganizing as one does research. Students come to realize that not only is this revision okay, but that it is often the most productive element of critical learning experiences. For some students, who in the past have viewed library research as a matter of luck, the revelation that success is going to depend on planning what they do and how they do it is a powerful one. At this time, the students receive the final assignment of their information literacy component, a culminating exercise that they must complete independently.

The Final Culminating Exercise

The final exercise that we require the students to complete is intended to incorporate the concepts and understandings that they have built in the first two sessions and requires them to synthesize this knowledge to produce new knowledge on their own. For this exercise, we have the students examine a Web site that is quite controversial (without telling them that this is the case) and ask them to make their own conclusions about the purpose and reliability of the site (see Appendix E). We ask the students to summarize the content of the Web site, give their own analysis of its content (*e.g.* do they agree or disagree with the information and why), and provide supporting documentation in the form of resources (three of which must be traditional print resources) which confirm their own evaluation of the site. The site we use is a

Holocaust revisionist Web site published by Arthur Butz and located at: http://pubweb.acns.nwu. edu/~abutz/di/intro.html.

This exercise is intended to allow the students independently to put to use all that they have learned about locating, selecting and analyzing resources and also allows them a wide range of possibilities as to which resources they choose to utilize. Students are allowed and encouraged to revise their assignments after they have been graded (although few elect to do so) in order to encourage them to make reflection and revision a piece of their own scholarly habits of mind. The assignments are graded using a scoring rubric and students are provided with samples of work that would be considered excellent, acceptable, and unacceptable so that there are no surprises as to what the expectations are of the final product. The quality of student work on this final assignment has fallen along a wide continuum from those who didn't understand the actual assignment, to those who have thoroughly digested all that came in the first two sessions and will recognize the repugnant intent of the Web site and find good resources to refute its claims. We have had students voluntarily sign an informed consent form that allows us to retain copies of this final assignment as yet another piece in the assessment puzzle we seek daily to solve.

Problems and Conclusions

Just as we have pushed the students continuously to reflect, revise, and refine their own work, we have also held ourselves to these same principles as we seek to make our instruction more effective over the course of time. This type of instruction requires intensive collaboration (among ourselves and with our faculty), team teaching is time consuming and requires an inordinate amount of patience and revision. Good luck to us! We have run up against most of the day to day issues that all teachers face, ranging from the myriad of excuses for not showing up to sessions or turning in work on time, to the fallibility of the technology in use and our own exhaustion and frustration when things don't go as well as expected. One thing we have certainly learned is that continuous assessment is not only helpful, but also very necessary in order to forge a reflective teaching practice for ourselves and in order to create meaningful learning opportunities for our students. The crises that we face ("Ack! The video won't work!" or "where are the books we were going to use?") force us to learn just as mightily as the crises that we design for our students force them to learn. Allowing our students to make mistakes as they construct their own worlds of knowledge is a scary process and sometimes makes us want to return to the old days of "oh, just do this" when we were directing everything that took place.

The point here is that perfection is not the expectation and that guided failure can sometimes have very positive outcomes, even for us. Sometimes we feel very frustrated when students seem to have entirely missed the point of different exercises; this experience does not negate the usefulness of the exercises, but rather reinforces their absolute necessity. If a student is going to radically misinterpret a Web site, or search the completely wrong database, or pull their hair out trying to find a misplaced journal issue, better that they do it with us to scaffold the experience, than the night before the final history paper is due. Feedback at every point along the way is essential. For every major assignment our students complete, we structure a feedback memo for them that addresses major issues that came to the fore during the evaluation process. We also allow for the option of revising final assignments for students not satisfied with their evaluation. This cycle of feedback and revision parallels our process as instructors as we alter our instruction to address the real issues that the students are experiencing, and helps keep our curriculum and teaching vital.

—ESME DEVAULT, AMANDA GLUIBIZZI, AND ANN GLANNON—

Appendix A: Mini Bibliographies

What are some of the predominant symbols used in the *Scarlet Letter*?

Bloom, Harold. *Nathaniel Hawthorne*. New York: Chelsea House Publishers, 1986.
813 H31zbl

Kreger, Erika M. "Depravity Dressed Up in a Fascinating Garb: Sentimental
    Motifs and the Seduced Hero (ine) in The Scarlet Letter." *Nineteenth-
    Century Literature* 54 (1999): 308-332.

"Nathaniel Hawthorne." *Dictionary of Literary Biography*. Volume 1, 1978.
R810.9 D56 v.1

Santoro, Gene. "Scarlet Letter's Last Blush." *The Nation* 272:9 (March 5, 2001):32.

Is Alice Walker considered a feminist writer?

Clark, Suzanne. *Sentimental Modernism : Women Writers and the Revolution of the
    Word*. Bloomington: Indiana University Press, 1991.   **809 C54s**

Ferriera, Patricia. "What's Wrong with Miss Anne? Whiteness, Women and
    Power in Meridian and Dessa Rose." *Sage* 8 (1991): 15-20.

Roden, Molly. "Alice Walker." *Contemporary African American Novelists*.
    Ed. Emmanuel Nelson. Westport, CT: Greenwood Press, 1999.
R 812.09 W67c

Taylor, Carol Anne. "Critical Essays on Alice Walker." *African American Review*
    35:3 (Fall 2001):489.

What are the major arguments for and against the death penalty?

Costanzo, Mark. *Just Revenge : Costs and Consequences of the Death Penalty*.
    New York: St. Martin's Press, 1997.   **364.66 C82j**

"Death Penalty Update." *The CQ Researcher*. Volume 9, 1999. **R070.442 C83 1999**

Dolinko, David. "Justice in the Age of Sentencing Guidelines." *Ethics* 110 (2000):
    563-580.

Shapiro, Bruce. "Dead Reckoning: A World effort to Force an End to the U.S. Death
Penalty is Gaining Strength." *The Nation* 273:5 (6 August 2001): 14 .

Appendix B: Assignment Sheet

ENG 111 Library Instruction Session II Worksheet:

Names: **Date:**
English Instructor:

Part I:
Use this space to write down
1) Some of the ways in which the resources you have collected are similar and/or different. You might want to consider:
- how the information is organized physically in the resource
- how much information there is
- the depth to which the information is presented
- the difficulty of the material
- whom the information seems to be intended for
- if the information might lead you to other resources
- where the resource comes from
- and any other details that you notice.

2) See if each of the resources contains a citation to something else (another book/article) and decide if that resource would be useful.
3) Decide which resource best addresses the research question and explain why.

—ESME DEVAULT, AMANDA GLUIBIZZI, AND ANN GLANNON—

Appendix C: *Inspiration* diagram

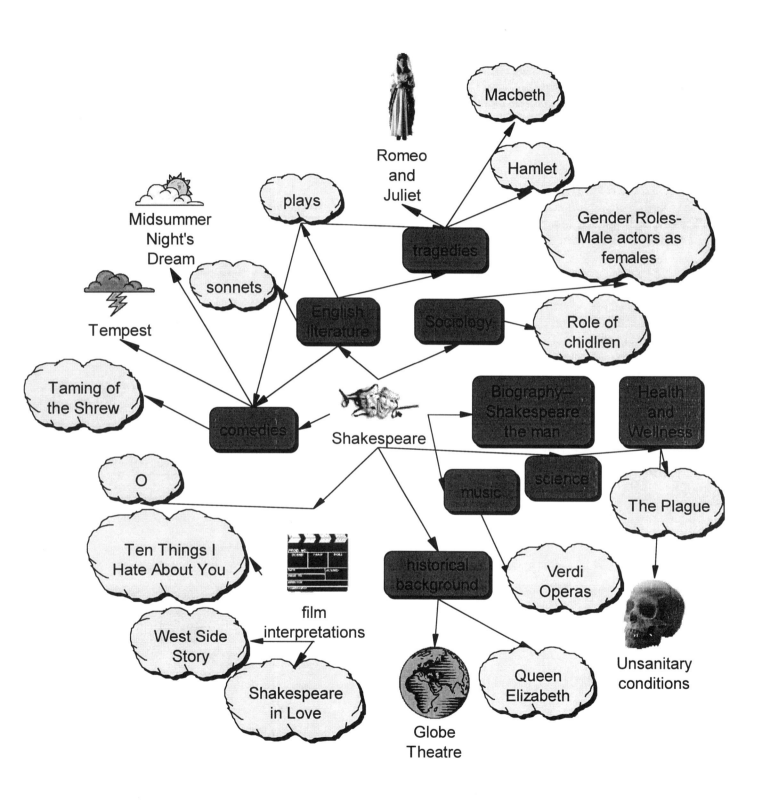

Appendix D: Reflections Sheet

Name:

Section:

Research Reflections
What information is important or useful?

Now that you have searched for resources, you need to reflect on your research.

- First, write down 3 citations that you might wish to use for your paper.
- Then, please <u>write a paragraph or two</u> about the process so far and what you have learned.
- *Reflect and evaluate,* don't just list titles, don't just answer the questions below in checklist fashion. These questions are to <u>stimulate your thinking</u> and identify elements of the research process that may be pertinent to your reflections. You may have other relevant observations, and those should be noted here.

Have I been able to identify some sources to start my research? If I haven't, how can I?

Have I been able to locate sources I've identified? If I haven't, how can I?

How useful are the sources I've found? Are they appropriate to my needs?

Do these sources lead me to other sources?

Have I found any new terms that can help me with my search?

Is there another database I might try for other information?

Do I need or wish to revise my question?

—ESME DEVAULT, AMANDA GLUIBIZZI, AND ANN GLANNON—

Appendix E: Final Assignment—Conclusions

ENG 111
Information Resources -- Final Assignment

DATE DUE:_____

Research is a process of evaluation and decision-making. As you work your way through the process you must continuously figure out if the material you have found is relevant and reliable. The "Research Reflections" you were asked to complete in the second session was an exercise that guided you in this process.

For this assignment you will use the research tools and strategies we have discussed in the two previous library sessions to evaluate a resource. This assignment is to be completed *individually*, <u>not</u> collaboratively.

Please visit the web site
    <u>http://pubweb.acns.nwu.edu/~abutz/di/intro.html</u>

to answer the question:
    Can I verify the content of this web site?

This is a **three-part** assignment.

- For the **first part** <u>summarize</u> the content of the site and <u>explain</u> your conclusions about the web site's *intent.* What is the site about and what is the author's purpose in publishing this page?
- For the **second part**, <u>give evidence</u> to support your assertions and conclusions. How could you tell? <u>What resources did you use</u> to *verify* information in the site? Do your sources <u>substantiate or refute</u> the information on the web site? Acceptable evidence can include reference books, general books, articles, and other web pages if appropriate. *You **must** use at least **three** print resources as evidence.*
- For the **third part** you must supply **documentation** of your evidence by <u>attaching photocopies or printouts</u> of the first page or title page of <u>each source</u> you provide as evidence.

This must be handed in to the ENG 111 box at the Reference desk on floor 1M of the Library by <u>***Monday, March 25.***</u> **LATE ASSIGNMENTS WILL NOT BE ACCEPTED.** Remember, the library component is **10 percent** of your total ENG 111 final grade. Please see samples below for examples of acceptable and unacceptable assignments.

Be sure to have your full name, your ENG 111 instructor's name, and your section number on the paper, to ensure you get credit for your work.

THE ROLE OF A COMPETENCY TEST IN SUPPORTING AND PROMOTING THE INTEGRATION OF INFORMATION LITERACY IN THE UNDERGRADUATE CURRICULUM AT JAMES MADISON UNIVERSITY

Kathy Clarke and Rebecca Feind

The Library Instruction Program at James Madison University is a comprehensive, multi-faceted program that reaches students at two levels: basic instruction during the first year and advanced instruction in the major. This presentation will discuss our work in reaching students at each of these levels, our online competency test, and our collaborative effort with faculty to further enhance our program. On a campus of 13,706 FTE, the Library Instruction Program at James Madison University reaches approximately 10,000 students each year, with about 3,000 completing "Go for the Gold," a Web-based program with online exercises, and some 7,000 receiving course-related instruction taught by fifteen liaison librarians. The Library Instruction Program begins in the freshman year with basic instruction in information literacy integrated into the General Education program using "Go for the Gold." This program is coupled with course-related assignments designed to give students experience in finding and evaluating information, employing the skills demonstrated in "Go for the Gold." Librarians provide formal training to General Education faculty to insure successful integration of information literacy objectives into course work. All first-year General Education students must pass an online Information-Seeking

Skills Competency Test by the end of the year.

In the early eighties, reference librarians developed a self-paced, individualized library skills workbook that was used for all first-year students taking English 101. In the mid-eighties, the library instituted a library liaison program in which librarians from all departments within the library were assigned to work with academic departments to provide instruction, work with faculty to develop the collection, and communicate important information about collections and services. From the beginning of the liaison program, the goal of the instruction program has been two-fold:

- To teach all beginning students basic library skills

- To teach all students in the major the sources and research strategies important to their field through course-related instruction performed by liaison librarians.

In the early nineties, JMU began planning a new General Education program, and librarians were a part of the planning process. The new competency-based curriculum included information-seeking skills as formally stated objectives. These objectives are:

- Formulate and conduct an information search that includes a variety of reference sources, such as encyclopedias, library catalogs,

Clarke and *Feind* are librarians at James Madison University, Harrisonburg, VA.

indexes, bibliographies, statistics sources, government publications, and resources available on the Internet.

- Evaluate information sources in terms of accuracy, authority, bias, and relevance in written and oral contexts.

These objectives became two of nineteen common objectives for basic skills courses in General Education. The basic skills are writing, communication, critical thinking, information-seeking, and technology. The General Education program consists of five clusters of objectives that cover important subject areas. Basic skills are taught in Cluster One and are considered to be foundational to the students' subsequent work in General Education and their major or preprofessional program. Once the information literacy objectives became an integral part of General Education, librarians and faculty wrote more specific information literacy skills into their courses. Using these specific local items as a basis, the library developed a Web-based instruction program called "Go for the Gold," which replaced the library workbook.

"Go for the Gold" is a series of Web-based instructional modules designed by the Carrier Library reference staff to introduce students to the services and collections in Carrier Library and to teach students basic information-seeking skills. The modules are organized in the following order:

Module 1 — Orientation to Carrier Library
Module 2 — An Introduction to the Information World
Module 3 — Searching an Electronic Database
Module 4 — Finding Information Resources: Using LEO: The Online Catalog, Locating Background Information, Books and Non-Print Media, Periodical Articles, Biographical Information, Primary Sources, Critical Reviews, Government Information, Statistical Information
Module 5 — Using Internet Sources
Module 6 — Evaluating Sources of Information
Module 7 — Information Ethics: Citing Sources and Fair Use
Module 8 — A Search Strategy for Research Papers and Speeches

Each module concludes with online exercises that are scored electronically so that students receive immediate feedback. Student scores for all eight sets of exercises are stored in a database that can be viewed by faculty. "Go for the Gold" has been refined and improved each year to reflect changes in the library, changes to our online database offerings, and to improve the quality of instructional delivery. This Web-based instruction program is assigned to all first-year students taking introductory General Education courses and serves as the primary method of delivering information literacy instruction to the 3,000 students enrolled in Cluster One. This online program can be viewed at: http://www.lib.jmu.edu/ library/ gold/modules.htm.

Along with development of the online program, the change to General Education also provided momentum for additional faculty collaboration and training. The new structure of General Education created interdisciplinary packages within each Cluster. The four packages of Cluster One are:

A: Writing, Communication, Critical Thinking
B: Writing, Communication, General Business
(Package C is still under development)
D: Writing, Communication, History
E: Writing, Communication, Introduction to Media Arts

The creation of these interdisciplinary clusters brought faculty together across departmental lines. In the changing seas of curriculum and technology, information literacy has provided a common ground for dialogue. The General Education office has facilitated this opportunity to integrate information literacy into the curriculum of Cluster One by providing yearly grants for faculty training.

Another core aspect of General Education, besides interdisciplinarity, is competency testing. James Madison University has been heavily invested in assessment efforts for many years, with faculty and staff in the Center for Assessment providing leadership and assistance with developing tests. Librarians at JMU have assessed library skills of freshmen since the late 1980s, originally using a multiple-choice paper and pencil test developed locally by reference librarians in consultation with assessment specialists. This test was administered to a random sample of students annually, and was revised and improved over the years to increase its reliability. In 1998, an online test in a Web-based format with frames was developed. Using several questions from the paper and pencil test as a starting point, questions were added that require students to find answers in the online catalog, in databases, and on the Internet. Librarians composed test questions, with input from teaching faculty and assessment specialists.

Once the 53-item online test was developed, it was piloted during 1998-1999 on several hundred students gathered by random sample. Pilot test results enabled us to make revisions and improvements that increased reliability. The Information-Seeking Skills Test (ISST) became a required competency test for Cluster One students in 1999-2000; the 2000-2001 academic year was the second year of implementation

After the decision to make the ISST a competency test, the next step was to set a standard for passing. The Center for Assessment invited 12 faculty and librarians to participate in two half-day sessions to set a passing score for the test. Participants represented General Education, Carrier Library, Speech Communication, History, Business, and Writing. The group set two cut scores, one for "Meets the Standard" and one for "Advanced". Using the "Bookmark" procedure,[1] participants examined the 53 test items that had been ordered by difficulty according to examinee performance on the ISST during the 1998-99 academic year. Based on the judgments of participants, the recommended cut score for "Meets the Standard" is 42 correct items. For "Advanced," the recommended cut score is 48 items correct out of 53.

The ISST is administered in a secure testing lab, staffed by the campus Center for Assessment. The test resides on the Assessment server and is password protected. Students may come in as individuals and take the test, or General Education faculty may schedule whole classes to take the test at once. Students receive immediate feedback on their scores and sub scores.

Maintenance of the test itself is an ongoing responsibility shared by librarians and assessment staff. Questions that require students to apply knowledge by finding answers in online sources are particularly challenging to maintain, as answers may change as databases constantly add and drop records, and access to databases changes over time. Databases may also be down temporarily, interfering with students' ability to complete the test. Proctors in the testing lab are usually the first to detect problems with questions, and they quickly communicate these to the librarian and assessment staff member who resolve them as quickly as possible.

Students who do not pass the ISST are offered the opportunity to attend small workshops led by librarians or meet individually with librarians for assistance. These sessions focus on the test questions that students most often miss:

1) Locating a journal article
2) Using Boolean operators
3) Understanding the difference between keyword and subject searching
4) Developing effective search statements
5) Identifying different types of citations

Librarians teaching these workshops incorporate instruction methods that address several learning styles, including demonstration, discussion, and having students write out search statements on a marker board before trying examples on the computers. Supporting materials included a map of the library, a list of library terminology, and a search statement worksheet.

Besides fulfilling its role as a competency test, the ISST also serves as a platform for subject area liaison librarians. The skills developed in "Go for the Gold" and tested with the ISST are reinforced and furthered in the major. Liaison librarians can assume students have a basic level of information literacy competency. This is significant for large gateway courses with research particular to a discipline. For example, COB 300 is a gateway course required of all business majors. High enrollment (700 students in Fall 2001), the specificity of the assignment (creation of a business plan) and limited class time devoted to library instruction (two fifty minute class sessions) make time of the essence. These sessions focus on the basics of business research with research basics woven in as review. Liaison librarians offer similar instruction in gateway courses for History, Health Sciences, English, Business, Psychology and Theater. Programs with specific research methods courses are another avenue for targeted instruction in the discipline and liaisons actively work with these courses. Having a basic program that tests first-year students' knowledge of information literacy allows us to plan a more sophisticated approach to library research in the major. The ISST also serves as a springboard for developing subject specific assessment tests. For example, Computer Information Systems 320 is an introductory course for computer and information systems majors that includes a research paper assignment on telecommunications trends. The majority of students in this class are transfer or older returning students who bypass General Education requirements. Most have limited information seeking skills and little experience in our library or with databases. This lack of skill was evident in papers that were less than satisfactory. The CIS faculty member and the liaison librarian worked together to redesign the flow of the assignment, building on basic research skills while focusing on particular sources for the assignment, the reverse of what happens in a gateway course. A test, designed by a librarian and based on the ISST, is used to assess the research skills taught in this course. The liaison librarian also reviews student presentations and final projects.

Several liaison librarians have developed information literacy objectives for specific majors. The Information Literacy Test for Psychology is administered to psychology seniors during the Spring semester. This online test consists of 43 multiple-choice items that measures knowledge in four areas: basic skills, database searching, Internet, and evaluation of sources. The Health Sciences and Health Services Administration majors take the Information Literacy Test for Health Sciences. This paper and pencil test is composed of 45 test questions and 15 survey questions. At this writing, other liaisons are developing objectives and assessment tools for major programs.

The incorporation of a competency test into our information literacy program for General Education has been an evolutionary process that has spanned more than a decade. Although the test was challenging to develop and is time intensive to administer and maintain, we have experienced significant benefits from this initiative. The relationship between the library and the General Education program has been strengthened. Liaison librarians and faculty are collaborating more closely than ever on delivering instruction and designing assignments to further develop the skills measured by the test. Students, knowing they will be held accountable for learning important skills, are taking information literacy seriously. The resources we have put into the competency test and the liaison program have been well worth the outcomes for JMU students.

ACKNOWLEDGEMENTS

As Coordinator of Library Instruction, Lynn Cameron has made significant contributions to the development and growth of information literacy. Her collaborative work is a key part of the role of information literacy in General Education and James Madison University and this report is made possible by her efforts.

We would like to acknowledge the expert assistance we received from the JMU Center for Assessment and Research Studies, particularly from Christine DeMars and Steve Wise.

NOTE

1. D.M. Lewis, D.R. Green, H.C. Mitzel, K. Baum, and R.J. Patz, "*The Bookmark Standard Setting Procedure: Methodology and Recent Implementations. Paper Presented at the Annual Meeting of the National Council for Measurement in Education,*" (San Diego, CA), April, 1998.

Tier One: Instruction at the freshman level

General Education Objectives for Cluster One related to Information Literacy:

- Formulate and conduct an information search that includes a variety of reference sources, such as encyclopedias, library catalogs, indexes, bibliographies, statistics sources, government publications, and resources available on the Internet.

- Evaluate information sources in terms of accuracy, authority, bias, and relevance in written and oral contexts.

These objectives are part of the Cluster One curriculum via Web based library instruction (online modules called "Go for the Gold"), library assignments given by Cluster One instructors, and are measured by the Information Seeking Skills Test.

Information Literacy Skills for General Education

Identify and locate the following services and collections in Carrier Library:

o   Reference Desk

o   Electronic Reference Area

o   Interlibrary loan/document express

o   Current and bound periodicals

- Government documents
- LEO
- Media Resources

- Describe how information is organized in libraries.

- Given a need for a particular type of information (i.e. overview, research report, news), identify an appropriate type of source (i.e. encyclopedia, scholarly journal, newspaper).

- Characterize the quality of information found on the Internet vs. in libraries.

- Define the terms database, record, and field.

- Define 3 types of information databases: bibliographic, full-text, numeric.

- Determine the subject scope and years of coverage of a given database.

- Identify the main concepts of a research topic and generate a list of search terms.

- Build a search strategy using Boolean operators.

- Compare and contrast a free text search with a controlled terminology search.

- Define truncation, nesting, field-specific searching, and phrase searching.

- Use LEO to locate materials held by Carrier Library (including books, nonprint media, and government documents)

- Find relevant background information on a topic.

- Locate and effectively use the following types of information sources:

Tier One: Instruction at the freshman level (continued)

o   Periodical Articles

o   News Sources

o   Biographical Information

o   Primary Sources

o   Critical Reviews

o   Government Information

o   Statistical Information

- Define Internet, World Wide Web, browser, and Internet search engine.

- Locate a specific Web site given an Internet address

- Conduct an Internet search on a given topic

- Compare and contrast a database search with an Internet search.

- Evaluate information using the following criteria:

    o   authority of the publisher, author, producer, etc.

    o   appropriateness of the date of publication or release of the item

    o   supporting documentation

    o   purpose of the work

    o   review process

- Identify the bibliographic elements essential for properly citing an information source

- Apply appropriate ethical guidelines to the use of information.

- Cite information sources using a standard bibliographic style.

- Define and apply an efficient search strategy for a research paper to include:

    o   Choosing a topic and identifying its main concepts.

    o   Narrowing the focus of the topic.

    o   Identifying appropriate reference books, indexes, and Internet sites.

    o   Using a variety of sources.

    o   Evaluating the sources for appropriateness and quality.

—KATHY CLARKE AND REBECCA FEIND—

Tier Two: Instruction in the major

Librarian led instruction takes place in the major, in gateway courses and research methods courses. Liaison librarians assist departments in developing Information Literacy objectives in the major. Assessment efforts in the major are underway for some subject areas.

Carrier Library Instruction page, maintained by Lynn Cameron:

> http://www.lib.jmu.edu/staffWeb/ps/instruction/

"Go for the Gold": http://www.lib.jmu.edu/library/gold/modules.htm

WHAT STUDENTS REALLY CITE: FINDINGS FROM A CONTENT ANALYSIS OF FIRST-YEAR STUDENT BIBLIOGRAPHIES

Lisa Janicke Hinchliffe, Christine Kubiak, Stephen K. Hunt, and Cheri J. Simonds

Introduction

Examining the sources used in student work can reveal student understandings about information sources and the research process. This chapter details the methodology and findings of an assessment project at Illinois State University designed to investigate the kind and quality of sources first-year students use in an introductory communication course. Student portfolios were collected and retrieved from a sample of students and the sources cited in two speech bibliographies. Each item on the bibliography was assessed, and the bibliography was also considered as a whole. Key findings relate to material types used (more books and less Internet sites than expected), instructor feedback practices, source use in the speeches themselves, and preliminary indications that students are using public libraries rather than the university library to complete their research assignments.

Curricular and Course Context

Illinois State University implemented a new General Education Program in Fall 1998 and with it came a new General Education Library Instruction

Program.[1] The General Education Program is characterized by the sequenced and integrated approach attempted in the curricular design of the program. The previous "cafeteria" style approach to general education only required students to take a certain number of hours in various categories of courses at some time during their college education. The new General Education Program requires students to take very specific courses early in their college careers and has an established pre-requisite structure similar in some ways to the structure found in a major or minor program of the student.

An emphasis on assessment and student learning outcomes accompanied the implementation of the new General Education Program.[2] Various efforts have been undertaken at all levels: individual student learning outcomes assessment, course assessment, and program assessment. This study is one part of a multi-part project assessing *COM 110: Language and Communication,* which is the basic communication course that students are required to take in their first or second semester as an undergraduate student.

The Assessment Project

Language and Communication has six course goals:

1. Apply the rhetorical principles informing effective formal communication.
2. Accommodate rhetorical principles to different speech situations, both formal and informal.
3. Conduct background research necessary to develop well-informed presentations.
4. Evaluate the oral presentations of others according to rhetorical principles.

Hinchliffe was the Library Instruction Coordinator at Illinois State University and is now the Coordinator for Information Literacy Services and Instruction at the University of Illinois at Urbana-Champaign. ***Kubiak*** is the Music/Communication Librarian at Illinois State University. ***Hunt*** and ***Simonds*** are co-directors of the *Language and Communication* course at Illinois State University.

5. Apply rhetorical principles critical to effective communication in small-group discussions.

6. Demonstrate openness, intellectual tolerance, and civility in the exchange of ideas and the resolution of conflicts in small-group settings.

The final assignment in *Language and Communication* requires each student to create a portfolio of materials including: speech materials—speech outlines and bibliographies; artifact papers—short essays linking communication concepts to an observation of communication outside of the classroom; the student's speeches on videotape; the Communication Improvement Profile—a paper in which the student identifies personal learning goals for the semester; and a synthesis paper in which the student considers his or her progress during the course. The portfolio was designed as a summative assignment through which students would demonstrate attainment of course goals.

As mentioned above, the study reported here is part of a larger assessment project. The initial phase of the project investigated whether the extent to which the student portfolios could be used as an effective tool for demonstrating student learning relative to course goals. That study found that "student portfolios are an effective tool for gathering evidence that students have accomplished course goals" and that "materials that students generated during the semester provide rich data for investigating student insight, observation, experience, and performance."[3]

Having shown the efficacy of student portfolios for assessing student learning relative to course goals for *Language and Communication*, follow-up projects were undertaken to assess student achievement of the course goals. This study pursued course goal #3: conduct background research necessary to develop well-informed presentations.[4]

Hypotheses

Other studies have documented the types of sources cited by undergraduate students in their papers. Davis and Cohen analyzed undergraduate term papers in micro economics and reported that citations to books decreased while citations to newspaper articles and Web sites increased from 1996 to 1999. Their study also showed that the students cite a greater percentage of periodical articles than books. Popular sources, magazines and newspapers, were more commonly cited that journals.[5] Malone and Videon's survey of students found that students reported that 28.5% of their sources were electronic. An analysis of the bibliographies revealed that the citations themselves indicated that 7% were electronic, indicating that students may not always cite

electronically-retrieved sources as electronic.

The following hypotheses were developed, related to the course goal being investigated and the specifics of the informative and persuasive speech assignments. They are based on findings reported in the literature, anecdotal observations at the reference desks and in instruction sessions, and the findings of the initial phase of the assessment project of which this study is a part.

Hypothesis A.   Undergraduate students cite more Internet sources than any other category of sources in their bibliographies.

Hypothesis B.   Undergraduate students cite more periodical literature sources than monographic literature sources in their bibliographies.

Hypothesis C.   Undergraduate students cite more popular sources than scholarly sources in their bibliographies.

Hypothesis D.   Undergraduate students cite sources published within the last five years more frequently than sources published more then five years ago in their bibliographies.

Hypothesis E.   Undergraduate students do not differentiate when citing the electronic version of a resource in their bibliographies. Students incorrectly cite electronic versions in the same format as the print version of the resource.

Hypothesis F.   Instructor comments on undergraduate student bibliographies are primarily on citation format rather than on the source quality or use.

Methodology

The initial sample of portfolios consisted of approximately 10% of the student portfolios available at the end of Spring semester 1999. In order to control for instructor influence on the findings, the sample was taken across all sections of the course.[6] After excluding those utilized in the initial phase of the assessment project, and then excluding those used in developing the specific content analysis coding template for this study, 123 portfolios remained for the analysis reported here.

—LISA JANICKE HINCHLIFFE, CHRISTINE KUBIAK, STEPHEN K. HUNT AND CHERI J. SIMONDS—

For each portfolio, speech materials (outlines, bibliographies, and instructor feedback forms) for the informative and persuasive speeches were coded using two coding templates: one template for each speech as a whole and one template for each individual item listed in the bibliographies. As such, the resulting data set consisted of 246 speech level entries and 1246 item level entries. In addition, unlike many other citation analysis studies, an attempt was made to retrieve all items cited in the bibliography,[7] integration of the sources into the written work was reviewed, and instructor feedback about sources was analyzed. This approach was selected in order to provide a more complete picture of students' experiences of research and source use.

The coding templates were developed by a team of librarians who used the coding template from the initial phase of the assessment and then expanded and refined it using a iterative process of applying the template independently to assess the usability of the template and then discussing changes. The process also resulted in a rubric for coding data using the template so that the template would be applied consistently.[8] After one librarian coded all of the data, a student assistant entered the information into a Microsoft Excel spreadsheet which was then transferred to Intercooled Stata 7.0 for statistical analysis.[9]

Findings

The results of the data analysis revealed interesting patterns related to the type of sources cited, the quality of those sources, and the kinds of comments instructors provide as feedback to the students. Unexpected findings include the number of sources students cite in the bibliographies but do not use in the speeches and the preliminary indications that students are using public libraries rather than the university library to complete their assignments. The discussion of findings will first focus on the specific hypotheses for the study and then conclude with the unexpected findings.

Hypothesis A. Undergraduate students cite more Internet sources than any other category of sources in their bibliographies.

Hypothesis B. Undergraduate students cite more periodical literature sources than monographic literature sources in their bibliographies.

Publication Type	Percent
Article - Magazine or Journal	34.45
Book	27.36
Website	24.51
Other	3.75
Pamphlet	3.50
Article - Newspaper	3.09
Personal Communication	2.77
Chapter	0.57
Total	100.00

Unexpectedly, both articles from magazines or journals (34.45%) and books (27.36%) were cited as sources more often than Websites (24.51%). Though this is somewhat explained by the directions for the speech assignments which state that "no more than half of the sources you use should be taken from the Internet," students as a whole used fewer Internet sources than the assignments would have allowed. There were students who disregarded the directions for the assignment and cited all Internet sources; however, there were also students who used no Internet sources. Students do appear to be using appropriate and varied types of sources for their speeches.

Though the hypotheses that predicted more citations to articles was confirmed, we were surprised by the number of books cited in the bibliographies. Given the time frame of the assignments it seemed unlikely that students would have sufficient time to read whole books and incorporate them into their speeches and so we are puzzled by the high usage patterns. We suspect that students may be retrieving books and then utilizing a chapter or quotation but then citing the complete work; however, the data analyzed here does not allow investigation of this hypothesis and instead only points to a potential follow-up study.

Hypothesis C. Undergraduate students cite more popular sources than scholarly sources in their bibliographies.

Though students are citing a proportionately large number of magazine and journal articles, the type of articles cited confirmed our hypothesis. Of the articles cited in the speech bibliographies, 77 % were from popular sources and 21 % were from scholarly sources (the type could not be determined for 2% of the articles). Trade and professional publications were coded as scholarly in keeping with the way that the different types of sources are discussed in the *Language and Communication* course. One factor possibly influencing the types of articles cited are the speech topics. Some of the topics students select are ill-suited to research in scholarly databases. Further investigation is needed to determine whether students are not selecting the scholarly databases or whether they are locating scholarly sources but then not citing them.

Hypothesis D. Undergraduate students cite sources published within the last five years more frequently than sources published more then five years ago in their bibliographies.

Sources published between 1994 and 1999 accounted for 75% of the sources cited in the speech bibliographies. The general pattern of students citing more 1994-1999 sources than pre-1994 sources was also true of each publication type category with the exception of books for which the pattern reversed (62% were pre-1994 and only 38% were 1994-1999). Of the pre-1994 items, 21% were magazine or journal articles, 66% were books, and the remaining percentage was distributed across the other publication type categories.

Hypothesis E. Undergraduate students do not differentiate when citing the electronic version of a resource in their bibliographies. Students incorrectly cite electronic versions in the same format as the print version of the resource.

Very few articles cited pre-date the date coverage of general article library databases. Interestingly though, given librarian and instructor observations of student research behavior, no article citations in the speech bibliographies indicated that an article was retrieved from a full-text database. Of course, it is not possible to determine conclusively whether students retrieved the full-text of an article from a database from the student portfolios; however, using clues such as unusual page references (e.g., page 14++) and references to paragraphs rather than page numbers, it is conservatively estimated that over 50% of the magazine and journal articles were retrieved from electronic databases rather than from print copy. Given Malone and Videon's findings that students self-report including more electronic sources than their bibliographies reveal,[10] consistent with the data reported here, it seems likely that students in *Language and Communication* would benefit from specific and explicit instruction about when and how to cite sources retrieved electronically.

Hypothesis F. Instructor comments on undergraduate student bibliographies are primarily on citation format rather than on the source quality or use.

Instructor comments on student sources were found to be the reverse of what was predicted. Instructors made comments about source quality, content, or use on 61% of the speeches. Of these, 39% were positive comments, 51% were negative/constructive, and 10% contained both positive and negative/constructive elements. Instructors made comments about citation format on 35% of the speeches. Of these, 11% were positive comments and 89% were negative/constructive.

We were pleased to see that students are getting feedback on the more substantial issues of source quality and integration into the speech; however, the analysis of student performance with respect to citation formatting and correctness raised some additional concerns related to instructor feedback. Examining each citation in the speech bibliographies revealed that only 13% of the citations were formatted correctly (following the *Publication Manual of the American Psychological Association*—the required format for the course). The remaining 87% were not formatted correctly. Additionally, at least 36% of the items were cited incorrectly— meaning that at least one element in the citation was incorrect (e.g., publication title or author name). Given this data, it seems likely that students would benefit from more explicit feedback from instructors about citation format and the correctness of the citation elements.

Unexpected Findings

The data analysis revealed some unexpected findings as well. Though the informative and persuasive speech assignments specifically state that "all of the sources that appear in the reference page must be incorporated into the speech and identified" through an explicit mention of the source details, the data analysis revealed that 31% of the sources listed in the bibliography for a speech were not mentioned in the speech itself. This may indicate that students are adding citations to the speech bibliographies in order to meet the requirements of the assignments (four sources for the informative speech and six for the persuasive) or that students have difficulty sign-posting source use in the text of their speeches. Further investigation is needed to explore this issue.

Students are also re-using research materials collected for previous assignments (e.g., composition paper from the previous semester) and making use of information that is available to them from other sources (e.g., parents files of information about illness their children had). Approximately 9% of the bibliographies contained items that appeared to have been "recycled" in these ways. Depending on the extent to which the speech text itself therefore represents work previously submitted in another

—LISA JANICKE HINCHLIFFE, CHRISTINE KUBIAK, STEPHEN K. HUNT AND CHERI J. SIMONDS—

course and whether the "recycling" was approved by instructors, this re-use of source may indicate a violation of the *Code of Student Conduct* which states that "submitting the same paper for more than one course is considered a breach of academic integrity unless prior approval is given by the instructors." Even if not an indication of a violation of academic integrity, this finding raises the question of whether students can be said to accomplish course goals if they do not conduct research specifically for the course.

Finally, of the books cited in speech bibliographies, attempts at retrieval revealed that only 61% are owned by Milner Library at Illinois State University. The remaining 39% are not owned by Milner Library. Of the 61% the library does own, it is, of course, not possible to determine whether the student who cited the book checked out Milner's copy. Though not conclusive, coupled with the general notes made about the titles by the librarian who coded the bibliographies and the knowledge that many first-year students return home each weekend, this seems to suggest that many students are using their public libraries rather than the university library to complete their assignments. Further research is needed to investigate this tentative conclusion; however, the difficulties of doing college-level research in a public library are well-known to public and academic librarians alike and may account for some of the patterns of source type and quality discussed previously in this chapter.

Discussion

An analysis of the student bibliographies and sources cited reveal that many students are conducting appropriate background research in completing the informative and persuasive speech assignments in *Language and Communication*. The research demands of the assignments are not complex and sophisticated; however, the assignments do set clear parameters and expectations related to source type, quality, and integration. The primary areas of concern with respect to course goals and assignments relate to citation practices – following a specific formatting style and assuring the correctness of the citation elements – and integrating sources into speeches. Instructor feedback related to both of these areas needs continued attention as well.

Attempts to address the findings of this study are already underway. The course co-directors have established a rubric for evaluating information and persuasive speeches. They also provide training on how to apply the rubric as part of the instructor training for the graduate teaching assistants who teach *Language and Communication*. The rubric includes specific criteria for determining whether references

are correct/sufficient, whether the sources are well-integrated, credible and cited fully in the speech itself, and how well the speech meets the criteria (grades A-F). In addition, efforts have been made during the librarian-led portion of the instructor training to address issues related to giving feedback about sources and helping students conduct research. Finally, a pilot project was conducted in which librarians provided feedback to students about the research process after the library instruction session for the course but before the student wrote his or her speech.

Future Research

This study has raised many questions for future research including: why and how students use books as research materials, particularly for assignments with short time frames; whether students are using scholarly databases; how students make decisions about whether to use scholarly databases and articles; how students integrate sources into written work; and why and how students use different types of libraries for college research assignments.

In addition to future research about student research patterns, this study raises questions about citation analysis as a research methodology. Further discussion is needed about adequate sample size, reliability of coding, and how certain criteria are best applied (e.g., scholarly vs. popular articles).

Conclusion

Analysis of bibliographies continues to serve as a valuable approach for investigating student source use and citation patterns. This study contributes to the literature by coupling citation analysis with source retrieval, analysis of the integration of sources into written work, and examination of instructor feedback. The findings demonstrate that this approach to content analysis provides a more complete picture of the experiences students have relative to research and source use than bibliography analysis alone. Most importantly, as an assessment project, this study demonstrates that investigations into student learning and experience can provide clear direction for improving course delivery and design.

WORKS CITED

1. For a complete overview of the General Education Library Instruction Program, see Lisa Janicke Hinchliffe and Patricia Meckstroth, "The Principle is Partnership: General Education Library Instruction at Illinois State University," in *Library User Education: Powerful Learning, Powerful*

Partnerships, edited by Barbara Dewey (Metuchen, NJ: Scarecrow Press, 2001).

2. See http://www.assessment.ilstu.edu/resources/ for examples of the assessment projects undertaken related to general education or the first-year experience.

3. Stephen K. Hunt, Cheri J. Simonds, and Lisa Janicke Hinchliffe, "Using Student Portfolios as Authentic Assessment of the Basic Communication Course," *Journal on Excellence in College Teaching*, 11 (2000), 71.

4. Other follow-up projects include analyses of the artifact papers, the Communication Improvement Profile papers, and the synthesis papers, as well as a study of instructor feedback on speech evaluation forms.

5. Davis, Philip M., and Suzanne A. Cohen, "The Effect of the Web on Undergraduate Citation Behavior 1996-1999," *Journal of the American Society for Information Science and Technology*, 52 (2001): 309-314.

6. For details on sampling and, see Hunt, Simonds, and Hinchliffe, 61-62.

7. For books, the record from the online catalog rather than the book itself was retrieved.

8. The authors wish to thank Pam Werre, previously at Illinois State University and now the Public Services Librarian, Minnesota State University – Moorhead, for her assistance with the template, rubric, and hypotheses development.

9. The authors also wish to thank Joseph Hinchliffe for his assistance with the statistical analysis and the University Assessment Office at Illinois State University for the 1999-2000 Assessment Small Grant which funded the student assistance for source retrieval and data entry.

10. Debbie Malone and Carol Videon, "Assessing Undergraduate Use of Electronic Resources: A Quantitative Analysis of Works Cited," *Research Strategies*, 15 (1997), 154.

—LISA JANICKE HINCHLIFFE, CHRISTINE KUBIAK, STEPHEN K. HUNT AND CHERI J. SIMONDS—

WHO WANTS TO BE INFORMATION LITERATE

Susan S. Drummond

Knowing the importance of information literacy is easy when you're an academic librarian. You see the need for it everyday at the reference desk when students ask those questions that make you cringe. It often begins with, "My professor told me to come to the library and get two articles out of 'the' academic journal, where do you keep it?" College professors often assume that their students are as information literate as they are. They asked their students to get two articles out of "an" academic journal, while their students interpreted that request in a very different way. The problem is more than just one of poor communication.

College professors are information literate and find it very hard to remember what it was like when they weren't. Frequently professors are willing to share their stories of the trials and tribulations of dissertation research with only the slightest bit of encouragement. Often in these tales, the help of a reference librarian is described as being one of the essential elements to their success, if not the most essential element. What happens to that reliance on librarians and the information available in libraries after they obtain a position at a university? Why does this relationship with librarians seem to stop? Their students are sent to the library for information not understanding anything about how information is organized or how to access it. Often they arrive with assignments that have not been updated in years and are shocked to hear, when told by a librarian, that the only format a particular database comes in is no longer CD-

ROM, but Web based. How often have we heard, "but my professor said it was on CD-ROM and that's what I am supposed to use."

In order to introduce information literacy at Indiana University of Pennsylvania, a daylong information literacy think tank seminar was held in February 2000 sponsored by the University Library, the Office of the Provost and the Center for Teaching Excellence. The result of this seminar was the creation of a university-wide information literacy task force. The purpose of this task force was to examine information literacy and bring forward recommendations for implementation. Using as a reference point, *"Information Literacy Competency Standards for Higher Education,"* adopted by the Association of College and Research Libraries, this task force developed a one-page version of the ACRL standards, performance indicators, and outcomes. (See: IF Task Force standards summary attachment) The task force recently developed an assessment tool to assess the current skills of IUP students. The results of the assessment will help support the task force's efforts to promote information literacy and hopefully generate commitment among the faculty for its inclusion across the curriculum. Currently, the task force is developing faculty workshops to be presented in the Fall of 2002 and also providing funding for twenty-five mini-grants for the implementation of information literacy into the subject curriculum.

Along with the task force, of which I am a member, I started an information literacy teaching circle. The circle consists of three librarians and two faculty members from the nursing department. A Web page was developed and a presentation was given in

---

Drummond is an Instruction Librarian at the Indiana University of Pennsylvania, Indiana, PA.

October 2001 for sixty faculty members of Reflective Practice, a cross-disciplinary teaching group supported by IUP's Center for Teaching Excellence. (See URL page and Webliography) The purpose was to introduce and educate faculty about information literacy and the ACRL standards and outcomes, as well as providing a fun learning experience through the playing of a game, and how these standards could be incorporated in their curricula. A revised and updated presentation is what has been planned and submitted for LOEX.

The goal of the presentation is to introduce subject faculty to the concept of information literacy and get them interested in incorporating it into their curricula. It begins with examples from actual reference interviews to illustrate how their students often misinterpret their assignments and requests. The frustration the students feel is also illustrated when asked to retrieve items no longer available in old formats. The program consists of a PowerPoint presentation that begins by answering the question, "What is information literacy?" A brief history of the development of information literacy, the ACRL standards, performance indicators and outcomes and examples of ways information literacy is already being implemented at many universities serve as the introduction. The focus of the presentation is aimed at showing faculty how easy it is to incorporate information literacy standards, outcomes and assessment into their own teaching.

The questions from the presentation are based on each of the five ACRL standards and include the basic competencies that students should acquire by the end of their freshman year. The process that achieves this goal is accomplished by playing the game, "Who Wants to be Information Literate?" (See URL page at the end) Three volunteers will be chosen from the audience. Each contestant will be asked questions that illustrate one of the five standards. The monetary value of the questions increases with each standard. Contestants will have three lifelines that include: asking the audience, 50/50, and polling a colleague. The winner is the contestant with the most money at the end of the game. A small prize is awarded to all the volunteers, however the real prize is seeing the ease of implementing the information literacy standards.

The incorporation of information literacy into the subject curriculum at IUP is in its infancy. The goal of the information literacy task force and the Reflective Practice teaching circle is to make subject faculty aware of the need for information literacy and help them integrate it into their courses. If your institution has already adopted information literacy as an objective and has implemented ways to achieve it, then I thank you for paving the way for those of us just starting out.

The IUP Libraries offers three different courses on information access and digital resources for college credit each with a heavy emphasis on information literacy. These classes are taken as free electives, providing credit only towards graduation and are not required as part of any major course of study. Our goal is to make information literacy a required competency for all IUP students. There are many ways to achieve this with Web-based instruction, credit courses, collaborative teaching, etc. How it comes about should be an interesting course of events, one that will take the support of the administration and subject faculty along with the leadership of the information experts, the university librarians.

—SUSAN S. DRUMMOND—

URL Information for *"Who Wants to be Information Literate"*

This PowerPoint game is available as a link on the IUP Information Literacy Web Page at:

http://www.lib.iup.edu/infolit/infolitgame.ppt

The Webliography is available at
http://www.lib.iup.edu/infolit/Webliography.htm

A Review of the Information Literacy Competency Standards is available at
http://www.lib.iup.edu/infolit/ilintro.ppt
To learn more about Information Literacy visit the ACRL site at -
http://www.ala.org/acrl/infolit.html

IUP Information Literacy Competency Standards

Adapted 12/14/01 from the Association of College and Research Libraries, 2000.

Standard 1: The information literate person **determines** the nature and extent of the information needed.
Performance Indicators: The information literate person—
1. –defines and articulates the need for information.
2. –identifies a variety of types and formats of potential sources for information.
3. –considers the costs and benefits of acquiring the needed information.
4. –reevaluates the nature and extent of the information need.

Outcomes Include:
The person is able to identify and refine perceived information deficiencies, i.e., what information is needed; identify and analyze sources of information, i.e., where is the information located; analyze the financial and logistic implications of acquiring information, i.e., how will the information be obtained; and monitor the acquisition of information with an eye toward review and revision, i.e., when has enough information been gathered and evaluated

Standard 2: The information literate person **accesses** needed information effectively and efficiently.
Performance Indicators: The information literate person—
1. –selects the most appropriate investigative methods or information retrieval systems for accessing the needed information.
2. –constructs and implements effectively-designed search strategies.
3. –retrieves information online or in person using a variety of methods.
4. –refines the search strategy if necessary.
5. –extracts, records, and manages the information and its sources.

Outcomes Include:
Using efficient investigative methods, the person will implement effective information search strategies that will be beneficial in extracting and managing needed information. The research plan will utilize effective keywords, discipline-specific vocabulary, and a variety of search systems including library sources, online search engines, and other forms of inquiry, i.e., surveys and interviews. The person will evaluate the quality of the information and use correct citation procedures.

Standard 3: The information literate person **evaluates** information and its sources critically and **incorporates** selected information into his or her knowledge base and value systems.
Performance Indicators: The information literate person—
1. –summarizes the main ideas to be extracted from the information gathered.
2. –articulates and applies initial criteria for evaluating both the information and its sources.
3. –synthesizes main ideas to construct new concepts.
4. –compares new knowledge with prior knowledge to determine the value added, contradictions, or other unique characteristics of the information.
5. –determines whether the new knowledge has an impact on the individual's value system and takes steps to reconcile differences.
6. –validates understanding and interpretation of the information through discourse with other individuals, subject area experts, and/or practitioners.
7. –determines whether the initial query should be revised.

Outcomes Include:
The person will have an understanding of relevant information and the evaluation of the resource where the information was found as the first step to being able to then manipulate the information in various multimedia or software programs. The person will then determine supporting or conflicting information and viewpoints through comparison of information or discussion with others, in order to conclude whether or not the need for information has been satisfied.

Standard 4: The information literate person, individually or as a member of a group, **uses** information

 —SUSAN S. DRUMMOND—

effectively to accomplish a specific purpose.

Performance Indicators: The information literate person—

1. –applies new and prior information to the planning and creation of a particular product or performance.
2. –revises the development process for the product or performance.
3. –communicates the product or performance effectively to others.

Outcomes Include:

The person is able to plan and efficiently organize for an end result; incorporates all appropriate information (regardless of format); revises interim results(s) as necessary and is able to present the end result clearly and effectively to an intended audience.

Standard 5: The information literate person **understands context**, meaning, many of the economic, legal, and social issues surrounding the use of information and **accesses** and **uses** information ethically and legally.

Performance Indicators: The information literate person—

1. –understands many of the ethical, legal, and socio-economic issues surrounding information and information technology.
2. –follows laws, regulations, institutional policies, and etiquette related to the access and use of information resources.
3. –acknowledges the use of information sources in communicating the product or performance.

Outcomes include:

The person should know and respect privacy rights, etiquette, and copyrights. The person should also understand censorship and plagiarism issues. Finally, the information literate person must also know how to cite sources appropriately.

BUILDING A FAN BASE FOR
INFORMATION LITERACY

Carol Stookey and Lisa Roberts

Why build a fan base for information literacy?

It is vital that the entire campus be educated and work together to ensure students become information literate life-long learners. We'd love to share how we started the process and what we are learning along the way.

Three years ago we realized that perceptions about our library, the building, the collection and the instructional program were a bit out of date. We knew on the surface that we looked the same, but things were changing and changing dramatically. We had a homepage providing access to thousands of full-text articles—more than we ever had in print—we initiated a Reference One-on-One Program, and we were providing in-depth, course specific library instruction. But few knew it. We were out of touch with our administration, our faculty and our students.

To put this all in context, Principia College is a small (550 student enrollment) private liberal arts college for Christian Scientists located on the bluffs of the Mississippi River not far from St. Louis, Missouri. The institution was founded on the concept of whole-man education focusing on the spiritual, intellectual, moral, social and athletic development of each student. We offer 28 majors, support 19 varsity sport teams and have an average class size of 16. For an international perspective, Principia sponsors 4-6 study abroad programs annually with each having a specific focus (environment, music, language, WWII, etc). The Marshall Brooks Library contains approximately 200,000 volumes and provides access to over 90 electronic databases. We have 3.5 librarians and 2.75

adult support staff in addition to student workers. We work and play hard. Busyness can spawn a unique sort of isolation. And that's where we were.

Faculty members were certainly aware of the Internet information explosion, but few anticipated the extent of its impact on academics. Many were astonished with the realization that some students turn only to the Internet for information and never enter the library. Cut and paste plagiarism was being detected. The library could help, but how could we spread the word?

Where to Begin?

We started at the top. When Lisa interviewed for her position with the college library she asked the President and the Chairman of the Board to share their vision for the library. It became clear that the library could do even more than the administration had hoped for, but the library staff needed to communicate the possibilities in a tangible way. So this is where we began.

Carol had been reading the criteria for evaluating a college library in Peterson's *Smart Parent's Guide to Colleges* and our library compared very favorably. We decided to use these third-party criteria as a framework for a presentation to the college administration. Using PowerPoint to organize and deliver our message, we invited the College President, Deans of Faculty and Chairman of the Board to a presentation focusing on the strength and value of our library.

This was the first time they had ever been invited as a group to walk into the library and hear a presentation by the library staff. We described our vision for the library: an outstanding collection for undergraduates, premier service, and excellent training. When the criteria for evaluating the library

Stookey and *Roberts* are Librarians at Principia College, Elsah, IL.

shifted in their thought from the number of paper volumes in the building, to the access and services provided, we became an asset rather than a liability to the institution. We were perceived as small, but we were progressive and we were focusing our efforts in the right direction. We were asked by the administrators to share the presentation with admissions counselors, which led to a defined slot in freshman orientation.

While we were pleased with our initial success, we knew we needed to conduct a thorough assessment of our collection and services, and do a better job of reaching out to the larger college community. We asked ourselves the tough questions. Would our library be needed in 5 years, 10 years? If so, why? What would it look like? What would the collection be? What services would it provide? Would we be replaced by an online database?

We concluded that there was a place for our library in the future. But, it was clear that we would need to adopt a new collection development model, and the nature of instruction would certainly need to keep pace with the changes in the publishing world. We consciously set goals to advance the information literacy agenda with all our patrons: students, faculty and staff.

We began a review of our collection development policy, we updated our Web page and we placed a greater emphasis on instruction. In order to achieve our goals for information literacy several key pieces needed to be in place. Quality research required an outstanding collection (including quick, reliable access to subscription databases). In addition, we needed to provide reference services and bibliographic instruction that addressed the issues of information literacy. Finally, we needed a physical space that supported these key functions.

Goals Lead to Action

Our second "August Annual Report" to the administration used the same presentation technique as the first, and focused on a serials review project emphasizing our commitment to high academic standards and fiscal accountability; migration to electronic resources; improved reference services and our redesigned Web page. Challenges included the need for more computers, a teaching lab and remote patron access.

At this stage, serious planning for a teaching lab in the library began. Through the support of the administration and cooperation with CIS (Computer Information Services) we established an excellent lab. With the infusion of new computers, the library building now had more computers than any lab on campus. Inspired by a presentation at a LOEX conference we incorporated a Team Board in our lab design. Our teaching lab revolutionized the way we conducted bibliographic instruction sessions. It changed the community's perception of library resources, the physical space and the staff. For once, the library was on the cutting edge of technology and instruction.

Momentum was building. During these years we still worked intensely with individual faculty members to design instructional sessions, usually of the one-shot variety and had a loyal band of colleagues who were integrating information literacy expectations and skills into their course assignments. Collaboration in the development of capstone projects was a major endeavor. We worked side by side with faculty to design a research methods seminar for two individual disciplines. Senior capstone courses allowed us to hone higher-level research skills and emphasize the importance of critical evaluation of sources. We enjoyed great success with this core group of faculty, but we needed to reach a larger audience.

Raising the Bar

Our continued dialogue with the administration revealed the college President's desire to raise the research standard on campus. The administration turned to us as a partner and advocate for better, clearly articulated standards and the tools for achieving them. We shared a copy of the ACRL *Information Literacy Competency Standards for Higher Education* with the administration. We also distributed the document and articulated its goals in academic unit meetings and with Freshman Year Experience faculty. Our internal assessment of the library collection, services and facilities enabled us to speak clearly and plainly about our vision. It became the persona of the library. We stood for information literacy.

Our third annual session focused on research standards and challenges in the information age. We illustrated the relationship between good research assignments and good research products. We suggested techniques for setting a higher research standard while simultaneously pre-empting plagiarism. We also unveiled our new library home page. The page had been redesigned to facilitate an organized research strategy. Within the year we had an opportunity to address the entire faculty on the subject of plagiarism during a regular faculty senate meeting. In addition, the Deans who heard the message about assignment design asked us to conduct a workshop for all new faculty (those with three or fewer years experience at our institution). The workshop focused

—CAROL STOOKEY AND LISA ROBERTS—

on effective research assignment design. Our theme was "make it easy for students to do the right thing". We encouraged cooperative collection development, collaboration on research design, incorporation of library instruction and utilization of Reference One-on-One. It provided an opportunity to share our information literacy goals and the response has been positive and appreciative. With a renewed sense of vision we shared our message with others whenever the opportunity presented itself.

Developing Partnerships

We began to act as a partner with the Assessment Office in their efforts to conduct assessment in the classroom. Our faculty members are asked to assess their courses and the outcomes of their assignments, but to many, it is a daunting task. We provided the assessment office with criteria for good research assignments—elements that help the student on the path to information literacy. They took the criteria and produced a rubric for faculty to employ when designing and evaluating research assignments. It was a symbiotic relationship—they gained a valuable support tool for faculty and we were able to reach our target audience with our message. Faculty and students benefited from the improved research assignments. The success of this endeavor encouraged us to look elsewhere on campus for partners.

We finally realized that we needed to share our vision with the CIS department. Until then our communication had been limited to discussion of computer problems. We had never shared the big picture with them. We explained the importance of delivery time for our databases. Library databases were in direct competition with search engines. It was paramount that delivery time was not an obstacle. We wanted to make it easy and desirable for students to access the best information on a given topic. Now CIS better understands our demands on the server and the role of our Web page. They gained a better appreciation for our expertise and sent faculty our way for collaboration on academic information technology projects.

Branching Out

Individuals who attended our various presentations asked us to share with other groups on campus. All it takes is one inspired listener in the audience. We never say no to an invitation or opportunity to share our skills, message, vision, purpose, or opinion with individuals or groups. We do make office calls, and encourage phone-in questions at the time of need.

As a result, we have shared our message with a variety of departments and audiences including the Career Development Center, Development and Field Activities, and Staff Senate, to name a few. We made presentations during Summer session (for adult learners) and Alumni Week. Each time we customized our message, our slides and analogies to meet the needs of the audience. Our audiences left informed, interested and impressed. They often refer faculty our way.

Presentation Style

Using PowerPoint allows us to plan and script our messages so the presentation is succinct, well organized, and attractive. It keeps us focused on our subject and keeps us on time. We use PowerPoint for structure and impact but we never try to "read our slides." We do the talking and rarely provide handouts.

Team presentations have proven effective. We provide back up for one another in case a point is forgotten or needs clarification. We can stop each other from rambling. It brings energy to the presentation as the audience attention shifts from speaker to screen to different speaker. While one is speaking the other can assess the audience reaction and mentally prepare for the next segment. We can spontaneously respond when we see confused or questioning expressions.

Our message is always positive and our presentation style is informal and enthusiastic. When outlining the challenges of the information age we suggest practical solutions and explain how we implement those solutions in our daily work. In short, we don't whine. Our audience understands that we are approaching information literacy from a positive, energetic perspective. We see it as an opportunity for continued progress. We explore and propose solutions, share in and encourage brainstorming, and are not afraid to address challenges or concerns. The library is important, as are the services we provide and the skills we teach.

We are constantly working to inform simply with clearly defined concepts. Finding common vocabulary is paramount. We avoid jargon and consciously question and evaluate our use of "library lingo." Terms we have clarified include: online, electronic, catalog, OPAC/IPAC, Internet access, subscription database, migration, cut and paste plagiarism, and the most ubiquitous term of all "information literacy".

At its root, information literacy is not a complicated concept. People can relate to the objective when you employ analogies or give examples of the good and the bad. Everyone wants to connect with a positive, progressive vision. Our audiences were grateful to know that we are teaching the ethics of information and are expecting quality research at the undergraduate level. They felt good about our vision of the library in the information age, and as a result, became advocates for information literacy.

Why Build a Fan Base?

We learned that we couldn't achieve our goals for information literacy alone. We needed to work in collaboration with many others. In our case, the support of top administration has been key. They have provided funding for projects, endorsed our agenda and articulated their support to the faculty. They have provided forums with the faculty that we could not establish on our own. The support of CIS was, and continues to be critical. Without their technical support, our library services are crippled. The support of the Development Group has led to funding and donations. The staff senate presentation led to publicity for the library programs in the alumni magazine. Alumni groups became aware of our activities and their support impacts enrollment and perception of the institution as a whole. The job of assessment has become easier and more focused, more purposeful as a result of our collaboration. Our connection with the Career Development Center has

led to a regular slot in a two-day Career Camp seminar for juniors and seniors entering the job market. In short, our goals became shared goals. Through marketing our vision we found a common ground with new partners and ultimately the real winners are the students.

So where are we on the path to information literacy? We're still at the first curve in the road, but it is a good beginning. Our administration knows we're ready and willing to lead, and the climate is right. So, we keep offering and suggesting, teaching and smiling.

BIBLIOGRAPHY

Association of College and Research Libraries. *Information Literacy Competency Standards for Higher Education*. Chicago, IL: American Library Association, 2000.

Ernest L. Boyer and Paul Boyer. *Smart Parents Guide to College: The 10 Most Important Factors for Students and Parents When Choosing a College*. Princeton, NJ: Peterson's, 1996.

—CAROL STOOKEY AND LISA ROBERTS—

COMPARING TWO APPROACHES TO DEVELOPING INTERACTIVE TUTORIALS

Heather Cunningham, Margaret Cunningham, Rea Devakos, and Trudi Bellardo Hahn

As we step into the 21st century, librarians are seeking innovative pedagogical approaches for introducing the ever-increasing complexities of research to novice users. Interactive tutorials that appeal to the Web generation, are self-paced, and satisfy the needs of large numbers of commuter students for virtual and anytime access to library resources. In addition, they address the logistical challenges of limited staff and appropriate teaching facilities. This paper describes and contrasts two different approaches to creating and evaluating online tutorials for teaching information literacy skills to large first-year classes.

The Gerstein Science Information Centre at the University of Toronto (U of T) is creating a customized online tutorial to be integrated into *BIO 150 Organisms in the Environment* in the Fall of 2002. Students must complete the self-study exercise before their first major written assignment. This stand-alone tool will be intertwined with a specially developed desktop library.

The University of Maryland (UM) Libraries modified the open source code of the University of Texas' popular tutorial, *TILT (Texas Information Literacy Tutorial*: http://lib.utsystem.edu/). UM's *TILT (Terrapin Information Literacy Tutorial*: http://www.lib.umd.edu/UES/TILT) prepares students enrolled in *ENGL 101 Introduction to Writing* before

Heather Cunningham and *Devakos* are librarians at the University of Toronto Libraries, Toronto, Canada; *Margaret Cunningham* and *Hahn* are librarians a the University of Maryland Libraries.

before they attend *Library Day*, a lab session conducted by librarians.

University of Toronto: Project Planning, Implementation, and Evaluation

Since *BIO 150* is a prerequisite for additional undergraduate life science courses, there are approximately 1,500 students for the main academic year and 300 for the summer session. One course coordinator, six to eight faculty and 35 graduate teaching assistants (TAs) teach the course. Lectures and labs are supplemented by the innovative use of instructional technologies. The course's Web-based exercises are lab assignments and hence integrated into the grading structure (http://www.cquest.utoronto.ca/zoo/bio150y/labs/online.htm). The course's core nature presents a unique opportunity to reach large numbers of students, influential faculty, and TAs who in turn may further disseminate information about library resources.

Library instruction has been and will continue to be provided by an online *Library Clue* assignment; each student is randomly assigned an incomplete journal citation. Two hundred unique clues are generated and approximately ten percent are changed each year. Students must locate the article and photocopy the first page. Web pages explain how to use a periodical index and the catalogue (http://www.cquest.utoronto.ca/zoo/bio150y/labs/library00.htm). Most students find their journal articles within an hour. Students learn not only the basic steps in locating a journal article but are taught, through example, *what is* primary science literature.

Impetus for the current project came from the *BIO 150* course coordinator. When faced with developing a position on a controversial scientific topic, students needed skills beyond those covered in *Library Clue*. The initial meeting emphasized the need to link library resources and instruction. In addition, we chose to build on expertise gained in developing previous online tutorials and desktop libraries.

The core working group was comprised of two librarians and the course coordinator. The library matched funding received from the Provost's Instructional Technology Courseware Development Fund. The monies received were used for hiring a graduate assistant, Web designers, and an illustrator. The librarians created the content for the tutorial, the illustrator created graphics, the graduate student assisted in resource discovery, inputting of content, and text editing, and the course coordinator vetted content. Web designers were hired to create an XML template. All working group members except one librarian had a biology background. Development started in May 2001. To date, librarians have spent the equivalent of approximately two months full-time, and the graduate student accounts for another two months. Two intertwined tools are being developed and tested:

My Biology Library (http://eir.library.utoronto. ca/MyUTL/guides/index.cfm?guide=biology), using locally developed "my library" software, is a Web portal of highly selective and annotated collections of online site licensed resources, such as e-journals, periodical indexes, e-books and Web sites. It is intended to be a desktop library for the entire University biological sciences community.

The tutorial (http://www.cquest.utoronto. ca/zoo/bio150y/oif/) will demonstrate, through interactive exploration, how to effectively search and use the resources delineated in *My Biology Library* as well as propose strategies to evaluate the information retrieved. Three independent modules focus on Web, journals, and monographs. A biology example is used, hence the name "*Optimal Information Foraging*" (OIF). Upon completion, the OIF will be a required self-study lab with the same look and feel as the other online laboratory exercises.

In order to incorporate active learning and stretch limited funds, quiz content, games (Tiltometer, Think Fast, Library Squares), and images from Texas' TILT will be adapted and integrated. Graphics cleared for educational use as well as originally created images will also be used. The interactive features of Flash Animation and Java components illustrate and enforce concepts; hence, a text-based version was not considered. Students have access to library and other campus workstations that meet optimal technical requirements.

Implementation and formal usability testing will begin in summer 2002. Feedback will be gathered via focus groups, evaluation forms, and interviews with students and TAs. This will allow for modifications before fully integrating both tools into the fall curriculum and grade structure.

The working group faced many challenges. Deriving a storyline, or "hook," that would capture students' interests and make it appealing was a major obstacle. Early attempts involved controversial examples that would retrieve information with strong biases to emphasize the need for evaluation and selection. However, when the examples began to drive the tutorial, the working group decided that the instructional content should exist independent of the examples. This would facilitate future changes to the example in order to incorporate "hot" or innovative topics without having to reconstruct the entire tutorial.

It is a decided benefit for a librarian to have a subject background in biology, particularly for resource selection and suggesting appropriate examples. In addition, knowledge of Flash, HTML, and XML coding are advantageous skills in order to modify TILT as well as incorporate new content.

The project and approach have been time consuming. Close collaboration between the librarians and *BIO 150* course coordinator has been required; the meshing of time schedules has been difficult. Many discussions between the librarians and faculty members appeared to reveal conflicting viewpoints. Later, however, we realized that the views were similar but expressed in different terminology. Besides a great deal of time, capital is also required to create a customized tutorial. We have also learned to delineate task responsibility clearly in contracts. For example, Web designers and librarians were both under the impression that the other would encode in XML; the task ultimately fell on the librarians.

University of Maryland: Project Planning, Implementation, and Evaluation

Since the early 1980's, the UM Libraries has provided instructional support for the English Department's Freshmen Writing Program. *ENGL 101* is required for all entering freshmen; each year it is offered in the Fall, Spring and Summer semesters to approximately 3,300 students in 180 sections. A director manages the program; graduate teaching assistants or instructors teach individual sections. Each section comes to the library on their *Library Day* for information literacy instruction. Until three years ago, library staff trained *ENGL 101*

 —HEATHER CUNNINGHAM, MARGARET CUNNINGHAM, REA DEVAKOS, AND TRUDI BELLARDO HAHN—

teaching assistants how to teach library research skills. In recent years, however, TAs have found it increasingly difficult to master the rapid changes and proliferation of information resources. In 1999, the library received a modest campus grant to hire three special lecturers to teach most of the *Library Day* sessions. In a typical session, students learn about using information resources to choose a controversial current essay topic, select databases, construct search strategies, and evaluate Web sites.

Librarians initiated the tutorial project by soliciting the help of the Freshmen Writing Program director in rethinking *Library Day*. In addition, the newly hired special lecturers provided timely recommendations. The goals of the 50 or 75-minute sessions, to introduce a wide range of information resources as well as demonstrate specific tools to research individual topics, were too ambitious. Special lecturers were spending precious class time covering *what is a catalog*, *what is a periodical database*, and *how to read an LC call number* rather than helping students find keywords and create effective search strategies. Librarians proposed an interactive tutorial to introduce a broader range of information literacy skills as pre-work to *Library Day*. Options for creating the tutorial ranged from in-house production to outsourcing, either to campus computer center programmers or outside (non-university) programmers.

Fortuitously, neither of the local options was required; the University of Texas made TILT available via open source code. This acclaimed instructional tool contained the critical features needed. If TILT could be successfully adapted, *Library Day* could be assignment driven, focusing on specific resources and search strategies for students' individual paper topics. TILT was downloaded onto the library's server in March 2001 with few problems. The major obstacle was using the campus' LDAP server to store information about students as they logged into TILT. The LDAP server worked fine but there were numerous problems getting TILT's php3 scripts to relay or "talk to" it properly. This issue was resolved by converting all php3 scripts from LDAP to MySQL, an open source database package. Because Maryland decided to track a different set of data about students than Texas (name and ID barcode number), most of the cookies had to be redone. Changes were made so that quizzes could be taken an infinite number of times and a student could e-mail all module quiz scores at one time to the *ENGL 101* teaching assistant.

In April, a working group was formed to adapt TILT. The adaptation and implementation occurred in four phases:

Phase I. A working group of ten was formed consisting of seven librarians, two graduate students from the College of Information Studies, and one programmer. For two months, the group examined TILT page by page. Although the essential content was retained, some pages were edited, reordered, or omitted and some new pages were developed. By June, the working group was reduced to two librarians and the programmer. TILT was introduced to eight *ENGL 101* sections (181 students) during the summer. The students commented, via TILT, on each of the three modules. The majority liked TILT and enjoyed the games, images, and interactivity. Fortunately, they reported few technical problems. However, some commented that TILT took too long to finish, some of the quiz questions were tricky or confusing, and the third module was the most difficult.

Phase II. (August to December 2001) Based on student feedback, the librarians and programmer spent a large part of August and early September modifying TILT. The Freshmen Writing director mandated that students must take TILT as a prerequisite to *Library Day*. At the Fall orientation for *ENGL 101* TAs and librarians introduced TILT—what it is, how to access it, when to assign it, what to do if there are technical problems. They also discussed how it supports *Library Day* and how it should be incorporated into the syllabus. During the Fall semester, students were surveyed about TILT use and integration with *Library Day*. Of the 1,123 evaluation forms collected at the end of *Library Day*, 67% had completed TILT, 11% partially completed and 22% had not (most in this last category said that TILT was not assigned). Of the students who had completed both TILT and *Library Day*, 38% said they worked well together, 54% gave no response, and 8% disagreed. Not one student thought TILT should replace *Library Day*.

Meanwhile, a graduate student in the College of Information Studies worked on a 3-credit independent study, analyzing Maryland's TILT to see how particular pages could be shortened and made more readable and appealing to freshmen by using recommended Web design principles.

Phase III. (January to April 2002) The graduate student's recommendations, as well as the results of the librarians' close analysis of TILT in relation to the ACRL Information Literacy Competency Standards for Higher Education (http://www.ala.org/acrl/ilstandardslo.html) were applied to yet further revisions. Librarians also created a pre-and post-test to assess what students were learning from TILT alone and what they were learning from the combination of TILT and *Library*

Day. The tests were piloted with 176 students in eight sections. Even though the pilot revealed some problems with the test instruments, the results offered insights into which information literacy skills were not being covered adequately in either TILT or *Library Day*. The pre-test was given about one week before students experiencing TILT or *Library Day*. The post-test was given to half the students immediately prior to *Library Day* and the other half was administered one week after *Library Day*. The mean score of the pre-test was too high; the questions are probably too easy or guessable. We are currently analyzing the learning curve of individual questions. So far, we are seeing improvement on identifying the best type of source to use for specific information needs, use of different Boolean operators, and LC call number sequencing

Phase IV. (May to August 2002) The pre-and post-tests will be revised and used again. Rearranging, revising, deleting, and adding new TILT pages will continue. Librarians will work on building their own advanced skills to design new graphics and Flash animation, to be able to improve TILT without having to depend upon the programmer. A decision will be made whether to revise or drop TILT Lite (a less interactive version).

Conclusions and Lessons Learned

There are similarities and dissimilarities between projects. A number of key differences cannot be attributed to differing project time lines. At the U of T, the result is a customized tutorial and desktop library. Usage of the *OIF* and *My Biology Library* is intended not only for the *BIO 150* community, but for the natural progression of life science courses. Content is new but the instructional and design "template" was taken from the course, not library tutorials. UM did not have to invent from scratch an interactive tutorial that introduces basic information literacy and library terminology; Maryland adapted content from an existing library tutorial to leverage traditional in-person instruction. The combination of tutorial plus live class enabled *ENGL 101* students to receive a basic information literacy foundation and instruction pertinent to their assignments. Librarians had the necessary HTML skills to modify TILT and could rely on in-house programming to troubleshoot technical problems.

The similarities are perhaps more telling. Both projects are immediately relevant to the needs of a specific group of students and integrated into the course curriculum. The U of T and UM tutorials share short time lines and mainly use existing staff. Both projects do not build on work previously done, both in online tutorials and in fostering strong faculty relationships—neither the ENGL 101 director nor the BIO 150 course coordinator could to be persuaded about the value of library instruction. The most critical element for successful development and implementation of a Web-based tutorial is buy-in from faculty who understand the value of information literacy skills for their students and the relationship of these skills to their curriculum goals. Interactive Web tutorials can successfully teach basic information literacy skills. Whether creating a tutorial from the start, or modifying a ready-made one, the task is extremely time-consuming if one wishes to link it closely to local curricular needs. Either way librarians will need to develop technical skills for writing or modifying code. User testing and feedback help ensure that a tutorial is meeting users' needs and preferences.

—HEATHER CUNNINGHAM, MARGARET CUNNINGHAM, REA DEVAKOS, AND TRUDI BELLARDO HAHN—

DIFFERENT MODELS, COMMON GOALS: INFORMATION LITERACY ACROSS THE LIBERAL ARTS CURRICULUM

Jessica Grim, Susan D. Scott, Julia Chance Gustafson, Jasmine Vaughan, and Cynthia H. Comer

Introduction

In 1999 the Five Colleges of Ohio (The College of Wooster, Denison University, Kenyon College, Oberlin College, and Ohio Wesleyan University) were awarded a major grant from the Andrew W. Mellon Foundation for support of a three-year program called "Integrating Information Literacy into the Liberal Arts Curriculum." The work of the grant focuses on building collaborative partnerships between librarians and faculty members at each of the campuses, with the ultimate goal of increasing undergraduate students' information literacy (IL) skills and capabilities. A Steering Committee and an Information Literacy Committee made up of members from across the consortium are responsible for oversight of the grant and consortial planning. Campus Committees on each campus oversee grant-related projects and activities at the local level.

Specific project goals include:
- Increased awareness on each campus of the need for and importance of IL
- Incorporation of IL content into the curriculum in significant ways

---

Grim and *Comer* are librarians at the Oberlin College Library, Oberlin, OH; *Scott* is a librarian at the Denison University Library, Granville, OH; *Gustafson* is a librarian at The College of Wooster Libraries, Wooster, OH; *Vaughan* is a librarian at the Kenyon College Libraries, Gambier, OH.

- Sharing of local experiences among librarians across the consortium
- Improved faculty communication on issues of pedagogical techniques for incorporating IL
- Improved faculty and librarian skills for teaching IL
- Improved mechanisms for sharing instructional materials relating to IL
- Increased use of Web resources to facilitate the development of IL skills
- Sharing information about the project through national-level conferences and publications

At each campus, curriculum development incentives in the form of stipends or course-release are made available to teaching faculty, who then, in conjunction with librarians, develop proposals for incorporating IL into new or existing courses.

Two years into the program our collective experiences across the five colleges, which have involved over 40 separate curriculum development projects, 60 faculty members, and 24 librarians to date, have provided us with much to learn from, think about, and share with others. These first two years of the grant have been among the busiest that any of the librarians involved in instruction at the five colleges can remember, in no small part due to increased activity, excitement, and involvement stemming from the grant.

The following comments focus on four topics central to the program: cultivating faculty interest in the curriculum development aspect, collaborating with faculty on course development, methods for teaching IL content, and assessment and outcomes.

Recruiting Faculty

While faculty recruitment at each of the five colleges looks similar in many ways, the process at each campus has unique aspects. Getting the course development projects off on the right foot was a major goal for each Campus Committee, thus most of the pilot projects were hand-picked. Selection was based primarily on pre-existing relationships between librarians and faculty that had been developing over time. On some campuses an opening event also played a role in the selection of the pilot project.

Events to encourage faculty to submit curriculum development proposals are, at some institutions, scheduled on a regular basis at the beginning of each semester. At other campuses publicity events are more sporadic. For example, the College of Wooster's librarians hosted an Information Literacy Grant workshop, with dinner served, at the beginning of the first year of the grant, and in subsequent semesters have held workshops with brown-bag lunches or teas. Ohio Wesleyan University kicked off the grant on their campus with an all day program that included an address by a nationally known speaker.

Overall, the strategies employed to encourage faculty to apply for information literacy curriculum development grants are similar to those typically used to entice them to take advantage of our larger instructional programs:

- Workshops (organized at the campus or consortial level)
- E-mail broadcasts
- Library newsletter articles and reminders
- Flyers
- Campus newspaper articles
- Library Web page announcements
- Enhancing and expanding pre-existing working relationships with faculty
- Using the liaison system as a vehicle to begin conversations
- Announcements and reminders at departmental meetings

Successful Recruitment Strategies

Several symposiums have been organized for faculty and librarians from across the five colleges. One workshop focused on assessment, and featured Debra Gilchrist, a nationally recognized expert on the topic in the library field. Another symposium targeted faculty members in the sciences and included activities and demonstrations focused on the science disciplines. Symposiums typically include a panel discussion featuring faculty members who have received a curriculum development grant and the librarian working with them. Hearing about successful experiences creates interest such that new grants are generated following each of these symposiums.

Librarians have also used the opportunity of local library-sponsored workshops, on topics such as cybercheating or copyright, to speak to faculty about the available information literacy curriculum development grants.

At colleges using a liaison librarian system, librarians working closely with departments have capitalized on already forged relationships to promote information literacy as a concept, which has led to a number of grant proposals.

In addition to targeting specific groups, such as mentioned above, with the workshop for science faculty, targeting specific individual faculty members serves two positive ends. First, building on an existing teaching relationship can smooth the grant application process as well as the teaching of the revised or new course associated with the grant. Targeting individual faculty members can also facilitate the distribution of information literacy throughout the academic divisions.

In some cases, faculty members who are already developing new courses or who are contemplating doing so, hear about the curriculum development grants and are motivated, because the timing is right, to apply for a grant. These new classes, with information literacy concepts as major teaching objectives, have been some of the most innovative classes developed under the grant.

Library directors have also played a significant role at each of the five campuses in recruiting faculty. Some directors have spoken at departmental meetings, while others simply take the opportunity to share success stories at the many informal occasions they have to interact with faculty.

Collaboration with Faculty

The collaborative role of librarians working with faculty on information literacy projects under the grant can best be represented as a continuum, running from very minimal collaborative input to complete team-teaching. The models described below represent the range of that continuum.

Levels of librarian collaboration in projects vary from librarian to librarian, faculty member to faculty member, and course to course. Involvement levels depend on local guidelines in place at some institutions; the comfort level, persistence, and experience of the librarian; the commitment to the project on the part of the faculty member; and the nature of the course itself.

Librarian as Consultant

The Consultant Model involves librarians working with faculty members at a number of stages including syllabus planning, assignment design, and assessment design. Some librarians create assignments or assessment instruments, and others assist faculty members in creating Web sites. These projects do not involve classroom teaching on the librarian's part.

One weakness of the Consultant Model arises when the results of assessment are not shared fully with the librarian or when the assessment instrument is not well-designed, creating an environment where the librarian lacks enough feedback to know whether the project has been successful. A positive aspect of this model is the emphasis on the librarian-faculty interaction at the syllabus planning stage, when the librarian has an opportunity to help the faculty member integrate IL in the most appropriate places in a given course.

Librarian as Consultant/Instructor

Librarians working with faculty using the Consultant/Instructor Model typically do some or all of the tasks described above, with the addition of teaching responsibility for up to several class sessions. Some librarians in this collaborative model create assignments or assessment instruments and Web sites or tutorials to accompany the sessions they teach. Others utilize pre-existing Web sites such as the Five Colleges of Ohio Information Literacy Tutorial (http://www.denison. edu/ohio5/infolit/).

The strengths and weaknesses of the Consultant/Instructor Model echo those of the Consultant Model. All of the Five Colleges report that some of their librarians work within this model. While the local guidelines at the College of Wooster state clearly that the librarians will serve as consultants in the grant projects, they also allow the faculty member and the librarian to decide together how many class sessions, if any, the librarian will lead.

Librarian as Team Teacher

The Team Teacher Model incorporates all of the activities in the Consultant and Consultant/Instructor models, but includes additional in-class observation and more opportunities to participate in the teaching of the course. There is also more librarian involvement in the design, implementation, and reviewing of course assignments (see Appendix 1). Librarian involvement

within the Team Teaching Model ranges from teaching three or more class sessions and/or labs, to observation/participation in half the class sessions, to attending all class sessions.

For a project in Economics at Denison University, a librarian team-taught the course and contributed to every class session. At Ohio Wesleyan University, all project librarians are required to teach four or more class sessions per project. Some librarians attend each class session and some attend only the classes in which they are the featured instructor, as determined by the faculty-librarian team.

One weakness of this model is librarian stress and overwork as a result of the significant time and energy commitment. The benefits of this model include a significant increase in demand for information literacy advice and integration into the curriculum, an increase (at some institutions) in demand at the reference desk and for individual research appointments, and wide-spread visibility on campus for the library's efforts in the area of information literacy.

Teaching Models

Many methods for teaching IL concepts and skills have been used across the campuses. Some methods rely on leadership by the instructors. These methods include lectures by the faculty member and/or librarian; in-class discussions about the research process; local information resources, and the ethical and legal uses of information; and hands-on instruction or lab sessions.

Other methods rely on assignments to reinforce IL concepts. Some examples of written assignments are worksheets, annotated bibliographies, literature reviews, research papers, and research logs which are kept by students and e-mailed to the librarian for feedback (see Appendix 2).

Faculty-librarian teams have sometimes employed collaborative learning techniques. These techniques have included peer-review of written assignments, group evaluation of print and electronic resources and Web sites, and critique of peers' research processes.

In addition to employing a number of in-class and take-home activities, faculty-librarian teams have produced a variety of online materials to support IL instruction and assignments, including guides, bibliographies, tutorials, bulletin boards, and chat environments often employing courseware.

Factors Influencing Selection of Methods

Selection and implementation of these teaching models are influenced by a combination of factors, including: degree of librarian involvement; role of the librarian in collaboration and instruction; faculty member's knowledge of information literacy principles and information resources; goals of the course; amount of time available for in-class IL instruction; language of instruction; number of students; physical location of students, *e.g.* study abroad or on-campus; technology skills of faculty member and librarian; and availability of technology resources.

Examples

The following case studies highlight some of the unique teaching methods employed in funded projects:

In a **First-Year Studies Seminar** at Denison University, students were required to maintain a research log. Initially, the librarian requested weekly updates from the 18 students in the seminar, though the frequency was later reduced. Students were required to complete a standard list of questions addressing such things as database used, search terms and results, and evaluation and planned use of the resources. Depending on the quality of work the librarian made anywhere from one to many replies, and even required in-person meetings for some students. The research log was intended to hold students accountable and keep them on track for completing a research paper over the course of the semester.

In **Psychology 101: Introduction to Psychology**, at Kenyon College, a psychology-specific tutorial, http://www2.kenyon.edu/depts/psychology/psychtutorialdraft/, was modified from the general tutorial mentioned above, to introduce students to IL concepts. The tutorial was designed both to introduce IL concepts and to reinforce them as follow-up to librarian-led instruction sessions on OPAC and database searching. The tutorial and instruction session equipped students to complete a series of worksheets leading up to a comparison of claims in a popular source and three scholarly articles. At Kenyon there are three sections of Introduction to Psychology, with a total of about 200 enrolled students. Many of the students are non-psychology majors, taking the course to fulfill general education requirements.

In support of the **Rhetoric & Composition** curriculum and new **First-Year Seminar Program** at Oberlin College, one faculty member, in consultation with a librarian drafted a print guide for faculty called "Integrating Research and Information Literacy into Rhetoric & Composition Colloquia and First-Year Seminars." The guide includes practical suggestions, pointers, and advice based on the faculty members' direct experience. Sections in the guide include: "Why integrate information literacy into the colloquia?" "How to integrate IL", "Guiding students in Web-based research", "Options for working with a

librarian", "Suggested in-class activities", and a bibliography of IL articles and Web sites.

Assessment and Outcomes

Student Learning

According to the grant proposal, one measure of the project's success would be the improved information literacy skills of students, as determined by participating faculty. Although the proposal did not specify methods of assessing student learning, it was understood that course evaluation data would be collected from student participants, including self-assessments of whether or not their skills improved.

The Steering Committee developed a student evaluation questionnaire as a guideline for use in individual courses (see Appendix 4). This instrument is primarily a self-assessment tool that asks students to indicate whether their IL skills improved as a result of taking the course. Many participating faculty have used this form as is, some have adapted it to their own needs, adding checklists or converting questions to Likert scales, and still others have developed their own tools to more fully assess what and whether students are actually learning.

Some instructors have used simple feedback gathered throughout the semester to determine the levels of student comfort with the material, while others have developed more elaborate methods of assessment. Various course assignments, some of which are described in the section above on teaching models, form the basis for effective evaluation of student learning. Examples include graded exercises, research logs, critical analyses of journal articles, literature reviews, research papers, presentations to peers describing research projects, and final exams. In several courses students were administered a pre-test at the start of the semester, and a post-test at the end. For example, a targeted pre-test was used in a Chemistry course at the College of Wooster (see Appendix 3), with the intention of giving the same or a parallel test at the end of the course. Results of these tests are encouraging; faculty report improvement on post-test scores. In the case of a First-Year Seminar course at the College of Wooster, there was marked score improvement (the test used as pre/post-test, complete with outcomes and answers is found at: http://www.wooster.edu/library/oh5/literacy/assessment/pretestwithanswers.html).

Overall Grant Program

The grant proposal explicitly states that the program overall must also be assessed. The primary basis for this assessment will consist of the success in meeting stated outcomes, as described in the introduction. As the end of the grant period approaches, it is clear that substantial progress in meeting the initial goals of the proposal has been made. Faculty awareness of information literacy issues has increased significantly on our campuses. Currently there are more than forty individual projects completed or in progress. Hundreds of students have benefited from these revised curricula.

Several symposia sponsored by the consortium have brought librarians and faculty together to discuss course revision, new course development, and pedagogical techniques. The project Website, http://www.denison.edu/ohio5/grant/, reflects the activities of the faculty-librarian teams in many efforts: syllabi, assignments, handouts, guides, and links to outside resources. Faculty-librarian teams have delivered papers about their information literacy collaborative efforts at two disciplinary conferences, and presentations have been made at various local and regional meetings as well.

Reflections

In the beginning of the program, many librarians lacked confidence in conducting effective assessments. To address this a symposium was organized that included both an outside expert on the topic, and several faculty-librarian teams from the first round of projects who presented initial assessment results. Faculty with a stronger interest in assessing student opinions and behaviors are often more engaged in the information literacy aspects of their courses than other faculty. When pre-tests are given, many faculty express surprise at the knowledge gaps in their students' understanding of basic information literacy concepts. The realization that students are not as adept at these concepts as faculty had assumed has sometimes resulted in new faculty-library collaborations.

This program continues to be a "work in progress." It is too soon for comprehensive, final assessments. Even after the grant period has ended, the work of collaborating with faculty to integrate information literacy into the curriculum will continue. Both faculty and librarians realize that the assessment process must be refined, based on student experiences as well as campus needs.

Conclusion

Although the Mellon grant provided the impetus for the activities described in the sections above, in large measure the success of the program has depended upon a general readiness "on the part of both librarians and faculty" to move the IL agenda forward. While we suspect the stipend offered for course development served as the primary motivator for a few faculty proposals, in most cases the motivations to apply for a grant were pedagogically based on: 1) faculty seeing more and more students who simply don't understand how to do effective research; 2) concern over plagiarism and intellectual property issues; and 3) frustration with student use and misuse of the Internet. Faculty at many institutions were, in short, ready to hear about information literacy, and ready to see its potential for providing valuable solutions to these problems.

The grant provided us with a highly visible platform from which to promote IL on our campuses. It also served to push along the IL agenda within our libraries, where librarians were suddenly more engaged with discussing and thinking about IL issues. Yet without the readiness of faculty, the perception that *something* needed to change, *and* the readiness of librarians, the project would have fallen flat.

There was a small amount of librarian release time built into the grant (approximately .3 FTE at each institution), and this unique aspect of the grant is one of its strengths. Yet the time and energy being put into grant-related work by librarians across the five campuses is such that it is often hard to fit everything else in, and it has become clear that the released time built into the grant only partially addresses the need.

Assuming we can find methods of off-setting schedule demands for librarians, the major question to address as we move into the final phase of the grant program is how can the largely successful efforts to incorporate IL into the curriculum be continued into the future? How can we ensure that the far-reaching curricular impact that has developed under the grant will be built upon? The answers to these questions will ultimately have to be worked out on each campus, factoring in the subtleties of campus climate, faculty culture, and library culture. Determining levels of support both within the institution and the library administration will also be key in helping set the long-term post-grant IL agenda on each campus.

Additional information about the background, structure, and workings of the grant, as well as materials such as assignments, syllabi, and library skills tests, can be found on the grant Website: http://www.denison.edu/ohio5/grant/

The authors would like to thank Danielle Clarke, Ohio Wesleyan University, for her valuable input in the course of writing this paper.

Appendix 1: Team Teacher Model

Education 312 Fall 2001   *Teaching is Transformative*
(a page from the syllabus for Education 312, Dr. Lyn Robertson & Susan D. Scott, librarian, Denison University)

Class	Lab	Readings	ISTE Standards	ACRL Standards & Objectives

September 3
Discussion:
 	
- 30 years of literacy research
  - schema theory
  - metacognition
  - theory into practice
 	
Susan Scott on information literacy:
- equity, ethics, legal and human issues concerning technology & computer use
- technology and lifelong learning
	September 4
	Classroom management tools:
	
	Word
	Excel
		Read:
		■ Rosenblatt (Eres)
		■ Praxis III, Domain C
		Set up a grade book for one of your student teaching classes; use it to track your students' progress through the lessons you teach this semester.
		
		In preparation for 9/11 lab, choose an issue in reading and/or writing relevant to your discipline. Find & bring to class Monday an article referencing these issues.
			1.2.1
			1.2.6*
			1.2.7*
			2.2.1*
			2.2.2
			2.2.4
			3.1.2*
				<u>Standards</u>
				
				Three: 6*
				
				Five: 1*
				
				Two: 3
				
				<u>Objectives</u>
				
				3.4.g

September 10 Discussion: The transactional model: a new paradigm - meaning & purpose - reading & writing - theory into practice Praxis III: Domain C Susan Scott on information literacy: - Finding the literature of schema & transactional theories - Introduction to field experience in the course (see guidelines in syllabus packet; lesson plans & reports due as you complete the teaching of targeted lessons)	**September 11** Powerpoint in the classroom	Read: Vacca, part I Find an article about reading in your discipline in which schema theory and/or transactional theory are discussed. Communicate about your article on *Blackboard* by noon on September 17 and bring to class a copy of your article and your thoughts about the information presented in the article. Powerpoint presentations: Prepare a Powerpoint presentation (5-7 minutes) for a future lab session.	1.2.2 2.2.7* 2.4.10 3.1.4* 2.4.6* 1.3.1 2.3.2* 2.3.3* 3.1.5* 3.1.6* 3.1.8*	<u>Standards</u> One: 1* Three: 7* Four: 2* <u>Objectives</u> 1.1.e 2.2.d

*denotes standard continues throughout the course

Standards referred to:
  ISTE (International Society for Technology in Education) Standards for Initial Endorsement in Educational Computing and Technology Literacy
  ACRL (Association of College and Research Libraries) Information Literacy Competency Standards for Higher Education
  ACRL Objectives for Information Literacy Instruction: A Model Statement for Academic Librarians

Appendix 2: Teaching Techniques

Teaching Techniques: from Denison University First Year Seminar
Developed by Mary Prophet

Research Log
Use only those parts below that are needed to report research activity since last log entry.
Reports may be e-mailed to librarian as text or as an attachment.

Name: _____

Date/time: _____

Action: _____

- **Index, Catalog or Web Search engine Used:** _____

- **Search Strategy:** _____
  Show search terms, how the term was used (i.e.. keyword, subject, author, etc.)
  connecting terms or symbols used (i.e. OR, AND, NOT, +, -,=, etc.)

- **Materials Found:** _____
  Including notes on which materials are available at Denison, which can be/ have been
  ordered via OhioLINK and Interlibrary Loan, which are downloaded as full text. Be sure
  to include all information you will need for your bibliography.

- **Use of Materials:** _____
  This information may be included with the materials found. Some students have found it
  useful to include notes on how they plan to use the information in their research or
  paper.

- **Items Read:** _____
  - o **Useful – Why:**

  - o **Not Useful – Why:**

Future Plans: _____

Problems or Questions: _____

Appendix 3: Library Skills Test

LIBRARY SKILLS TEST
Organic Chemistry 212

Class: First Year_____Sophomore_____Junior_____Senior_____
Major:_____

Please indicate courses in which you have had previous library instruction, and whether the instruction was primarily given by a librarian or by the course instructor.

Please circle the correct answer to each of the following questions.

1. An example of a primary literature source in the sciences is:
    A. review article
    B. journal article
    C. textbook
    D. abstracts
    E. A and B

2. Which of the following would be the best place to look for physical property data for organic compounds?
    A. *Handbook of Chemistry and Physics*
    B. *Macmillan Encyclopedia of Chemistry*
    C. CONSORT
    D. *Hawley's Condensed Chemical Dictionary*
    E. MEDLINE

3. Which of the following series of call numbers is in the correct order?

A.	QH	QH	QH	QH	QK	Q
	42.1	52	421	421	421	421.5
	.B6	.A6	.A5	.A456	.A1 B4	.B6

B.	Q	QH	QH	QH	QH	QK
	421.5	42.1	52	421	421	421
	.B7	.B6	.A6	.A456	.A5	.A1 B4

C.	QK	QH	QH	QH	QH	Q
	421	421	52	421	42.1	421.5
	.A1 B4	.A5	.A6	.A456	.B6	.B7

D.	Q	QH	QH	QH	QH	QK
	421.5	42.1	52	421	421	421
	.B7	.B6	.A6	.A5	.A456	.A1 B4

4. Which of the following is the best place to look for reports on the most recent research on the design of anticancer drugs?
    A. *Merck Index*
    B. *Physicians Desk Reference*
    C. SciFinder Scholar
    D. CONSORT
    E. Index to Journal Articles

5. How would you determine whether the following article is available at the College of Wooster?

> Kolpin, Dana W.; Kalkhoff, Stephen J.; Goolsby, Donald A.; Sneck-Fahrer, Debra A.; Thurman, E. Michael. Occurrence of selected herbicides and herbicide degradation products in Iowa's ground water, 1995. Ground Water (1997), 35(4), 679-688.

    A. Conduct a Journal Title search in CONSORT, entering "Ground Water"
    B. Conduct a Journal Title search in CONSORT, entering "Occurrence of selected herbicides…"
    C. Conduct an Author search in Index to Journal Articles
    D. Conduct a Keyword search in CONSORT, entering "herbicide* and degradation and ground water"
    E. Conduct a Subject search in Index to Journal Articles, entering "Herbicides, degradation of"

6. How would you determine whether the following item is available at Wooster?

> Bailey, D. K., 1987, "Mantle Meta-somatism--Perspective and Prospect," *in* Fitton, J. G., and Upton, B. G. J., eds., Alkaline Igneous Rocks, Geological Society of London Special Publication 30: Oxford, Blackwell Scientific Publications, p. 1-14.

    A. Conduct a Title search in CONSORT, entering "Mantle Meta-somatism perspective"
    B. Conduct a Title search in CONSORT, entering "Alkaline Igneous Rocks"
    C. Conduct an Author search in CONSORT, entering "Bailey, D. K."
    D. Conduct an Author search in CONSORT, entering "Fitton, J. G."
    E. Either B or D

7. How would you obtain an article from a journal that is not available in any format at the College of Wooster, but is available at the Ohio State University?
    A. Request the journal volume using the CONSORT "Request This Item" option
    B. Request the article using the OhioLINK "Request This Item" option
    C. Request the journal volume using the OhioLINK "Request This Item" option
    D. Request the article using the WebZap form
    E. Request the journal volume using the WebZap form

Adapted from a test developed by Donna K. Jacobs at the College of Wooster.

Appendix 4: Suggested Questions for Student Evaluations

The Five Colleges of Ohio
Andrew W. Mellon Foundation Grant
Integrating Information Literacy into the Liberal Arts Curriculum
Suggested Questions for Student Evaluations

Information literacy is a set of abilities requiring individuals to "recognize when information is needed and have the ability to locate, evaluate, and use effectively the needed information."

- One of the goals of this course was to increase your skills and capabilities in using library and information resources. How successful was this course in helping you to reach that goal?

- In what ways has this course helped you to understand better the research process?

- In what ways has this course helped you understand how to locate, use, and evaluate sources of information available electronically? Please be specific.

- In what ways has this course helped you understand how to locate, use, and evaluate sources of information available in print? Please be specific.

- The Internet offers a wealth of materials that vary widely in quality and scope. What strategies have you developed that help you evaluate and make appropriate use of them?

- The development of sound information literacy skills should be an integral part of a liberal arts education. Do you agree or disagree with this statement, and why?

[This document can be found on the grant Web site, at http://www.denison.edu/ohio5/grant/development/stueval.htm]

"Inch by Inch, Row by Row..."Growing an Information Literacy Program

Joanna M. Burkhardt and Mary C. MacDonald

Creating an Information Literacy Plan for your institution is like creating a garden. It requires short and long range planning, a vision for the future, attention to detail, cooperation from many different sources, hard work, stamina, diversity among the crops, the ability to assess what works and what doesn't, the ability to weed out what is not doing well, and knowledge of what will flourish in the local environment. Using this organic metaphor throughout the process of developing an information literacy program can help your institution to "grow" a successful plan.

At the University of Rhode Island, a small group of librarians worked for 18 months to make our plan or IL a reality (http://www.uri.edu/library/instruction_services/infolitplan.html). Our experiences taught us to think broadly, to keep open minds, to ask questions, and to be persistent. If your institution is working toward, or is in the midst of, developing an information literacy program, careful planning will save time, lend credibility and provide a clear process for all involved.

Creating an information literacy plan is a multi-step process. Taken one step at a time, the sense of being overwhelmed can be avoided. The steps below are based on our experience in creating the Information Literacy Program at URI, but can be generalized to pertain to almost any institution and almost any situation.

Burkhardt is the Head of Providence Campus Library at the University of Rhode Island. *MacDonald* is the Information Literacy Librarian at the University of Rhode Island.

Collect Information/Read the Garden Catalogs

The ACRL Information Literacy Competencies will give you guidance as to the only national standard in place so far for academic libraries. Your institution may want to accomplish only some of the information literacy (IL) competencies ACRL lists. The competencies are the backbone of IL in the United States academic libraries. (www.ala.org/acrl/ilcomstan.html) You will need to find other institutions that have plans, and get them. It will be enormously helpful to identify similar institutions, whether by size, curriculum, or funding levels. Knowing how others are approaching the same problem may save you some time and give you some good ideas. Other plans and programs can provide you with ammunition you may need to convince people at your institution to give you support, staff, money and offer other unexplored ideas that may serve you well. They can warn you of potential problems and/or suggest possible solutions to problems you have already foreseen.

You will need to look at the organization of your own institution and discover its idiosyncrasies. Who belongs to what department, division, or college? Who supervises each unit? What is the reporting structure? You will need to know the chain of command. Who can present a new program for approval? To whom is it submitted? How long will it take to get approval? What committees have to agree? Does the approval process go outside the institution? How are programs made known on campus? How are programs described in your course catalog? Can you "own" the program, or will you need to partner with someone else? The answers to these questions are what will guide your planning process.

At URI, a small committee of library faculty members met to brainstorm what options might be available to us on our campuses for developing an information literacy program, what the needs of our students and faculty were, and how information literacy could be delivered to all interested parties. The results of this meeting were sent, as a written report, to the larger Public Services Department for discussion, review, and revision. Once approved by the Public Services Department the draft plan was sent to the Library Curriculum Committee for review. The revision process continued. After being approved by the Curriculum Committee is was sent to the Library Faculty–more revisions. When the faculty approved it, the plan was sent to the Dean. When the Dean approved it, it was finally posted on the Library Web Site.

Important pieces of the plan had to be approved by other governing bodies at the University. For example, establishing the credit-course was as big a job as developing the plan. In order to propose the course, it was developed in house, approved by the Library Curriculum Committee, Public Services Department, and Library Faculty. Then it left the Library, to go through the Curriculum Affairs Committee (CAC) of the University and finally on to the Faculty Senate.

Proposing the accepted credit-course as a General Education option for undergraduates meant going through this process again with justification and explanation as to how and why it qualified for such a designation. The experience at your institution may be very similar or very different. The point is that by identifying the organizational scheme, the governing bodies and supportive individuals you will improve your odds at successfully establishing any program.

Thinking About Your Students/Prepare the Earth

Think about the student population you serve. What is their level of need? At what point in their academic program is the best time to give IL instruction? Do you want to be comprehensive, or supply just the basics? Do you need to reach distance students who are not physically on your campus? Assessing who your users are will help you to build a program specific to your needs. At a two-year junior college or community college, it may not be necessary to teach research tools that are relevant to graduate students. Your assessment will tell you how many levels of instruction you need. Thinking about the progress of students through their degrees will also

help you determine when they should receive instruction. A first-year music student may have no need to use the library during that year, as performance may be the focus for beginning students. Design your program so that you will reach the students when the information is relevant to them.

URI is a medium sized public research and graduate institution with a healthy undergraduate program. As such, we saw the need to create a plan that would answer the information literacy needs of students and faculty at many levels. We identified the introductory college programs as well as the largest colleges as places where the need was greatest and worked from there. We agreed that specialized sessions would be useful for people who have already declared a major. We also thought that faculty might benefit from education and training in Information Literacy as well. How many different ways will you reach students? What do you already provide in terms of instruction? Will you continue what is already in place? Will you add to it? Do you plan for instruction in the library, or will you take it to the classroom? Will instruction be in-person, or via distance education or Web tutorials? Will you offer a for-credit course, workshops, or one-shot sessions?

Some of our biggest opportunities for information literacy instruction were developed from our already established First-year Student programs. Using these as a basis, we incorporated information literacy standards into those modules and promoted the benefits to the University administration.

Our credit courses were established and continue to grow. We did not discard any of the programs already in place. Instead, we built on those established teaching opportunities, adding, and revising as needed. We also began promoting the new segments of the plan to the faculty and administration, with presentations and demonstrations, corridor discussions and liaison meetings with our departments.

Who will partner with you on campus? Who will support your plan? What routes do you have for contacting faculty on your campus? Is there a library liaison program? Are there institution-wide committees with representatives from the library? Are there faculty convocations? Are there orientation sessions for new faculty? Are there social gatherings where you might be asked "So what's new at the Library?"

At URI, librarians found answers across the campus. We are all subject selectors and curriculum liaisons to departments. We are all representatives on various campus committees. These responsibilities offer endless opportunities for introducing information literacy to our colleagues and

—JOANNA M. BURKHARDT AND MARY C. MACDONALD—

in turn, finding the necessary support for our initiative. We also made personal contacts with the faculty—from lunch dates to university functions. We made a presentation to the Council of Deans at one of their meetings, and were overwhelmed by their enthusiastic response.

Once you have asked all these questions and have some idea of where you would like to go, you can begin to lay out your plan.

Defining Information Literacy/Decide What Will Grow

Make sure your definition clearly states what information literacy means (or will mean) at your institution. Do not assume that everyone at your institution understands the concept, or knows what *you* mean when you use the term. Make sure that you have an in-house agreement about your definition before you offer it to the general public.

To put your plan in perspective, you may want to explain how libraries and library users have changed with technological changes. People used to stand at the Reference Desk and ask questions. Now they call, e-mail, chat, *and* stand at the desk. They used to use a fairly limited set of resources—books and journals in paper format. They needed to be where the resources resided. Today, there are many choices of format, many options for access and delivery, and sometimes no need to be on site to use the materials. The content of many available resources are beyond the control of the library and/or academic community. The Web for example, is a source of information that many students use. The quality of the information available is very uneven, and not always suitable for academic purposes. The content of this resource is out of the control of any library, but it may contain many good and useful sites that are acceptable in an academic setting. Students must be taught how to evaluate what they find, so they can identify appropriate sources of information.

The increase in demand for "teaching" in the library and/or from the library has increased exponentially. Describing this change should make obvious the need for your program. Do not be afraid to restate the obvious! Inform readers of the changing nature of library use, user education, and reference. Describe what you do, how it has been accomplished in the past, and why you need to shift those tasks to a program which better meets the needs of today's users. It is important to set the stage, so readers understand the need for your program.

Be sure to explain who will administer your program. If the library is to "own" the program, it will be administered by the library. If you are collaborating with another department or departments on campus, explain who will be in charge, and who will bear the responsibility for the program.

Implementing the Plan/Plant the Crops

Create a document that explains the reasons and the need for the program. Spell out what this program is designed to do. Any terms that are not part of the average non-librarian's vocabulary should be defined.

Be as clear and as detailed as possible in describing the various pieces of your plan. Lay it out so that it is both easy to read and easy to visualize. Explain where each segment and each option fits in the students program of study. Discuss what students will learn in each segment.

Plan for as many delivery options as possible. Be flexible. Methods for achieving competencies may include: in-class exercises, homework assignments, papers, projects, on-line/off-line work, credit courses, workshops, and Web tutorials. Build on what you already do and call on local experts to help you expand from that base. Suggest places (courses, programs, special projects) where pieces of your information literacy plan might be useful.

Make your offerings incremental and modular. This will allow implementation of your plan one piece at a time. While it is wonderful to think about dropping an entire plan into place and making all parts of it run at a selected point in time, it may be necessary and perhaps even desirable to introduce parts of your information literacy plan individually over a period of time. In practical matters such as personnel, funding, and space, this may be the only way in which the entire plan can be completed.

Link exercises, tutorials, activities in each piece of your plan to the ACRL competencies and make sure to state which competencies are addressed with which parts of the plan. In creating your classes, tutorials, modules, etc. try to balance what students like to do with what they need to know. Students enjoy learning information literacy via active learning techniques. Consider designing the delivery of your program using active learning, resource based learning or problem based learning.

Remember, just because we told the students how to be information literate, does not mean they really "got it". Everyone you talk to will want to know how you know if your program is successful. Develop and include measurable outcomes for each segment and each delivery option you plan to offer. Assessment can also take several forms, including surveys, opinion polls, student evaluations, and other formats. But measures of whether students are achieving the competencies you have targeted will be necessary to "prove" the effectiveness of your program to skeptics and believers alike.

Build methods for educating faculty and administrators about information literacy into your plan. You will want to encourage faculty to incorporate information literacy into their curriculum, send students to your classes and/or tutorials, and get them up to speed on how the world of research has changed during the past 10 years. You may want to build tutorials, exercises, bibliographies, and other tools specifically for that audience. You may want to tailor what you have already created for students for your faculty. Offer workshops, and exclusive and intensive sessions for faculty. Ask to be part of new faculty orientations. Create new avenues for reaching the non-students on campus.

Putting Your Plan in Place/Sow, Water, Fertilize and Weed

Once your plan is drafted, share it with people who you feel are supportive of the concept of an information literacy program. Ask them to read through your plan and offer feedback. Start with concerned parties in the library. Once you have consensus within the library, share it with those outside the library who you know will offer constructive criticism. Listen to their ideas and concerns. Look for ways to incorporate your plan into their curriculum. Revise, revise, revise.

When your plan is complete, send it through the approval process for your institution. Do your homework and make sure you do not miss any steps. Do not be afraid to ask questions. Stay on top of where your plan is and on whose desk it might be sitting.

Take your opportunities as they arise. Not everything will fall into place at one time. You may have to choose one small project and stick with it. You may be able to implement pieces of the plan earlier than anticipated, or in a different order. You may be presented with multiple opportunities during the same semester. Don't promise more than you can deliver.

Preparing for the Future/Watch the Weather

Have a game plan for implementation. Know what you are going to need for each piece of your plan. More staff? More space? More money? Make sure it is going to be there when you need it. Perhaps promises were made about resources, which cannot be delivered. Scale back your plan and implement it one module at a time. Think about alternate ways to get the job done using only what you already have. Be creative. Remember to be flexible as well. You may have to revise your game plan in the ebb and flow of opportunity.

How will you tell people about your plan? Once it exists, sharing it with as many people as possible should be a goal. You must determine with whom you want to share it, and how to put it in their hands. Think outside of the box. Of course, you want your students, faculty, and administrators to know. What about alumni, the Board of Governors, local employers, college recruiters, prospective students and their parents, other libraries?

Once approved, be sure to inform all interested parties about the plan. Post it prominently on your Web page. Send copies out via e-mail. Send paper copies. Write a story for the student newspaper. Announce the plan in the faculty newsletters and departmental meetings. Have library liaisons meet with their departments to discuss and plan. Make sure people know and remember that your plan is in place.

Savoring Your Accomplishments/Reap the Harvest

Your completed plan will be a major accomplishment. It will serve you and your community for many years to come. It will provide vital skills for your students and increase the Library's role in the education of students at your institution. Your garden will flourish and your produce will be of the highest quality. Remember to feed and water, weed and fertilize. With your careful attention, your harvest will be abundant.

—JOANNA M. BURKHARDT AND MARY C. MACDONALD—

IS THIS ASSIGNMENT *REALLY* NECESSARY?: THE EVOLUTION OF A FIRST-YEAR EXPERIENCE LIBRARY RESEARCH ASSIGNMENT

Carolyn Frenger

The Background
CCAS and FAW

Each Fall semester, as part of its programming to acquaint freshmen with college academic and campus life, The George Washington University's Columbian College of Arts and Sciences (CCAS) has a mandatory, one-credit course, CCAS 001-Freshman Advising Workshop (FAW), which all CCAS freshmen must take their first semester at GWU. The six-week course meets once a week for 75 minutes and provides CCAS first-year students with advice and skills in areas of time management, study skills, picking a major or a minor and how to adjust to being on their own for the first time. Another requirement of the course is an orientation to Gelman Library, GWU's primary research facility.

The Origins of the Current FAW Gelman Library Research Assignment

Prior to my arrival at Gelman Library, the FAW library assignment consisted of providing FAW advisors with four printouts: two book citations from Gelman Library's online catalog, ALADIN, and two article citations from the database Periodical Abstracts. Students were to receive bibliographic instruction from their workshop advisors, not from the library. However, many faculty members found that they were either uninterested or unequipped to provide this

---

Frenger is the User Education Librarian at The George Washington University, Washington, DC.

instruction and would invariably try every way conceivable to get the library's small instruction staff to teach these sessions, many without any prior notice. Obviously, something radical needed to happen to improve this situation for all parties involved.

The Evolution

Fall 1997

When I arrived at Gelman Library in the Fall of 1997, the FAW assignment and instruction had already taken place. I was already aware of a need to retool the assignment to make them substantive and to alleviate the instruction department's burden of being asked to teach over fifty library orientation sessions with 25 students in each class within the first three weeks of the Fall semester.

However, as with all good intentions, my efforts were side-tracked with other pressing projects and the retooling had to be put on hold for nearly a year, until right before the beginning of the Fall 1998 semester.

Fall 1998

The first element in the retooling of the FAW library assignment was the instruction. Gelman Library hired a freelance contractor to teach the 50+ sessions during the second and third weeks of the Fall semester, which were coordinated with the FAW section advisors. These sessions were lecture/demo in format and were intended to equip students with the library skills necessary for them to complete the library assignment, which still comprised the four citations from the previous Fall semester. The experience was an eye-opener to say the least. Our instructor was teaching up to five classes per day, including sessions over the lunch hour, since the FAW classes were scheduled between 9 a.m. and 4 p.m. Monday through Friday. Needless to say, she was exhausted and we were left with a huge dilemma, what to do to radically improve the situation before next Fall.

Fall 1999

Gelman Library underwent an organizational change during the Summer of 1999 and the Education and Instruction Group (EIG) was formed. Under this new group's leadership, the instruction program at Gelman also began a transformation. Part of that change included the creation of an actual library research assignment, not just finding citations, which EIG felt was a complete waste of time and not a proper orientation to using the library for research. Collaborating with the FAW administrative staff and CCAS' Associate Dean for Undergraduates, EIG created a full-scale library research assignment. The assignment consisted of five research tasks:

- locating books
- locating magazine and journal articles
- locating newspaper articles
- locating information on the World Wide Web, and
- ordering a book from another consortium school.

CCAS Associate Dean Kim Moreland wanted FAW students to have a key experience using both print and electronic resources in the library. Therefore, the article parts of the assignment involved utilizing print indexes. In addition, the group provided FAW advisors with a list of 28 topics to assign to the students, ranging in scope from the women's movement to censorship in motion pictures to the impact of computers on society. The assignment was intended to be self-paced, done on a student's own schedule and turned in on the last day of their FAW sessions. No formal FAW section instruction was planned to help the students with the assignment. Instead, I planned 26 hands-on library research instruction sessions, which were held in the PC/Multimedia lab in the lower level of the library during weeks three through six of the Fall semester. Students were required to preregister for these sessions, which they did by e-mailing a special e-mail account, by phoning the reference office's main phone number and signing up with the office assistant or by

coming in person to the reference office. Two other librarians and one paraprofessional helped me teach the sessions. In addition to these sessions, I offered two one-hour, drop-in clinics per week during those weeks that the instruction sessions were held. These clinics were staggered over different hours in the day in an effort to make sure that students had many opportunities to ask for help. Finally, for the students who attended the research instruction sessions, I created a library assignment tips handout. Midpoint through the semester, I put it up on the Web and had paper copies available at the reference desk for distribution to any students who might ask for help with the assignment. This change came because of the feedback I was getting from the desk staff about the students and the assignment.

Lessons Learned

I learned many lessons from this first attempt at a new assignment and method of instruction. First off, unless students are required to attend a library instruction session, they will not come. Of course, now that the entire enrollment for the workshop had grown to about 1350 students, I wasn't sure if I was upset or relieved. Of the 26 sessions I offered, I canceled more than half for lack of enrollment and the majority of the others had three or fewer students in attendance, which was a huge waste of the staff member's time and energy. The clinics didn't fair much better. Of the eight clinics offered, less than five people total took advantage of them. Yet another drain on the staff's time. The place that had more than enough traffic was the reference desk. During the entire semester and, in particular, around the end of the FAW course schedule, the desk staff was inundated with students who needed help doing the assignment and some who wanted the staff to do the assignment for them. Many of the students hadn't read the assignment before coming to the desk to ask for help and even when armed with the assignment tips, they still required significant hand holding. Finally, many students seemed perturbed that they had to do the assignment at all, often referring to it as "this lousy library assignment" or far more colorful remarks. This was hardly the outcome that I had hoped for and one that didn't seem to demonstrate the students' successful orientation to the library, except perhaps where the reference desk was located. I was determined to improve upon this first experience and make it a better one for everybody involved during Fall 2000.

—CAROLYN FRENGER—

Fall 2000

The library assignment and accompanying instruction underwent some overhauling for this year's FAW sessions. In addition, the size and number of the FAW sections continued to grow to accommodate 1500 students. The CCAS FAW staff wanted to add another exercise to the assignment, locating refereed journal articles using a scholarly index. The magazine and journal article exercise would be limited to just popular literature. After some negotiating about increasing the length of the assignment, both parties agreed it would be a good addition to the overall assignment. In addition, the wording of the assignment was tightened up and made more explicit, at the recommendation of the reference desk staff. Also, the entire workshop had its own Web site, linked from the library's course-related Web page, which had links to the assignment, the schedule of instruction sessions and the assignment tips handout, all of which were widely publicized to workshop participants. Based on the low attendance of last year's instruction sessions, I tried to work with the FAW administrative staff to better market the in-person instruction sessions to FAW advisors and students alike. They were offered twice a week during weeks two through seven of the semester, and still required preregistration to attend. One of the two major changes I made for these sessions was to make them more interactive with lecture/demo as well as active learning 'games' including team call number arranging and putting parts of a citation together, just to name a few. I gave out prizes and candy to students for participating and asking questions. Never underestimate the power of bribery to help gain and keep students' attention. The other change was surveying a random sample of the students during their spring semester about their experiences with the library assignment. It was Web-based and, as an incentive, I offered a random drawing for four $25 Borders Bookstore gift certificates to all students who responded to my survey. Of the 227 students I surveyed, I got one-third of the surveys back.

More Lessons Learned

Print indexes aren't as resilient as one might imagine. The magazine article part of the assignment, as it had in the previous year, asked students to look for an article on their topic written BEFORE 1980, necessitating the use of the *Readers' Guide to Periodical Literature* to locate citations. The same went for the newspaper article exercise. Students used either *The New York Times Index* or *The Washington Post Index* to locate a newspaper article on their topic written before 1980. By the end of the semester, the indexes looked bad, pages torn, and spines of the volumes well creased. Also, many of the magazine citations students found were for publications that our library didn't own, demonstrating the value of vetting the topics of an assignment against your own collection before putting it into practice.

The scholarly index citation question presented additional problems. The assignment mentioned a few online article databases as examples of sources for scholarly articles, but absent any instruction to know which database to use for their specific topic, students tended to use ONLY those databases mentioned in the questions, which proved frustrating for them and the reference desk staff alike. In addition, students were unaware of what the differences between popular and scholarly publications, further complicating their abilities to do the assignment on their own and adding to the reference desk's transactions. Finally, the assignment's length and amount of time it took students to do was discussed and alternative plans for the future were considered. All of these lessons were used to take a huge step forward in the next year of the library assignment's evolution.

Fall 2001

The Education and Instruction Group began migrating its entire instruction program to an information literacy focus during 2001 and the FAW library assignment was a part of that migration. It underwent some drastic modifications, but kept its central goals intact. The group considered what was the main purpose of the assignment. At its heart, it was a library orientation assignment and could serve the same function with fewer questions and no in-person instruction at all, especially now that the number of FAW students had grown to 1700. Thus, the online FAW library assignment instruction was added to the already existing course Web site. This instruction can be viewed at http://www.gwu.edu/gelman/instruct /course/faw.html Essentially, it took what was taught in a regular live library session and compressed it into digestible 'chunks' of instruction, broken up by one of four library exercises: searching for books, searching article databases, searching newspaper databases and how to use myALADIN, the Washington Research Library Consortium (WRLC)'s online patron portal. Students would read each section of instruction, and then do the required exercise. All of this self-paced assignment, with the exception of photocopying the title page of a book, could be done anywhere a student had access to the Internet, creating a remotely accessible project that provided students with a realistic library research experience, a goal of EIG's for this revamped assignment.

Final Lessons for the Future

We still have improvements that we can make. The elimination of using print indexes and specifying an article database to be used during the assignment, not to mention tightening up the assignment overall were excellent steps, as was putting all of the instruction on the Web. However, students still seem reluctant to use it unless it is visually engaging, leading EIG to decide that Fall 2002's FAW assignment will feature an interactive online tutorial as its instruction component, which it hopes will be attractive and conducive to today's visual learners, and enable them to gain a solid orientation to Gelman Library.

Practical Applications

Here are some tips and hints about implementing a library research orientation assignment in your institution's first year experience program:

- **Be flexible.** Your assignment will evolve as the first-year program does as well as your library does. Don't be afraid of trying new things or completely changing the assignment.

- **Know who your allies are and use those relationships effectively.** Establishing a library assignment within a first-year experience may seem daunting at first, so try to make gradual in-roads with those faculty members and administrators of the programs that you are already acquainted with.

- **Keep in touch with your collaborators (faculty, administrators, etc.).** Regular contact throughout the year with those people you are working with to create and administer the assignment is essential and keeps you fresh in their minds.

- **Ask many questions.**

- **Know your instructional audience.** By being aware of first-year students' information-seeking behaviors, interests, attention spans, and other factors, you can design assignments and instruction components that have a better chance of being used and appreciated.

- **Don't try to teach them too much!** Keep your instructions focused and concise. If you offer an online instruction option, mix up the text with graphics and where text is needed, keep it short.

- **Know your library's collections, especially its limitations.** Students don't like not finding articles for the citations they have, especially for an assignment they really don't want to do.

- **Use the Internet creatively.** Create online tutorials, course Web pages, and other visually stimulating materials to supplement the assignment itself.

- **Make your Web site user-friendly.** Too many bells and whistles can be distracting, but don't make it too plain or your students won't give it a second glance. Trial and error seems to be the best way to find out what works best.

For the texts of the library assignments, topics, student surveys, and online instruction mentioned above, please visit the Web page I've created for this presentation:http://www.gwu.edu/gelman/instruct/faw/loex2002/index.html

—CAROLYN FRENGER—

THE CSU FULLERTON INITIATIVE: INTEGRATING INFORMATION COMPETENCE INTO THE CURRICULUM

Ellen Junn, Suellen Cox, Patricia Szeszulski, and Sorel Reisman

Background and History

In 2001, California State University, Fullerton (CSUF) was awarded a CSU Chancellor's Office grant to systematically implement campus-wide information literacy standards. This award was unique because it was a collaborative effort including the Vice President for Academic Affairs, the Faculty Development Center (FDC), and Pollak Library.

As an institution, CSUF is poised particularly well for this type of initiative for the following reasons:

- CSUF has a Faculty Development Center (FDC) charged with supporting faculty and serves as a central, highly visible, and highly regarded source of faculty support and training, particularly in the area of instructional technology. While IL is not synonymous with instructional technology, there is overlap; thus for example, in the last three years, the FDC has trained over 450 faculty who have enhanced a total of 900 courses with WebCT, BlackBoard, or FrontPage, involving over 20,000 students.
- CSUF's Pollak Library is a state-of-the-art facility complete with more than 400 computer workstations, as group study rooms with laptop docking stations, and library instruction classrooms that allow for hands-on student learning with

Cox is the Instruction Librarian at California State University, Fullerton. *Junn* is the Associate Dean of the College of Human Development & Community Service; *Szeszulski* is a professor in the Department of Child and Adolescent Studies; and *Reisman* is the Coordinator of Academic Technology. They all work at California State University, Fullerton.

regards to library resources and web based technology. In addition, the Library provides remote access to electronic databases and full text resources via a proxy server for faculty and students, which supports both on-campus and distance education programs.

The Library has a very vigorous and proactive, instruction program that emphasizes student-centered, technology-based learning that reaches over 16,000 students each year in approximately 300 course-related library instruction sessions per semester. The classes involved cut across most disciplines and occur at all levels from remedial to master's level. Librarians often work with faculty to tailor the sessions in order to meet the research needs of the class, create effective library research assignments, and develop useful in-class exercises. In addition to these faculty requested library instruction sessions, a variety of other learning opportunities are also offered each semester, including electronic resources workshops, one-on-one research consultations, point of need instruction at the Reference Desk and Electronic Resources area, and online subject specific Library Research Guides accessed via the Library Home Page.

The CSU system has provided a strong incentive to incorporate information competence into the curriculum. All instruction at the Pollak Library, whether faculty requested, workshop-based, or one-on-one consultation, has its foundation in the core information literacy competencies outlined in the ACRL National Standards.

Information literacy is also promoted on our campus through individual consultation and instruction for new and part-time faculty in each of the colleges.

Librarians have also worked on developing a more integrative approach aimed at improving information literacy by working in close collaboration with faculty from departments such as Anthropology, Biology, Child & Adolescent Studies, Communications, and Nursing. An information literacy library component is also imbedded in the Fullerton First-Year program, which has been in existence for five years and reaches 150 first-year students each year.

CSUF Information Literacy Initiative and Participants

Our approach to implementing information literacy across the entire campus curriculum was to encourage, assist, and support departmental teams in infusing these skills into their department's curriculum. The campus received funds from the CSU Chancellor's Office for the first year, with second year funding coming from the CSUF Vice President for Academic Affairs to support departments participating in this initiative. Participating departments were asked to identify two core courses in their program, one at the entry level and one capstone course and to develop syllabi and assignments designed to promote students' information literacy skills. The original grant called for the creation of a Website for posting the required deliverables: (1) a list of the department's student learning outcomes including the skills of information literacy; (2) syllabi for two courses which identify assignments to facilitate information literacy; and (3) representative assignments that demonstrate student acquisition of information literacy skills. This Website, which includes the initial grant proposal, is available at: http://www.library.fullerton. edu/information_comp/.

Last year this initiative hosted three activities: (1) a day-long campus retreat during Spring 2001 for departmental teams that was convened by the Vice President for Academic Affairs in collaboration with the Library and organized by the FDC; (2) provision of ongoing Summer consultation and assistance by Library faculty for participating departments; and (3) a follow-up Fall 2001 meeting for departmental progress reporting prior to submission of final deliverables.

The day-long campus retreat was attended by department chairs and teams of 2-3 faculty from the departments listed below, as well as nine librarians. The purpose of the retreat was to provide faculty with an overview of information literacy, the grant guidelines, and give them an opportunity to explore ways to explicitly integrate information literacy into their departmental curriculum. The retreat featured a keynote address by Dr. Susan Curzon, Dean, University Library, California State University, Northridge and Chair of the CSU Work Group on Information Competence. Dr. Curzon provided the history and evolution of the concept of Information Competence within CSU. Attendees also participated in an exercise to identify, frame, and discuss the ACRL Information Literacy/Competency Standards within the parameters of their respective disciplines. Additionally, the nine-minute video *e-literate* was shown, and librarians held a short panel discussion on creating effective library assignments. (The video is a production of the Pacific Bell/UCLA Initiative for 21st Century Literacies, available on the Web at http://newliteracies.gseis.ucla.edu/video/index.html)

For a very modest investment (retreat costs, plus $1,000 per participating department), this project attracted substantial faculty interest and involvement and permitted a systemic approach to facilitating student information literacy. During year one, the 20 departments listed below volunteered to participate.

1. Accounting
2. Afro-Ethnic Studies
3. Biology
4. Child and Adolescent Studies
5. Chemistry
6. Computer Science
7. Economics
8. Foreign Languages
9. Geological Sciences
10. Gerontology
11. Human Services
12. Information Systems and Decision Sciences
13. Marketing and Business Writing
14. Mathematics
15. Nursing
16. Psychology
17. Science Education
18. Sociology
19. Speech Communication
20. Women's Studies

Outcomes and Assessment of the Information Literacy Initiative

Of the 20 departments that volunteered to participate during the first year of the initiative, 15 submitted the required deliverables. A review of the submitted materials supported two general conclusions. One, the project did succeed in its primary goal to initiate serious dialog about and replicable processes for the infusion of information literacy across the curriculum. Two, the practices reflected in the submitted materials made it clear that participating departments are at various stages of

—ELLEN JUNN, SUELLEN COX, PATRICIA SZESZULSKI, AND SOREL REISMAN—

development in implementing information competency standards. While two-thirds of the participating departments submitted materials in all three of the required categories that addressed topics related to information literacy, there was considerable variation in the number of standards included as well as the correspondence between outcomes expectations listed on syllabi and the class assignments purported to foster course goals associated with information literacy.

The materials presented by several participating programs demonstrate a coordinated approach that makes information competency central to instruction and ongoing evaluation and establishes benchmarks for levels of accomplishment at different phases of learning. The fact that implementation of the initiative is in its infancy may explain why many departments, who routinely include references to IC standards as program goals on paper, have not yet transferred these goals to department Websites. Across departments, Standards 1-4 were the most likely to be included and addressed in assignments. However, we must underscore both the lack of correspondence between specified learning goals and assignments as they apply to particular assignments as well as the lack of increased expectations for IC between entry and capstone courses within departments. A key feature of the initiative was promoting greater collaboration between library and discipline faculty to make information competency a central outcome of student learning. Indeed, the best predictor of inclusion of IC standards on syllabi and the utilization of high-quality assignments in order to foster student learning outcomes was attendance at the library instruction sessions.

Second-Year Information Literacy Initiative and Participants

As specified in the original grant proposal, the CSUF Vice President for Academic Affairs has provided second-year funding in the amount of $31,000. In initial planning, the second-year activities were to be identical to the first year: (1) a day-long campus retreat; (2) provision of ongoing Summer consultation and assistance by Library faculty for participating departments; and 3) a follow-up Fall 2002 meeting for departmental progress reporting prior to submission of final deliverables. However, one modification to this plan has been made, a half-day retreat was planned instead of a full-day retreat. The expected deliverables remain the same.

A second year retreat has been held. During year two, the ten departments listed below volunteered to participate in the retreat. The deliverables for these departments are due in December 2002.

1. Anthropology
2. Asian Ethnic Studies
3. Civil Engineering
4. Communications
5. Electrical Engineering
6. History
7. Mechanical Engineering
8. Music Education
9. Political Science
10. Visual Arts

Conclusions and Lessons Learned

This initiative has been successful in a number of ways. There is increased campus understanding of, and appreciation for, the concept of Information Literacy. Prior to this initiative, many CSUF Information Literacy efforts originated in the library, or as library responses to CSU system-wide initiatives. There has been increased collaboration between discipline faculty and library faculty in integrating information literacy into course curriculum. This is especially the case with the departments of Business Administration, Biology, Child Adolescent Studies, Marketing, Nursing, Science Education, and Women's Studies. This past year, there has been increased student attendance at, and participation in library instruction as a result of this systematic approach to involving faculty and departments. Lastly, the quality of many library and/or research assignments has improved. There are fewer ineffectual library scavenger hunts.

The following lessons were also learned and may be useful for others contemplating a similar approach:

☐ There must be a clear commitment, funding, communication, and collaboration among multiple, related units for a successful institutional initiative of this kind.

☐ Funding matters. The importance of flexible funding as an incentive cannot be over emphasized.

☐ Do not allocate funding all at one time (up front). Allocate some seed money, and then provide the remaining funds when all deliverables have been submitted.

☐ Implement an organized, sequential series of supports and events.
For example, formally evaluate the proposed deliverables mid-way through the process and ask the following questions:

o   Are the department learning goals consistent with the ACRL standards?

o   Are the standards clearly articulated on the chosen course syllabus, and integrated appropriately into the course?

o   Do the assignment(s) allow students to demonstrate acquisition of information literacy skills?

☐   Have deliverables revised as needed before final submission.

☐   Create strategies to deal with courses that are taught by adjunct faculty who may not teach from year to year. What happens to their courses, syllabi, and assignments should they leave the institution?

☐   Strong, ongoing, consistent leadership is essential at the Administration, Dean, and Department Chair level.

☐   Having a campus-wide Information Literacy requirement is the ideal. There is no requirement on our campus.

—ELLEN JUNN, SUELLEN COX, PATRICIA SZESZULSKI, AND SOREL REISMAN—

Checklist for Measuring Assignments for Information Competence

PLEASE CONSULT DEPARTMENT, COMPLETE FORMS, & BRING TO RETREAT.

Information competency is a set of abilities requiring individuals to "recognize when information is needed and have the ability to locate, evaluate, and use effectively the needed information." An information literate individual is able to:
- Determine the extent of information needed
- Access the needed information effectively and efficiently
- Evaluate information and its sources critically
- Incorporate selected information into one's knowledge base
- Use information effectively to accomplish a specific purpose
- Understand the economic, legal, and social issues surrounding the use of information, and access and use information ethically and legally

Choose one early entry core course and one senior level capstone or equivalent course (use separate sheets for each course) that either currently includes student information competency goals and assignments or would be amenable to information competency goals and assignments. For these 2 courses, please consult with your departmental faculty before filling out the checklist below.

Department: _____

Departmental Team Members: _____

Course Name/Number:_____

Does this course explicitly state learning goals that focus on student information competency in the course description or on the syllabus? YES / NO. If yes, please list these learning goals:

_____

Does this course require:

1.___assignments that ask/encourage students to articulate a research or theoretical question issue or problem? Describe and/or list assignments:

2.___assignments that ask/encourage students to make multiple and different determinations about the types of sources? Describe and/or list assignments:

3.___assignments that ask/encourage students to conduct research using scholarly sources such as books, journals, etc.? Describe and/or list assignments:

4.___assignments that ask/encourage students to conduct research through electronic data retrieval systems? Describe and/or list assignments:

5.___assignments that ask/encourage students to analyze and evaluate the credibility of information sources? Describe and/or list assignments:

6.___assignments that ask/encourage students to make selections from, integrate, and synthesize information retrieved in their search? Describe and/or list assignments:

7.___assignments that ask/encourage students to utilize computer literacy skills to communicate their results of their assignment? Describe and/or list assignments:

8.___assignments that ask/encourage students to demonstrate an understanding of fair use of copyrighted material and intellectual property (e.g., plagiarism)? Describe and/or list assignments:

9.___assignments that ask/encourage students to develop long-term, adaptable, cross-disciplinary scholarly and/or creative activity skills? Describe and/or list assignments:

INFORMATION COMPETENCE

Survey

This for-your-eyes-only survey asks you to report your views about information competence of students' in your department.

Please circle your response, on the rating scales. Feel free to attach an additional sheet of comments.

1. To achieve academic success, how important is competence in conducting research using library resources and information technology.

| Not at all important | | | | Extremely important | |
| 1 | 2 | 3 | 4 | 5 | 6 |

2. To achieve academic success, how important is competence in evaluating the quality of a source of information?

| Not at all important | | | | Extremely important | |
| 1 | 2 | 3 | 4 | 5 | 6 |

3. To what extent do you require your students to be information competent in order to successfully complete your courses?

| Not at all | | | | Require very high literacy | |
| 1 | 2 | 3 | 4 | 5 | 6 |

4. Please rate your students' competence in researching topics using library resources and information technology.

| Very Poor | | | | Very Good | |
| 1 | 2 | 3 | 4 | 5 | 6 |

5. Please rate your students' competence in evaluating the quality of a source of information.

| Very Poor | | | | Very Good | |
| 1 | 2 | 3 | 4 | 5 | 6 |

6. In what ways can the FDC and the Pollak Library assist you in incorporating information competence instruction in your courses?

Department_____

—ELLEN JUNN, SUELLEN COX, PATRICIA SZESZULSKI, AND SOREL REISMAN—

Choosing a "candidate course" for Information Competency integration

Identify two courses from your department that currently include, or could include student information competency goals and assignments.

The courses that you select should meet the following requirements:

- One course should be an **early entry core** course
- One course should be a **senior level capstone** or equivalent course
- Should be part of an incremental course sequence
- Are required for graduation
- Are frequently offered
- Assignment components can be framed in terms of specific skill-building tasks
- Suggest transferable skills (generic skills or discipline specific skills)

Applying ACRL Standards to Disciplinary Areas
This exercise asks questions to trigger your thoughts about applying the following ACRL Standards. (Refer to the "Summary of ACRL Standards" in your packet for a complete list of performance indicators.)

The information competent student:
1. *Defines the nature and extent of the information needed.*
2. *Accesses needed information effectively and efficiently.*
3. *Evaluates information and its sources critically and incorporates selected information into his or her knowledge base and value system.*
4. *Individually or as a member of a group, uses information effectively to accomplish a specific purpose.*
5. *Understands many of the economic, legal, and social issues surrounding the use of information and accesses and uses information ethically and legally.*

---

1. What are, or would be the department's information competency learning goals for students in an:

Early entry core course   **Senior level capstone course**

(OVER)

2. What **teaching methods** would you use in an early entry core course and senior level capstone course to help students achieve information competency?

Early entry core course   **Senior level capstone course**

3. What assignments would you use that allow students to demonstrate their level of mastery of information competency?

Early entry core course   **Senior level capstone course**

CSUF-CSU Information Competency Initiative for Department Chairs
Spring 2001

<u>Funding Support</u>

- Each participating department will receive a budget transfer of $1,000. Please fill out and submit the attached form and send it to Leticia Galvan (FAX: x5805 or lgalvan@fullerton.edu) with your departmental account number for the budget transfer and a brief itemized budget.

- Departments may choose to allocate these funds in a variety of ways so long as the funds are used to support faculty and the department in this project. Examples of funding allocations may include:
  - Independent contracts for participating faculty (see attached handout and contact Lou Hamby, x2412 for more information)
  - Hosting meetings or a departmental retreat for this project (e.g., room rental)
  - IMPORTANT NOTE: <u>meals/refreshments ARE NOT a permissible expense</u> from these funds, given the new Directive 11)
  - Student or graduate assistants for the project
  - Departmental O&E
  - Travel

CSU Expected Outcomes or Deliverables

1. A <u>list</u> of the department's student learning outcomes that include the skills of information competence.

2. Two syllabi (one entry-level and one senior or capstone core course) that specifically identify assignments that promote information competence.

3. Representative assignments indicating that students are being asked to demonstrate the various skills of information competence.

The above information should be provided in electronic form and will be posted on our CSUF Student Information Competency website at http://www.library.fullerton.edu/information_comp/.

Timeline and Important Due Dates

- Meeting 1: Departmental team participation at <u>Friday, April 20, 2001</u> symposium at the Marriott.

- Ongoing support and assistance from the FDC and the Library over the summer (e.g., individual consultations and occasional workshops). Also, the FDC will be building a Decision Support Center (with collaborative decision-making software) early this summer and those facilities will be available for departmental use when completed, perhaps August.

- Meeting 2: Follow-up progress report on <u>Friday, October 5, 2001,</u> 1-3 p.m. location tba.

- Project completion: The 3 deliverables listed above should be submitted to the FDC by <u>Monday, December 17, 2001</u> for inclusion on the website.

This past spring, the Faculty Development Center hosted a day-long, off-campus retreat on April 20, 2001 at which 20 department teams (department chairs, plus several faculty) across campus (see department list below) voluntarily convened to hear about and discuss the importance of enhancing student information competence. We were fortunate to have Dr. Susan Curzon, Dean of the University Library at CSU Northridge serve as the keynote speaker. Throughout the day, participants worked in large and small groups and with Library faculty on activities designed to assist faculty and chairs in developing specific ways to integrate information competence into the curriculum. Department teams will be expected to submit three outcomes at the end of this Fall 2001: (1) a list of the department's student learning outcomes that include the skills of information competence; (2) two syllabi (one entry-

—ELLEN JUNN, SUELLEN COX, PATRICIA SZESZULSKI, AND SOREL REISMAN—

level and one senior or capstone course) that specifically identify assignments that promote information competence; and (3) representative assignments indicating that students are being asked to demonstrate the various skills of information competence.

Work on this project will continue over this summer and fall. In addition, each participating department was assigned a specific Library faculty to assist them in this process. Later this Fall, the Faculty Development Center will convene a follow-up meeting of all participants on October 5, 2001 to discuss progress and assess the project. Departments will submit their materials for inclusion on this website by December 17, 2001 and the project should be completed this fall semester. Finally, CSU Fullerton hopes to continue and extend this project next year by asking the remaining departments on campus to complete the same process.

THE INFORMATION LITERACY TOOLKIT: FOSTERING CRITICAL RESEARCH SKILLS IN THE ONLINE LEARNING ENVIRONMENT

John T. Butler and Jerilyn R. Veldof

Introduction

For large research libraries, there are immense challenges in mounting a meaningful and comprehensive information literacy initiative. The enormity and diversity of need can be staggering. To illustrate, the University of Minnesota, Twin Cities campus offers 161 bachelor's degrees, 218 master's degrees, 114 doctoral degrees, and 5 professional degrees. Campus enrollment exceeds 46,000, with nearly 13,000 students at the graduate or professional school level. Over 14,000 faculty and staff support the University's land-grant mission of teaching, research, and outreach.

With this kind of scope, staffing levels (even if flush), could never come close to the ideal of reaching every student and working with every faculty member. In fact, to have a librarian to student ratio similar to that of a small colleges, such as Oberlin or St. Olaf, would necessitate the University Libraries hire 498 new librarians to liaison with faculty.[1] This will not happen.

Of the actual 71 librarians who do work with faculty, there is a wide range of instructional support offered. This situation is not unlike many other of Minnesota's peer institutions. On one side of the scale are librarians who respond to all course-related requests and may also actively market their instructional services. On the other side are those who choose to do absolutely no instruction or only selected instructional sessions for the upper levels and graduate students. Very few librarians report developing partnerships with

Butler is the Digital Reference Services Coordinator and ***Veldof*** is the User Education Coordinator at the University of Minnesota Libraries, Twin Cities.

faculty and providing curriculum design support. Gaps in instructional support are exacerbated by an extraordinary number of retirements in recent years (and economic challenges to fill those positions), leaving over a dozen academic departments without a library liaison. In sum, there is very little uniformity of instructional support across the campus. Some faculty and students get a fair amount, while others get nothing.

To add to these underlying challenges, the University has been moving to a more distributed model of instructional delivery. The University delivers instruction to students located in many states and countries, and a significant number of campus-based classes are delivering portions of their course content online.

The situation the University of Minnesota faces is not unlike other large universities struggling with low staffing levels, collection-centric (as opposed to education-centric) practices, and distributed models of instructional delivery. It is a situation, however, that needed to be addressed. Several years ago, the University Libraries identified the library's teaching role as one of five strategic goals:

> "Expand Libraries programs that teach and promote essential information skills required for success in the electronic environment."

Library staff were therefore challenged to devise scalable and practical ways to meet this goal in the face of circumstances such as those discussed above. Solutions would need to meet the following criteria:

1. *Adds value*–improves student learning and faculty effectiveness.

2. *Builds information literacy competencies*– provides faculty with plug-and-play information literacy tools.
3. *Builds worth*–helps faculty see the value of information literacy and the library's role.
4. *Curriculum integrated*–integral to students' success in the course.
5. *Easy and fast*–little or no work for faculty; technologically efficient processes for librarians.
6. *Scalable*–able to reach large numbers of students; as many benefit from the work of a few.
7. *Customizable*–learning resources should be modularized, available for tailoring and re-use.
8. *Supports distributed learners*–available to learners regardless of location and time of access.
9. *User-Centered*–conceived of and designed from the user's perspective.

Guided by these criteria and inspired by technological opportunity, the Information Literacy Toolkit was built incrementally over the past five years to meet the challenges of fostering information literacy in students of a large research university. A collaborative team of librarians, instructional designers, interface designers, Web programmers, and faculty are responsible for its ongoing development.

The Toolkit

The Toolkit currently consists of an integrated suite of six tools that support a wide range of learning activities and information research needs. The six components are the Idea Exchange; *CourseLib*; *QuickStudy: Library Research Guide*; the *Assignment Calculator*; *Research QuickStart*; and the *FAQ Database*. It is critical to note that the Toolkit, collectively, is designed to serve the needs of all three players in the information literacy enterprise—students, faculty, and librarians. What makes each a "tool" varies. That is, in some components, the tool-like attributes are most apparent to the librarian who benefits from an easy-to-use Web authoring tool that facilitates the rapid production of a customized library Web page for a course. With other components, students are the drivers and interact with the tool to generate pages or resources using parameters that they define on the spot.

The intended purpose and functional description of each Toolkit component is described below. The appendix provides screen shots of each tool's public interface, along with descriptions of each tools' administrative features.

1) Idea Exchange–http://www.lib.umn.edu/idea-exchange/

Turnover for instructors in the basic educational programs such as English Composition and Learning and Academic Skills is extremely high. The campus trend is also to hire more adjunct professors and fewer tenured ones. This amounts to a sizable pool of new instructors who are faced with designing a semester curriculum perhaps for the first time. They may only be teaching from that curriculum just a few times before they graduate or move onto another teaching position. Because there is not a lot of time for trial and error and revisions, getting their curriculum right the first time is important.

The Idea Exchange is designed to increase instructor's success in designing and/or choosing effective and tried-and-true lesson plans and assignments that help students increase their information literacy and writing abilities. Instructors can pick from a suite of curricular components as well as see how other instructors have pulled these components into a sequenced curriculum building towards a well-written and researched final project.

User Features
• Lesson plans, assignments and worksheets from across disciplines that are designed to improve research and writing skills.
• Reflections from instructors on how they build an effective sequence of assignments.

Statistical Profile
• No statistics available; still under development

2) *CourseLib*–http://courses.lib.umn.edu

Academic librarians have long seen the value of integrating their instruction program into courses and academic programs. But faculty haven't always. However, the recent surge of faculty activity in re-casting their courses for online delivery has presented an extraordinary opportunity for librarians to demonstrate how they can add value to the faculty member's primary teaching product—the course.

CourseLib is a Web-based authoring and database tool designed to support customized library page creation and instruction for specific courses and programs. The tool provides librarians with an easy-to-use authoring environment; and crosswalks to local database resources, such as online tutorials, course page templates and interfaces, e-resources, and service links. The design enables staff to create and maintain customized pages in the most efficient and scalable way possible. Most importantly, the tool has provided a vehicle for librarian-faculty collaboration resulting in opportunities to support the library's information literacy and distributed learning initiatives.

—JOHN T. BUTLER AND JERILYN R. VELDOF—

User Features

- From a single *CourseLib* page, students have direct access to the core library resources and services relevant to their course, including database and e-journal access, access to e-reserves, online reference services, key *QuickStudy* tutorial modules, specific FAQ records, and more.
- Customized library pages are linked directly from course Web pages or syllabi.
- Page links are drawn from a database with each page load, ensuring currency and appropriate proxy
- Pages are often used to support library instruction sessions, and remain available to reinforce the session's content throughout the term.

Statistical Profile

- Over 200 unique course pages created in the first 14 months.
- Five course pages each report over 500 hits to the main page and over 1500 hits to links on their respective pages.

3) *QuickStudy:* Library Research Guide— http://tutorial.lib.umn.edu/

With a ratio of one library liaison to 33 faculty, it is nearly impossible to work with all faculty or all students in a given department. *QuickStudy* is designed as an alternative to the "librarian in the classroom" and is intended to be assigned by faculty to supplement their own instruction on using the library and becoming effective researchers.

In eight modules with several lessons within each module, *QuickStudy* moves from "Starting your Research" through "Citing Sources." Guided Exercises allow students to try what they are learning and the module quizzes provide some measure for how much the students learn. Faculty are encouraged to have students e-mail their quiz results back to the faculty for credit.

Each of the lessons and quiz questions are matched with the information literacy standards they address.

User Features

- Includes lessons on: "Locating, Evaluating, and Using Statistics," "Finding Biographical Information," "Finding US Federal Legislation"
- Quiz answers are e-mailed directly to the instructor
- Guided Exercises show students how to learn by doing
- Information literacy standards are attached to content
- An Instructors Guide with sample lesson plans and assignments to supplement QuickStudy

Statistical Profile

- Hits from Jan 2001 to Dec 2002:
  - Main Page - 20,911
  - Module Level Pages - 24,730
  - Lesson Level Pages - 44,529
  - Specific Pages - 60,190

4)Assignment Calculator– http://www.lib.umn.edu/help/calculator/

Most reference librarians working the Sunday evening shift can recount horror stories of students coming in at the very last minute to do all their research from beginning to end in a scheduled one-hour period. The Assignment Calculator helps transform what would have been a last-minute panic dash to the library into a much more successful research experience.

The Assignment Calculator teaches students research is a process, that this process includes many steps, and time for these steps needs to be planned and managed. It also provides students with the resources and services they need during each step of the process. Step 6, for example, "Find, review, and evaluate journal/magazine/newspaper articles" points students to the appropriate module in the library's online tutorial as well as to *QuickStart*, our subject driven online pathfinders. Step 9, "Writing Your First Draft" points students to the Online Writing Center at the U of M, in-person writing centers, and links them to the Web site for reserving computer lab time. Note that the Assignment Calculator is centered on the student's experience of writing and researching for a paper. It does not force them to go to a particular tool for writing and another tool for research, but rather it weaves the research and writing process into one tool.

User Features

- Recommended due dates are presented for each step in the research process
- Access to writing and research support and resources from on-campus and beyond
- Ability to customize the resource list by topic area.

Statistical Profile

- Access to the Calculator peaked in February 2002 with about nine calculations a day
- 2001: July—311 (1411)/August—134 (1591)/ September—183 (3001)/October—176 (1372)/ November— 28 (1014)/December—146 (668)
- 2002: January—95 (409)/February—261 (931)

[Note: The first number reflects actual calculations; the second number shows the total hits to the home page and calculation pages.]

5) Research *QuickStart* – http://research.lib.umn.edu

Not many years ago, the main problem facing students in their research was coping with a scarcity of readily available information. This old problem has given way to its polar opposite. Now students face the challenge of making good information decisions while facing an overwhelming abundance of choices. Of course, the situation is exacerbated when students do not even recognize that there *is* a problem. However, it is widely acknowledged by librarians and increasingly by faculty that the sheer quantity of information resources so conveniently available to students has inspired a pattern of casual decision-making regarding appropriate, and even trustworthy resources. The problem facing students has shifted from "How do I obtain what I need?" to "What do I choose?"

Research *QuickStart* helps students focus the field of information choices by presenting them with key resources for *starting* their research in a particular subject area. It is a wizard-like tool that generates dynamic resource pages for over two hundred subjects. *QuickStart* is particularly oriented to undergraduates tackling term papers, developing speeches, or other class assignments requiring information research.

User Features
- Students select a subject, and then access a selective list of subject resources chosen by librarians who are experts in their discipline.
- *QuickStart* result pages contain links to both online subscription databases and Web sites, and listings of print resources.
- Resources in results pages often provide annotations that link to online guided exercises on how the resources can be searched or used.
- Students may also e-mail *QuickStart* pages to themselves or colleagues.

Statistical Profile
- Over 200 subjects are available to choose from.
- Main *QuickStart* page is accessed 180,000 times annually
- Most frequently accessed *QuickStart* subjects in current year are Psychology (3.62% of all subjects accessed), Current Issues (2.96%), Education (2.38%), Terrorism (2.01%), and English and American Literature (1.77%).
  38% of use occurs outside of "business hours" (9am – 5pm)

6) FAQ Database – http://FAQ.lib.umn.edu

A reference question is a teaching and learning opportunity. Yet, how many questions are never asked because reference librarians are not (and cannot be) at the point-of-need? Service available by phone, e-mail, and interactive digital formats addresses some of this need, but there remain times that students, by choice or circumstance, do not ask their question and the opportunity folds.

The FAQ (Frequently Asked Questions) Database is a growing archive of answers to common research and library use questions, available to users at all times. Beyond simply providing answers to questions, FAQ Database records are written to provide instructional guidance to those using this self-help resource.

User Features
- The FAQ Database provides three navigational options: 1) browsing by category and subcategory, 2) browsing alphabetically by index terms; and 3) keyword searching (simple and advanced options available).
- Individual records provide cross-references to other records in the database, as well as external Web resources.
- Each record also provides a link to the Libraries' *InfoPoint* digital reference service where e-mail, chat, and collaborative browsing services are offered (http://infopoint.lib.umn.edu/)

Statistical Profile
- Over 300 FAQ records created to date
- User statistics not available (module in development).

A Toolkit Scenario

How might the Information Literacy Toolkit make the faculty member's job easier while building information literacy skills in their students? The following is one scenario that pulls together use of all the toolkit components.

The Toolkit from the Faculty's Perspective

Early on in the development of the sociology course, "Public Ethics," the faculty member checks out a site called the "Idea Exchange" that she had heard about in a departmental e-mail message.

—JOHN T. BUTLER AND JERILYN R. VELDOF—

There she finds a wide range of assignments and exercises designed to help students develop critical thinking skills and become better writers and researchers. The first lesson plan she chooses addresses plagiarism, an issue she feels is critical to cover in this course. Written by an English Composition instructor and a librarian, the lesson plan includes a number of resources to help her teach the lesson. One of them is a module in QuickStudy, the Library's online research guide, which covers proper citation formatting. She works in the completion of this module and the online quiz as part of her syllabus. The Idea Exchange also alerts the faculty member to the possibility of having the library create a customized library page for her course called "*CourseLib.*" She e-mails the library about this and is directed to the library liaison for her department.

This e-mail sparks a series of conversations with the faculty member and her instructional designer about how the library can help in the development of her course. Aside from creating a *CourseLib* page and identifying the various resources available to support the assignments, the liaison mentions another tool that could help the faculty member scaffold her term paper assignment–the Assignment Calculator. The Calculator breaks down the research and writing process into 12 steps and assigns deadlines to those steps depending on when the paper is due. Along with input from the liaison, the faculty member uses this tool to decide which of the steps she would like to see evidence of students completing and use the suggested deadlines as milestones towards building the final paper. A link to the Calculator is also incorporated into the *CourseLib* page.

The Toolkit from the Student Perspective

From the online syllabus, a student in the Public Ethics course accesses *CourseLib*, the library page customized for his course. The page helps the student with the research he needs to do for his term paper assignment and gives him a link to submit any questions he has to the library, chat in real-time with a librarian, or check the FAQ database for answers to his questions.

When the faculty member explains the term paper assignment to the class, the first thing she does is to demonstrate the Assignment Calculator. She enters the deadline for the paper and then prints out and distributes the steps in the writing/research process and the deadlines for each step. The printout also includes the online and in-person resources and services that the library and writing centers provide to help students with each step in the process. The student now has a blueprint for the research and writing process including how he might pace himself.

According to the Assignment Calculator, in two weeks the students should be starting their review of the periodical literature. On that class day, the student participates in the library liaison's workshop designed to help him successfully complete this step. The liaison uses the *CourseLib* page as an outline for the workshop and all the students are able to use it during the workshop. The liaison also introduces QuickStudy, the online tutorial, and reminds the students that the professor is requiring that after the workshop they complete the assigned module and email her their quiz answers for grading.

Multiple Toolkit Paths

The scenario above describes specific ways in which faculty and students may connect with and use the Toolkit. In reality though, there are numerous different and often unpredictable paths through the Toolkit that faculty and students take. Figure 1–Faculty and Student Toolkit Interactions–illustrates

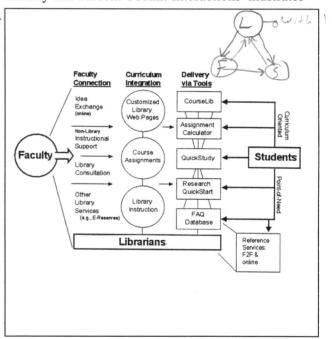

FIGURE 1: FACULTY AND STUDENT TOOLKIT INTERACTIONS

this. In their path, faculty often connect with a library liaison through a variety of channels. This in turn leads to a process in which strategies are made and actions taken to integrate library instructional content into the syllabus or curriculum. It is important to note that some faculty work independent of the liaison, electing to use many of the Toolkit components without librarian mediation. Student interaction with the Toolkit may begin with the path prescribed in the syllabus, but is likely more spontaneous and perhaps serendipitous. For this reason, Toolkit components are cross-linked. So that wherever the student "jumps in," other components are only a link away.

The Technology Behind the Toolkit

The Toolkit required a new technology strategy that was scalable, provided the capacity to customize resources, and presented an intuitive way in which Web pages are authored. Creating and maintaining flat HTML pages, therefore, would have been an unrealistic and unsustainable approach. Noting this, the technology design goals for the Toolkit were to:

- *Optimize use and re-use of data* (input once, use many).
- *Eliminate duplicate maintenance of Web pages* (use of dynamic updating).
- *Make authoring easy and intuitive* (forms-based and GUI interfaces; no code required).
- *Facilitate customization* (position existing resources for quick replication and tailoring).
- *Track use* (automated use data collection and report writing capabilities).

The initial solution involved the creation of multiple databases, actually one for each of the initial Toolkit components as they came on board. These databases included records for information resources, annotations, tutorial modules, guided exercises, library service locations, library subject specialists, page templates, images, and more. As the Toolkit expanded to include more components, "crosswalks" between databases were developed so that one Toolkit component could draw data from another.[2] The Toolkit is now being re-engineered into a data warehouse model. The basic concept of this model is illustrated in Figure 2. Here, data and files of all kinds are deposited into the warehouse through a host of easy-to-use input tools. Then, on the production end, authoring tools and/or algorithms (such as in the case of the Assignment Calculator and Research *QuickStart*) are used to generate end-user products and tools. Data are created only once, updated in only one place, but used in multiple instances. The use of static pages is minimized. The combination of database-delivered content and intuitive authoring tools provides a vehicle for rapid page creation and customization.

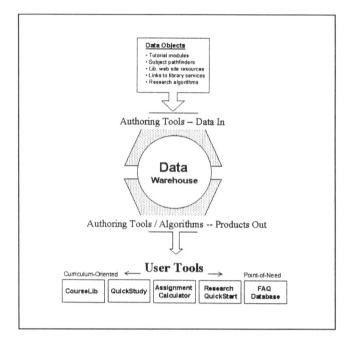

FIGURE 2: TOOLKIT DATA MODEL

Conclusion

Does the Information Literacy Toolkit work? A meaningful response to this question requires an evaluation of the Toolkit's performance from the perspectives of all three major players–students, faculty, and library staff. Such an evaluation is progressing incrementally, but remains at the very early stages.

For students, the main evaluation criterion is impact on learning. The plan for measuring impact is to deploy the "Kirkpatrick Model,"[3] which was chosen as a tangible framework for evaluating learning outcomes in progressive stages. The model, adapted for this purpose, is staged in four levels (noting that each level of measurement may be considered increasingly more important, but also increasingly more difficult to accomplish):

1) Reaction (do they respond favorably to the Toolkit and its various components?)
2) Learning (do they learn what we want them to learn?)
3) Behavior (do they apply their learning?)
4) Results (does it make a difference academically?)

With three of the six Toolkit components–*CourseLib*, *QuickStudy*, and *Research QuickStart*–formal evaluations have begun involving student and faculty respondents. The preliminary results from students demonstrate a high degree of success at level one–Reaction. This can also be said for faculty, whose initial response to the availability of these tools

—JOHN T. BUTLER AND JERILYN R. VELDOF—

for their students and in their courses has been overwhelmingly positive. A small amount of work has begun to measure the next level–Learning. This involves bench marking results of quizzing modules as well as involving faculty in evaluating the degree of information literacy competencies in evidence in term papers and other student products. Efforts involving the next two stages–measuring Behavior and Results–have not yet taken place.

For librarians, feedback has indicated that the Toolkit has been largely embraced for two key reasons. First, it has presented a means to efficiently scale up delivery of instructional and customized course support. Second, the Toolkit has provided a vehicle for librarian-faculty collaboration resulting in opportunities to advance the library's information literacy and distributed learning initiatives. The emerging irony of these successes has been increased numbers of faculty requesting services. While a good problem to have, it does intensify one of the original conditions that led to the development of the Toolkit—how to meet the library-related curricular needs of students and faculty at a large research university when the library staff is vastly outnumbered.

Ultimately, the Toolkit will need to be evaluated in terms of its return on investment.[4] While this cannot be determined now, there is considerable interest and will-power among library and other university administrators to undertake further development and deployment. Whether the specific solutions presented by the Toolkit are the right ones, time will tell. What is clear is that traditional strategies for coping with the institution's current needs don't have a chance.

Acknowledgments

Developing the Toolkit and its components has involved collaboration among librarians, faculty, students, and numerous campus units beyond the Libraries. These units have included the Digital Media Center, Java and Web Services, the Center for Teaching and Learning, the College of Liberal Art's Writing Center, and the Department of Rhetoric. Collectively, the expertise contributed to the project has included knowledge of bibliographic resources and search strategies, instructional design, interface design, graphic design, information design and technical communication, usability, and programming and database design.

While it is not possible to include all those who have played a part, the authors would like to acknowledge the key project leaders and contributors. Leading the project (or its components) at various points in its evolution have been Kay Kane, Chris Loring, Karen Beavers, Kate McCready, Gregg Richardson, Barbara Kautz, Jim Stemper, John Butler, and Jerilyn Veldof. Key contributors have been Ilene Alexander, Chris Ament, Kashif Asdi, Kate Gandrud, Malaika Grant, Laurel Haycock, Dave Johnson, Shane Nackerud, Travis Noll, Kate Rattenborg, Bill Tantzen, Jen Tantzen, Cynthia Teague, and Chris Tobkin.

NOTES

1. St. Olaf College Library, for example, has a librarian to faculty ratio of approximately 1:4 (58 liaison librarians who work with a total of 249 faculty). At the University of Minnesota Libraries, that ratio is closer to 1:32 (71 liaison librarians who work with 2275 tenured or tenure track faculty–this **does not** include the sizable number of non-tenure track instructors and TA's who also teach).

2. Research *QuickStart* was the first Toolkit component to be developed and it was designed as an MSSQL database using active server pages (asp) and vbscript. Other tools were developed using similar database models, and ODBC crosswalks have been developed between the separate databases. The Libraries' current project is to migrate all data into a single complex data warehouse.

3. Donald L. Kirkpatrick, *Evaluating Training Programs: The Four Levels* (San Francisco: Berrett-Koehler, 1994).

4. Jack Phillips suggests that "return on investment" might be the fifth level to Kirkpatrick's model. Jack J. Phillips, "ROI: The Search for Best Practices," *Training and Development*, 50 no. 2 (Feb. 1995): 42-47.

Idea Exchange **http://www.lib.umn.edu/idea-exchange/**

Administrative Features

- Note: The *Idea Exchange* is currently under construction.

- At this phase of development, all the materials in the *Idea Exchange* are published in html.

- Submissions are made through a Web form.

- Future development of a database will allow for indexing and querying by keyword and author.

Appendix: *CourseLib*

http://courses.lib.umn.edu/

UNIVERSITY**LIBRARIES**   LUMINA : DIGITAL LIBRARY GATEWAY

University of Minnesota

HOME   ASK US!   HOURS   HELP

Information Resources and Services for:

FINA 6322: Equity Security Analysis

Spring Semester : 2002
U of M, Twin Cities

Personnel:
Professor: David Runkle
Librarian: Judy Wells
Librarian: Mary Schoenborn

Contents:
- Identify Competitors in an Industry
- Find Industry Profiles: Sources to Help You Analyze Industries
- Find Financial Ratios for the Industry or Company
- Information about Companies
- Sources You Can Use to Analyze Public Companies:
- Find journal or magazine articles on a company or industry
- Other Web Sites for Company or Industry Information
- Welcome to Business Reference!

Administrative Features

- Full GUI, forms-based authoring; no knowledge of html or ftp required.

- Resources linked from resources/service database, supporting dynamic updating and centralized maintenance

- Multiple interface options to customize "look and feel." Interface "wrappers" can be changed instantaneously.

- Template function, enabling the creation of a new course page using other page in the course database as a template.

- Ability to add images (for screenshots, supporting graphics).

- Copy and paste utility, allowing the copying of a single resource or a hierarchical cluster or resources from one page for pasting on another page.

- Fully flexible content sequencing.

- Pages can be added to the database and not "published" until completed. Conversely, pages can be "unpublished" with one click, yet stored in the database for future offerings of the course.

- Fully integrated statistical analysis tool for measuring page and link hits, against date and time parameters.

- Extensive rights management system allows page authors to assign co-authors (e.g., other librarians, TA's, faculty, etc.). Author accounts tied to central campus authentication.

http://tutorial.lib.umn.edu/

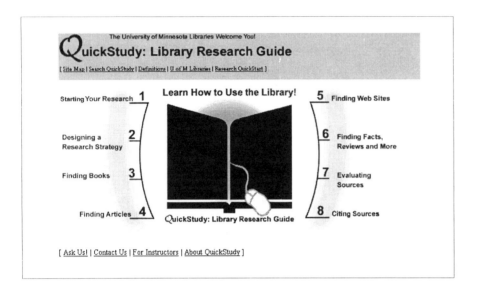

Administrative Features

- *QuickStudy* content is entered into a database that keeps the interface design consistent throughout the tutorial.

- Content can be added to the database and not "published" until completed.

- Textual content is entered using html tags.

- Quiz questions, guided exercises, glossary entries, external links, and information literacy standards are associated with either the modular or the lesson level.

- Lessons and the pages within lessons can be reordered at the click of a button.

- Other modules can be created in *QuickStudy*, but not appear on the homepage (such as a module on using MLA or on doing statistical research).

—JOHN T. BUTLER AND JERILYN R. VELDOF—

Assignment Calculator

http://www.lib.umn.edu/help/calculator/

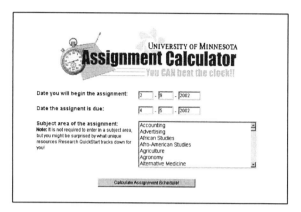

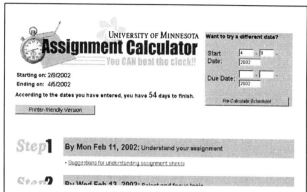

Administrative Features

- The subject list is pulled from the central data warehouse. Subject selectors do not have to customize this tool.

- Each of the 12 research and writing steps is assigned a deadline based on an algorithm created by librarians, writing center staff, and teaching center staff.

- Resources and services corresponding to each step are hot-linked in the second page version. Full URL's are included in the printer-friendly version.

- A future enhancement of the tool will send e-mail messages to the student to alert them to each deadline in the writing/research process.

http://research.lib.umn.edu/

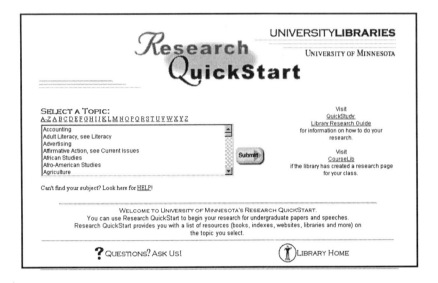

Administrative Features

- Full GUI, forms-based authoring; no knowledge of html or ftp required.

- Bi-directional authoring option where multiple *QuickStart* subjects can be associated with individual resources, or multiple resources can be associated with a single subject. The later option is offered through a feature called QuickPages, which allows authors to quickly select resources through a scrolling list of title in the database, enabling pages to be generated in minutes.

- Fully integrated statistical analysis tool for measuring page hits, against date and time parameters.

—JOHN T. BUTLER AND JERILYN R. VELDOF—

Frequently Asked Questions (FAQ) Database

http://FAQ.lib.umn.edu/

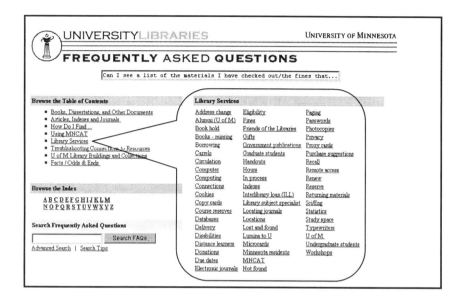

Administrative Features

- Full forms-based authoring; no knowledge of html or ftp required. Point and click indexing of FAQ records to support browsing navigation. Internal cross-references (i.e., referencing other FAQ records) are created through point and click function.

- Records in preparation can be hidden from public view until finished

- Page preview function

- Rights management system allows individual- and unit-ownership of records. Author accounts tied to central campus authentication.

Reaching Out to First-Year Students: The Passport to the Libraries of The Claremont Colleges Orientation

Gale Burrow, Carrie Marsh, Kimberly Franklin, and **Amy Wallace**

How It All Began

It was a dark and stormy night—it really was!—when the idea for Passport came to us.

In May 2000, three librarians, all members of the Instruction Group at the Libraries of The Claremont Colleges, attended the LOEX conference. The theme was freshman orientation, and we were keenly interested in getting more out of our 50-minute library research instruction sessions for first-year students by finding new ways of providing basic orientation outside of the instruction sessions. That day we heard several interesting presentations. One described a "scavenger hunt" that a group of private colleges had developed to orient the students from their institutions to the different libraries in the consortium. That session appealed to us because, like the librarian making the presentation, we in the Libraries of The Claremont Colleges are challenged to reach students in several different colleges.

The Claremont Colleges are a consortium of eight contiguous institutions (five undergraduate colleges—Pomona, Scripps, Claremont McKenna, Harvey Mudd, Pitzer; two graduate schools—Claremont Graduate University, the Keck Graduate Institute of Applied Life Sciences, and the Claremont University Consortium, the central institution providing coordinated support services for The Claremont Colleges). Libraries are the major academic support service, that is, we are "partners" with The Colleges in teaching and learning, but we "belong" to none of them.

Burrow, *Marsh*, and *Franklin* are librarians with The Libraries of The Claremont Colleges. *Wallace* is a librarian at the University of California, San Diego.

Back to the dark and stormy night. Our enthusiasm from a day spent listening to good ideas led to an evening of brainstorming, and the ideas poured forth; ways to introduce approximately 1,200 new students from five undergraduate colleges to the basics about the Libraries; ideas about what those basics should be; and plans to make the learning experience fun. As we talked, we threw out crazy ideas, and laughed. The idea of a passport book was born. When you travel, and explore the world, you carry a passport that is stamped in each country you visit. Why wouldn't that same concept work for students as they explored the resources and services of the libraries.

We had great fun discussing design, layout, activities, promotion, and prizes, and a rough plan, began to emerge. Students would acquire stamps on a passport by visiting service points and completing activities. Students who completed the passport would be eligible for fabulous prizes; prizes that would be big and 'cool' and provide enough incentive to entice all first-year students into participating in the program. We envisioned an ice cream party, with a deejay, where the prizes would be awarded. We were excited and ready to go.

Implementation of the Passport Orientation

When we returned to Claremont, after LOEX, our biggest concern was time. We wanted Passport to be fully implemented when the Fall semester began in just three months. Another concern was funding—especially for the big prizes.

The Instruction Group began by submitting a proposal to the Director of Libraries that outlined our plan for the Passport program; its value, funding needs, and our ideas for meeting some of the costs. At the same time, we began to develop the Passport activities. Once the Director approved our proposal, we were able to talk with the Deans of Students at the five undergraduate colleges, asking them to allow us to introduce and distribute Passports during orientation on each campus and requesting supplemental funding for prizes for each college's winners. With the Libraries' and the Colleges' support, "Passport to the Libraries" was inaugurated in the Fall of 2000.

The Passport orientation is about to enter its third year. What is involved each year in preparing for and carrying out this orientation? In the Summer of 2000, we created the Passport booklet. (See Appendix A). We decided that our Passport would resemble a typical passport. The booklet would be 5½ x 4¼ inches so that it would be easy for the students to carry around. We asked all library staff to contribute ideas for the activities. Sixteen activities were selected for the Passport. (See "Planning the Content," below, for details on development of the individual activities.) The Passport booklets and all Passport promotional materials are produced by the Libraries' copy center. Last year, the Summer of 2001, we began by reviewing student comments from Passport 2000. We asked Libraries staff for their suggestions. For Fall 2002, we will also be considering focus group discussions held in the Spring with first-year students and with faculty who taught first-year courses. Based on all these comments, we will discuss the content of Passport and revise it. We will also consider the implementation, look at what worked and what didn't, and consider how we can change our procedures to make it work more effectively—mostly, that means reaching more first-year students.

Because of the nature of The Claremont Colleges, we probably have more contacts to make than would be necessary for other college libraries. Our students come from five separate and independent colleges, so we must plan with each college how we will introduce and hand out the Passports. If we decide to hand them out to large groups during Fall orientation, we work with the Dean of Students offices. If we hand them out in the classes for which they will be required, we work with the faculty teaching freshman courses. Whether they are handed out during orientation or in class, we must also work with the faculty who have agreed to require Passport for their students.

Once all the campus details are worked out, we prepared in the libraries. The Passport activities introduce students to specific library resources and services. Some of the activities require students to use materials not contained in the booklet. These include using an item on reserve (Activity 6 and Appendix C), completing an exercise using the online catalog

(Activity 8 and Appendix D), and retrieving a book and a journal (Activity 10 and Appendix E). There are different versions of these activities, and each is reviewed and updated. For most interactions, students must get their Passport stamped at the appropriate service point to indicate they have completed the activity. In late Summer, just before orientation begins, we talk with staff at each service point to be sure they know what to expect from the students, provide the items the students will need, and provide stamping supplies. Finally, we put up posters about Passport in each of the Libraries and set up the travel trunk, where the Passports are turned in, at Honnold/Mudd Library.

During the two to three weeks when students are working on their Passports, we send occasional e-mails to student e-mail lists and to faculty who are requiring Passport for their classes, reminding them about deadlines, prizes, and the Passport prize party. Planning for the party, which is held about a week after the Passports are turned in, involves reserving a space, ordering the food, and organizing the entertainment. To prepare for the prize drawing, Passports are sorted by college and checked to be sure they are complete. Only completed Passports are entered in the drawing. We award identical "big" prizes to students at each college. The first year, one student on each campus won a Palm Pilot; last year we had three big prizes for each campus: a pair of ski lift tickets, a CD/MP3 player, and a gift certificate to Huntley, the Colleges' bookstore. Following the drawing for big prizes, all the remaining Passports are mixed together into one container and we draw for the smaller prizes, which are usually gift certificates from local merchants. Many merchants contribute prizes. Our goal is to award a prize to one out of every 6-10 students who participate in the Passport orientation.

Planning the Content

The goal of Passport is to provide first-year undergraduate students with vital information they need to know about the Libraries during the first weeks of their undergraduate career. It was conceived and designed as a creative alternative to the standard, not-well-attended library tour. More importantly, it was designed so that instruction librarians would not have to devote time in their 50-minute hands-on session to cover information that really could (and should) be delivered more effectively outside the classroom. How did we decide what to include in the Passport?

In consultation with the Libraries' Reference and Instruction Team, the Instruction Group brain stormed what we believed all first-year students should know

—GALE BURROW, CARRIE MARSH, KIMBERLY FRANKLIN, AND AMY WALLACE—

about the Libraries. We decided students should be able to:

- check out and renew library books
- access the Libraries' Web site
- get a copy card and use the Libraries' photocopy services
- access course reserves
- use our online catalog
- meet and talk with at least one librarian
- retrieve a book and a journal from the Honnold/Mudd collection
- be aware of resources and services like Interlibrary Loan, Special Collections, and Asian Studies
- be aware of and visit campus libraries (Denison, Seeley G. Mudd Science, Sprague)
- activate their college ID cards so they can be used as their library cards

Once we agreed on which topics needed to be covered, we set out to design the activities that would help introduce students to the Libraries. Design of the activities was guided by the following principles:

1. Passport must be interactive, because we know that students learn best when they are actively involved in their learning. Before the creation of Passport, instruction librarians at the Colleges had already had a number of discussions about the importance of incorporating active learning into our instruction program, and any library orientation we created had to include this critical element.

2. The activities must be fun and encourage students to be creative, hence the question about their funniest or most memorable library experience, and the rap/poem activity.

3. Students would not be penalized for wrong answers; we were more concerned that they complete all of the activities than that they answer everything correctly.

4. The activities must not be confusing or cause frustration. We tried to sequence the activities appropriately and to provide clear instructions.

5. The activities should encourage collaboration. Students were told that they could complete the Passport alone or in groups. We found that most of them worked in groups, thus Passport proved to be an excellent opportunity for students to engage in peer learning.

6. Passport must include both quantitative and qualitative mechanisms for evaluation. We gathered demographic information in the first group of questions (i.e. age, college and gender), and gathered qualitative data in the form of the poem, the two questions about the usefulness of Passport, and later, in focus groups with students and faculty.

7. Students must be able to complete the Passport in a reasonable amount of time. It was pre-tested with three students so that we could estimate how long it would take to complete all the activities. They accomplished everything within two hours.

8. Passport is more than a list of tasks and exercises; it is intended to be a positive, fun way for first-year students to *experience* the Libraries. A key element of that experience is students' contact with librarians and other Libraries staff as they move through the activities.

9. Passport must address information literacy competencies.

For some time before the inauguration of Passport, the Instruction Group had been working with information literacy competencies and incorporating them into instruction. The ACRL *Information Literacy Competency Standards for Higher Education* were available as we began work on Passport for 2001. The competencies addressed by Passport are these:

Standard One: The information literate student determines the nature and extent of the information needed.

Performance Indicator 2: The information literate student identifies a variety of types and formats of potential sources for information:

- Becomes familiar with in-person and online services and resources available at the Libraries.
- Recognizes that the Libraries provide immediate access to a variety of electronic resources via the campus network, which they may access in the libraries, computer labs, computer commons and in their dorm rooms.

Standard Two: The information literate student accesses needed information effectively and efficiently.

Performance Indicator 3: The information literate student retrieves information online or in person using a variety of methods:

- Uses specialized online and in person services available at the institution to retrieve information.
- Uses the Libraries' classification and location schemes to retrieve a book and a journal.

As the Libraries' orientation programming for first-year students evolves, we continue to focus on our guiding principles and the information literacy competencies and revise them as necessary.

Evaluation and the Future of Passport

One of the integral features of Passport is its evaluation component. A guiding principle in designing Passport was the need to build both qualitative and quantitative evaluation mechanisms into the experience. The first question in the Passport gathers demographic information such as students' age, gender, college, and the city, state or country in which they graduated high school. Toward the end of the booklet, students are asked to do the following: 1) write a short poem or rap on their Passport experience; 2) tell us something about the Passport experience that was especially useful and why; 3) tell us something about the Passport experience that was not useful and why; and 4) indicate their willingness to participate in a discussion about the libraries.

Using the feedback from these questions as well as from library staff has allowed us to revise the Passport. For example, the first version of Passport asked students for the city and state in which they graduated from high school. We noticed that someone had written in the name of their country because they had not attended high school in the United States. The next version of Passport included a space for country. It is important that the Passport experience is an inclusive one, and we must be attentive to such issues when we plan and design library programs. In another example, a word scramble with the names of various library service points was included in the Fall 2000 version of the Passport. Students commented that the activity was meaningless because they did not know why they would use those service points. For the Fall 2001 Passport, we changed the activity so that students matched a description of the service point with its appropriate name. We also found that when responding to the question about the usefulness of Passport, a student would say, "If I had not been forced to go to each library, I would not have known where they were," but would also comment that she did not like having to walk to each library. While such contradictory comments are confusing, they still provide good data if for no other reason than to indicate that we need to pay attention to certain activities.

We also made changes in the way we promote Passport. In Fall 2000, due to the very tight time frame, Passport was promoted directly to students through campus orientation, e-mail, posters, and handouts. The promotion focused on the incentives of the party and prizes. Fewer than 8 percent of eligible students completed the Passport in the first year of the program. To increase participation in 2001, we marketed directly to students, and collaborated with faculty in first-year seminars and classes. Members of the Instruction Group met with faculty coordinators on each campus to explain the Passport program and its value for first-year students. We also worked directly with the faculty who agreed to require Passport, coordinating time lines and answering questions. As a result, many more students participated in the second year of the program: 368 first-year students completed a Passport. Participation varied by college, ranging from a high of 52 percent to a disappointing 1 percent.

Decisions on how Passport to the Libraries will continue will be based on the hundreds of comments received from Activity 14 and Activity 15 in the Passport as well as on the series of focus groups held with students and faculty in April 2002. Our goal is to provide *all* first-year students with the information they need at the very beginning of their academic experience that will allow them to use library resources without anxiety and frustration, and with as much success as possible.

—GALE BURROW, CARRIE MARSH, KIMBERLY FRANKLIN, AND AMY WALLACE—

Appendix A: Passport Booklet

The Passport booklet is 5-1/2" by 4-1/4" and has 20 pages. The inside of the front and back covers are blank.

Back Cover   Front Cover

Printed by The Copy Center
Honnold/Mudd Library

Fall 2001

Passport
to
The Libraries
of
The Claremont Colleges

Passport to the Libraries

This is your Passport to the Libraries. Use it to tour the Libraries and acquaint yourself with the services and staff that will assist you this year and throughout your studies at The Claremont Colleges. As a reward for completing the Passport, you will be eligible to enter a drawing for some terrific prizes, provided that you follow the guidelines and rules outlined below. Welcome to the Libraries of The Claremont Colleges, and we hope that you enjoy your Passport experience!

ELIGIBILITY
1. The Passport program and drawing is open only to first-year undergraduates from Claremont McKenna, Harvey Mudd, Pitzer, Pomona, and Scripps colleges.
2. Students must complete **ALL** activities and get **ALL** required stamps in the Passport in order to be eligible for the prize drawing. Incomplete Passports will **NOT** be entered.
3. One entry per person.

DEADLINE
Completed Passports must be in the Passport Trunk in Honnold/Mudd Library by **5 p.m., Friday, September 28, 2001**, to be entered in the drawing for prizes.

COMPLETE GUIDELINES AND RULES
Before you begin your Passport to the Libraries, please read the complete guidelines and rules at the end of this booklet.

You may complete the activities in this Passport in any order. You may ask for assistance on Passport activities in any library.

---

1. Knowing who you are helps us to plan library services. Tell us about yourself.

Name:

_____

College:

_____

Age:

_____

Email:

_____

Campus phone:

_____

If Passport is required for your class, what is your professor's name?

_____

Where did you graduate from high school?

City: _____ State: _____ Country: _____

Circle one: female   male

Tell us about a memorable library experience you've had?

---

2. What's Your Research IQ?

Please check all that apply.
   I have used an online library catalog.
   I have written a research paper with a bibliography.
   I have used my high school library.
   I have used a public library.
   I have used a college or university library.
   I am comfortable using the Web.
   I am familiar with Web search engines.
   I have asked a librarian for guidance before beginning my research.
   I have attended classes on using library resources.

My favorite Web search engine is
   Altavista
   HotBot
   Excite
   Yahoo
   Ask Jeeves
   Google
   Dogpile
   Other: _____

---

3. Did you know that the same card you use to get meals in your campus dining hall gets you into the Libraries? Your student ID card will be your library card.

Activate your ID so that it becomes your library card. You have 2 options:

*   You can do this on the Web at http://voxlibris.claremont.edu/geninfo/activate.html.

NOTE: It takes about *24 hours* for your account to get into the system when you use the Web activation option. Wait at least that long to ask for your Circulation Desk stamp at one of the 4 libraries.

*   You can take your ID card to the Circulation Desk in any of the 4 libraries.

NOTE: You may activate or verify your student ID as your library card at the Honnold/Mudd Circulation Desk during all hours the library is open. At the 3 campus libraries, this service is available Monday-Friday, 8a.m.-5p.m.

Circulation Desk stamp (*after activating or verifying activation of ID*):

4. **Honnold/Mudd Library** is the largest of the Libraries of The Claremont Colleges. It has collections in humanities and social sciences. It also has a large collection of government publications, an Asian Studies collection, and Special Collections. There are 3 campus libraries. Visit all 3 campus libraries to decide why you might use them and to get a stamp.

1) **Denison Library**, Scripps College campus
   Library specialties: fine arts & humanities, women's studies, Rare Book Room, Scripps College archives

   Why would you use this library?

   Library Stamp:

2) **Seeley G. Mudd Science Library**, Pomona College campus
   Library specialties: biology, chemistry, geology, mathematics, astronomy

   Why would you use this library?

   Library Stamp:

3) **Sprague Library**, Harvey Mudd College campus
   Library specialties: engineering, technology, mathematics, and physics

   Why would you use this library?

Library Stamp:

5. What is the URL for the Libraries' web site?

_____

Can you access this web site from outside the Libraries? Yes / No

Since you will have to turn in this Passport booklet for the prize drawings, if you want a copy of the URL to keep, ask for a Libraries pencil at any desk.

6. To answer the questions below you need a copy of the reserve materials for the course called **Passport 101**. The instructor for this course is **Professor L.C. Dewey**.

- On the Libraries' Web home page, choose Research. Then choose Course Reserves. Finally, choose "Blais - Finding Print Course Reserves" and look up the course by Instructor Name or by Course Name.
- How many entries do you find for this course? _____
- Choose one of the entries and write the information you find for the reserve material for this course:

   _____

   _____

- This item is on reserve in all 4 libraries. Go to any of the libraries and ask for this reserve material. Use the item you find on reserve to answer these two questions:

   a) Do professors put materials on reserve in each of the four libraries? Yes / No

   b) Is the reserve material for Passport 101 available electronically? Yes / No

Reserves Desk Stamp:

7. At the Honnold/Mudd Information Desk or at any of the campus libraries, ask for the handout "Library Services for Undergraduate Students." Use that handout to answer the following questions.

How many books can you check out at one time?

_____

For how long can you check out a book?

_____

What are the 3 ways you can renew a book?

   a. _____

   b. _____

   c. _____

Stamp (any desk) (*for handout only, **not** correct answers*):

8. Blais is the Libraries' online library catalog. You will find a link to it on every page of the Libraries' web site.

Go to any of the libraries and ask for the worksheet called "Using Blais for Passport." Use Blais to answer the questions on the worksheet.

When you have completed the worksheet, fold it in half and staple it to this page of your Passport.

✈ ✈ ✈ ✈ ✈

My Blais, which you'll see at the top of the Blais main menu, allows you to view information about books you have checked out and on hold, renew your books, and save "preferred searches." During the year other options will be added that will allow you to customize many of the features of the online catalog. If you have already activated your library account (see Passport activity #3), explore *My Blais* now if you want to.

9. Go to the Honnold/Mudd Reference Desk and ask the librarian what her/his subject specialty is.

Librarian's Name: _____

Librarian's Subject: _____

Librarian's Signature: _____

What is a subject you're interested in?

_____

Which librarian is the Subject Specialist for this subject?

_____

(**Hint:** ask at the Reference Desk or look on the Web at http://voxlibris.claremont.edu/research/subjspecs.html for a list of the Libraries' Subject Specialists.)

Note: Honnold/Mudd Reference Desk hours:
   Mon-Fri, 8am-5pm, 6pm-10pm
   Sat, 1-5pm
   Sun, 1-5pm, 6-10pm

10. In Honnold/Mudd Library, go to the Reference Desk and get a "Find It" card. Follow the directions on your card to find the book and journal issue indicated. Bring the card, book, and journal issue back to the Reference Desk to get your stamp.

(**Hint:** Ask for a location guide. Then ask the librarian at the desk to explain it to you. It will help you find your items.)

Answer the following true/false questions:

• In our libraries most journals are arranged in alphabetical order by title.   True / False

• Many books near the one I chose were on the same topic.   True / False

Honnold/Mudd Reference Desk Stamp:

11. *The Library Blaiser* is a Web publication from the Libraries for students. You will find *The Library Blaiser* on the Libraries' web site in the "General Information" section. Choose "Publications." Use *The Library Blaiser* to answer the following questions.

a. On what dates is the workshop called "Doing Research in the Web Environment" offered?

_____

b. Who is the first speaker in the Claremont Discourse lecture series?

_____

c. What is the name of one exhibit at Denison Library?

_____

12. Other Passport activities take you to the Reference Desk and the Copy Center in Honnold/Mudd Library. There are also many more places in Honnold/Mudd where you can get assistance. By the name of each "service point" below, write the letter of the appropriate description from "Service Point Descriptions" on the opposite page.

(Hint: Anyone who works in Honnold/Mudd Library can help you with this!)

_____ **Interlibrary Loan**

_____ Asian Studies

_____ Special Collections

_____ Information Desk

_____ Search Center Assistance Desk

Service Point Descriptions

A. Houses unique and rare items such as medieval manuscripts, early printed books, modern fine printing, and the archives of The Claremont Colleges, and provides reference assistance in using these materials.

B. Service point for getting assistance with computer printers or finding general information on the Libraries web site.

C. Houses collections of material supporting research in Chinese, Japanese, and Korean social sciences and humanities fields and provides reference assistance in using these materials

D. Location for getting general information such as library opening and closing times or directions.

E. A service for obtaining items not owned by the Libraries of The Claremont Colleges.

13. Go to the Copy Center in Honnold/Mudd Library where you will receive a free copy card. Write your name on the back of the copy card.

There are three ways that you can add value to your card. Explain one.

List two services that The Copy Center provides.

Copy Center Stamp:

14. Write a short poem or rap on your Passport experience.

Feel free to attach extra pages if your poem is an epic!

May we publish your poem on the Libraries' web site or in one of our publications? Yes / No

May we use your name? Yes / No

15. We'd like to know how useful you found Passport to the Libraries. If you need more space, please use the last page of this Passport, which is blank.

a.   Tell us about something from this Passport orientation to the Libraries that was especially useful. Why was it useful?

b.   Tell us about something from this Passport orientation to the Libraries that was not useful. Why wasn't it useful?

16. Would you be willing to participate in an informal discussion about the Libraries next spring (2002)? Yes / No

Guidelines and Rules

Eligibility
1.   The Passport program and drawing is open only to first-year undergraduates from Claremont McKenna, Harvey Mudd, Pitzer, Pomona and Scripps colleges.
2.   Students must complete **ALL** activities and get **ALL** required stamps in the Passport in order to be eligible for the prize drawing. Incomplete Passports will **NOT** be entered.
3.   One entry per person.

Deadline
Completed Passports must be turned in at Honnold/Mudd Library by **5 p.m., Friday, September 28, 2001.**

Completing the Passport
1.   Passports will be distributed during orientation at each college. Anyone who did not receive a Passport may pick one up at the Honnold/Mudd Library Information Desk.
2.   Read these guidelines and rules, and all directions and questions in the Passport before marking your answers.
3.   Your name, college, email address and/or phone number must be printed clearly in the space provided; this information may be used to notify prize winners.
4.   Check all of your answers and make sure you have received all the stamps you need before turning in your Passport. It cannot be returned to you.

Selection of Winners
1.   A group of selected library staff will verify that all activities in each Passport have been completed.
2.   All completed Passports will be eligible for the prize drawing.
3.   The drawing will take place on October 11, 2001, beginning at 12:30 p.m. at Honnold/Mudd Library on the North Lawn.
4.   Winners do not need to be present. All winners must present their valid student ID to claim their prize.
5.   Winners will be posted on the Libraries web site.

Prizes
Grand prizes will be awarded by college. Dozens of other valuable prizes will also be awarded.

The staff of The Libraries of The Claremont Colleges strive to provide equal access for all users of the Libraries' resources, programs and services. If you have special needs for assistance related to this Passport program, due to disability or injury, please contact passport@libraries.claremont.edu.

DOODLE SPACE

THE LIBRARY LIAISON: INTEGRATING INFORMATION LITERACY INTO THE UNDERGRADUATE CURRICULUM ONE DEPARTMENT AT A TIME

Joe Jackson

Introduction

As more information becomes available online, and the library's traditional role as the sole campus information warehouse diminishes, outreach will be an important method for librarians to become more involved with faculty and departments, and retain a relevant role in the educational process. Library departmental liaison relationships can serve not only as an effective outreach tool, but also as an excellent means of delivering information literacy to undergraduates in four-year institutions. Liaisons are assigned specific departments to work with, a selection that would likely be based on a combination of a librarian's interest and academic background. The librarian's liaison duties are often accompanied by a library-specific task as well, such as instruction, access services, or cataloging. By examining the duties of a library liaison, as well as the potential challenges the establishment of a liaison program could face, the impact liaisons can have on the advancement of information literacy becomes more clearly visible.

Duties of a Liaison

Collections

While the liaison role consists of strong instructional, reference, and outreach elements, it grows initially out of collection development. The collection-based duties of a liaison can vary, but would include some or all of the following:

Jackson is a librarian at Winona State University, Winona, MN.

- Select material to be added to the library collection: in libraries where budget allows, the liaison would have discretionary funds available to address weaknesses in the collection for the assigned subject areas. Specific collections can be built with faculty participation in conjunction with course offerings.

- Act as information source for departments: first-hand knowledge of the resources available in specific disciplines makes it possible for librarians to create awareness for academic departmental members who often do not have the time to keep up on current publication trends in their fields. Catalogs and other promotional material for new products can be forwarded to relevant members of departments.

- Review material requests generated by teaching faculty: on campuses where discretionary funding is reserved for teaching faculty, the liaison can serve as a first point of processing faculty requests for materials. The liaison could be called upon to compare faculty requests to holdings in order to prevent unnecessary duplication, determine item availability, and repackage marked up catalogs, partial citations, and other problematic requests in a fashion more expedient to the acquisitions process. The liaison may even determine appropriateness of certain materials with respect to collection development goals, especially if requests exceed the available budget.

- Serve as electronic resource specialist for their particular departments: librarians often have knowledge of new database products as they become available. A liaison can help negotiate trial usage of the databases, facilitate access issues, and evaluate their quality with respect to existing collections and resources.

Instruction

Instruction plays a major role in connecting the liaison's role with the emergence of information literacy on campus. Armed with primary knowledge of subject-specific literature and resources, the liaison can work with departments in many important ways. To prepare students for higher-level research, one needs to cover the basics in specifically targeted introductory level classes, such as first-year composition and speech. These general education courses can serve as the instructional point of departure for finding and using information in an academic setting. This would include use of basic periodical indexes, online catalogs, and reference sources. At Winona State, a one-credit introduction to higher education class has also proven an appropriate venue to discuss where search engines and the World Wide Web fit into the academic research picture. As much of the material covered in these lower level classes is cross-curricular, any librarian on staff is able to supply the necessary introduction to research. The liaison's instructional role is more important for classes within majors. Ideally, students who come to the library for advanced instruction within their major fields will already have been to the library for an introduction to the basics, and so be prepared to tackle more specific resources related to the major. This diverges somewhat from many information literacy courses and tutorials in that students will work towards information literacy within the academic context of their majors. The relevancy of applying the principles of information literacy to real information needs produced from the students' existing course work is one advantage of this approach. For students who obtain work in their major field, or choose to continue their education as graduate students, this will translate into a solid foundation of information skills and strategies conducive to lifelong learning.

Reference

The liaison's knowledge of subject specific information resources and departmental needs could prove beneficial to reference services as well. Through appointments or with an on-call system, librarians could make use of extended knowledge of collections to help with reference questions of an involved nature. The emphasis would be on small-group or one-on-one reference assistance to both students and faculty in their departments. One concern about the liaison system is the amount of time necessary to do a proper job. One area where time can be freed up for liaison duties is the staffing of the reference desk by librarians. This is often an expensive solution for a job where a great number of the questions are of a basic nature, and could be easily negotiated by a well-trained student. When reference questions of a substantial nature do arise, the patron could either be directed to librarians who are scheduled to be available, or make an appointment with the subject-specialist librarian, who could keep posted office hours.

Implications for Information Literacy

The potential benefits a fully functional liaison program could bring to campus-wide information literacy objectives include the following:

- Librarians would have a collection development-based knowledge of subject specific resources that are available to students. This knowledge, combined with a librarian's familiarity with the curriculum, would allow instruction that introduces more advanced resources at appropriate moments to upper level students. Working with departments at all levels of instruction would preclude the necessity of the "one-shot" session; instead, resources and strategies could be examined in depth, with the knowledge that a return trip to the library is likely for the students as they continue through their major studies.

- Librarian and teaching faculty can share knowledge of collections to develop relevant assignments that make good use of available library resources. Instead of "treasure hunts" of dubious academic value, students would have assignments that introduce them to the best materials the library can make available or that have the greatest research value within the discipline.

- A strong liaison relationship with departmental faculty would likely promote greater input and participation on their part into the information literacy process. One objection raised by faculty to the entire notion of information literacy is the prescriptive nature of it, with librarians, not faculty, having developed the criteria. Faculty are generally quite information literate in their disciplines, and perhaps understand lifelong learning better than many librarians. To preclude faculty from participation in the formation of information literacy criteria makes their skepticism of information literacy as a legitimate academic discipline understandable. Inviting faculty into the development of information literacy goals and objectives would bring their considerable knowledge of the information process as it applies to their field into the discussion, and ultimately benefit the students.

- Students would assimilate the principles of information literacy within the context of their major course work. Their information needs will be real, not contrived by librarians, as is often the case with information literacy classes and tutorials. The principles of information literacy need not exist in a vacuum; instead, they could be worked into existing curriculum through the liaison's ability to interact with faculty, and thus achieve higher relevancy to students. The students' gradual incorporation of those qualities that define information literacy seems much more in line with the goal of helping people to become lifelong learners. In this manner, information literacy is earned through actual research experience, and thus is more likely to remain part of a student's intellectual formation than would a single library class or tutorial, which is often viewed by the student as unnecessary "busy" work.

- As students advance through their major field, additional resources can be introduced at relevant times. It is no longer necessary to cover it all in a single, one-hour session. A more programmatic approach to instruction ensures less repetition for the students; instead, they will receive instruction that follows a logical progression, from general to specific, that matches real information needs to available information resources. Information literacy goals and objectives could certainly be made explicit as part of this programmatic approach, or they could just as easily remain in the background. Students would learn a process that is transferable, and conducive to the lifelong learning objectives of information literacy.

- Faculty involvement in information literacy could spur greater interest and involvement in the library on their part. Departments that are actively involved with their library liaisons are more likely to be active in collection initiatives, and make better use of library services, such as instruction and interlibrary loan. At Winona State University, this has been the case with the History Department. The library's liaison, who

has a Masters level education in history and related fields, has been successful in getting history faculty actively involved in improving the library's collections. These improved resources are then introduced at appropriate times to history students, who often make several visits to the library's classroom, from introductory lessons in 100 level courses, to more advanced and specialized sessions for upper division classes. Instruction increases use of these resources, which justifies adding more to the collections. History faculty and students are also well aware of interlibrary loan, and know better than to limit themselves to what is locally available. Overall, an active liaison relationship has created a positive cycle of faculty involvement and interest in the library, which is passed on to their students through the assignments they create and their enthusiasm for the resources available. The result has been improved collections that better serve the needs of faculty and students, as well as increased use of those collections.

Challenges

Several challenges need to be overcome before a fully functional liaison system becomes a reality. One factor is librarian status on campus. A liaison program would probably be easier to create when librarians have faculty status. At Winona State University, librarians are members of the faculty union, serve as voting members on campus committees, and often occupy leadership roles on campus. Working with teaching faculty as peers has served as a natural stepping-stone to creating strong liaison relationships. This is not to say it is a required element, but rather a facilitating one.

Another obstacle for small to mid-sized libraries to overcome is the number of departments vs. the number of librarians available for liaison work. Winona State has 29 academic departments, but only eight librarians. While ideally librarians would work with one or two departments, this is not often going to be the case. One can overcome some of these problems by assigning all similar departments to an individual librarian. For example, foreign languages, English, and theatre all share certain resources, which could easily be encompassed by a single librarian. In similar fashion, finance, economics, business, and marketing all make use of a common base of resources, as well as resources individual to each discipline. Combined with the liaisons other more "traditional" library duties, this stretching of human resources constitutes one of the greatest challenges toward implementing a full-blown liaison program.

To make the liaison duties the focus of each librarian's job, as opposed to more traditional librarian roles such as "reference librarian," or "acquisitions librarian," requires perhaps the greatest challenge, the necessity of reorganization. To create a fully functional liaison system would require much of a librarian's time. In organizations that are often asked to do more with less, this is not a hurdle that is easily negotiated. One requirement is a support staff capable of moving into positions of greater responsibility, especially in the area of technical services, which could free up librarian time for liaison duties. Another potential obstacle is reaching consensus among librarians that liaison duties are the organizational focus they wish the library to take. It can be difficult to propose what may appear as radical reorganization plans that compromise traditional librarian roles and functions. In addition, some librarians may not want to perform all the liaison duties, instruction in particular. This can be managed in part through team teaching, where the subject specialist can work with other librarians in the classroom.

Conclusion/Outlook

In conclusion, there are some substantial obstacles to the implementation of a fully developed liaison program. It could require wholesale reorganization of existing staff, and reduction of traditional library services, such as staffing a reference desk. At Winona State University, the move to liaisons is currently a pilot program only for many of the reasons stated above: there isn't consensus among the librarians that this is the path we wish to take; budgets are tight, dimming the prospects of adding staff; not all departments show the same level of interest in working with the library, due in part to their heavy workload, but also lack of individuals who care enough about the library to try to improve the research experience for their students. In spite of these barriers, there are reasons why this model can work well at Winona State University, or other campuses, even on a limited basis.

A liaison plan can be partially implemented without additional librarians if the following is kept in mind: not all departments will respond with equal enthusiasm to library outreach initiatives, nor have the same information needs as others. As a result, it is perfectly legitimate to acknowledge that not all

departments will receive equal treatment. Concentrating one's efforts on those departments that do respond to library initiatives, and have concrete information needs that can be met by the resources the library owns or could add within budgetary constraints, will accomplish more than trying to spread such service across campus. It takes considerable time for a liaison to do a good job, and a liaison program would be better off doing a few jobs well, rather than many jobs poorly. Positive feedback and word of mouth reports may spread from one department to another, producing greater demand for the level of service liaisons could provide. If demand of liaison services were eventually to exceed the capabilities of existing staff, the library department would be in an excellent position to request additional positions at that point.

Finally, perhaps the greatest appeal of working closely with departments on a liaison basis is the potential involvement the librarian has at every stage of the student research process. The librarian knows the collection, and, through interaction with faculty on collection and curricular matters, knows how various resources are used within the discipline. This knowledge allows the librarian to help faculty design research assignments that make use of the best information resources available, and fulfill the pedagogical goals of the course. Through library instruction, the liaison can introduce the students to a progressive research method, the principles of which would be easily transferable to other topics. Follow-up reference interviews with individuals or groups of students can further refine the student's understanding of information generation and retrieval within their discipline. The interrelationship between collection development, instruction, and reference seems natural and logical when one has the chance to put liaison duties into practice. Liaisons provide academically relevant library services that extend beyond physical walls; as a result, departmental liaisons will continue to operate at some level at Winona State University Library. When one has the opportunity, through cooperation with faculty, to successfully guide students along the path of information literacy within their discipline, it is difficult to imagine a better method of working information skills into the curriculum.

THE QUEST TO UNDERSTAND K-16 INFORMATION LITERACY SKILLS

Marcia King-Blandford

This is a quest. It is not about answers. It is about the journey to learn to ask the right questions, at the right time and in the right place. Not as noble or as wise as Dante or Chaucer's undertakings, this quest seeks to know the community of information seekers on their journey from "teachable moment" into a lifelong learning. It is a quest to understand how to build a 'generation of information literate students.'[1]

The quest begins with questions. What do I really know about the students that I am teaching? What computer and information literacy skills do the students bring to their post-secondary education? Can they put their library experiences and research lessons taught during K-12 to use during their college experience? Are academic libraries, through their information literacy instruction initiatives, building lifelong learners?

This quest must start by acknowledging the public outcry for accountability in public education. This outcry has brought reform to K-12 education. It is no longer necessary to read professional publications like *Education Week* or *The Chronicle of High Education* to be familiar with the educational issues in the United States. The state of U.S. education is an everyday conversation. From *USA Today* to *Dateline*, the outcry about public education is being heard at the local, state and federal levels of government.[2] Ohio is not alone in overhauling its K-12 educational experience. For an Ohio student to successfully graduate from high school, the student is required to pass the state proficiency tests. The higher the percentage of students passing the proficiency tests the better the Ohio school district's 'report card.' The

better the school district's report card the more prestigious the Ohio school district. Committing to stronger licensure requirements for Ohio's K-12 classroom teachers, establishing Ohio's Education Strategic Plan and revising Ohio's Standard Operating Procedures should coalesce into the quality education being demanded by Ohio's constituents.[3] With the ultimate goal being quality K-12 public education, Ohio is hoping to follow in the footsteps of other states like Colorado or Washington.[4] The introduction of specific technology and information literacy competencies into the state's academic content standards is the necessary first step towards building a baseline for Ohio's K-12 educational experience.[5] This state driven weaving of technology and information literacy competencies into Ohio's K-12 education is the foundation for building a 'generation of information literate Ohio students.'[6]

Yet as public pressure forces an overhaul of Ohio's K-12 education, a recent revision in Ohio's Standard Operating Procedures, no longer guarantees the presence of either a school library and a certified school librarian in Ohio school districts.[7] Ohio's Standard Operating Procedures govern every facet of Ohio's K-12 education experience. The implementation of technology and information literacy competencies in the academic content standards may, by default, become part of the daily instruction performed by classroom teachers and not implemented by school librarians. Without giving value to the role of school libraries and school librarians in Ohio's new K-12 quality educational experience, how does life long learning and a generation of information literate students become a reality?

Examining the K-12 curriculum that college bound students experience before their arrival on campus is a crucial first step in knowing the community of incoming direct-from high school freshmen. In higher education, a post-secondary institution identifies itself

---

King-Blandford is a reference librarian at the University of Toledo's Carlson Library.

by its Carnegie classification, ' the framework in which institutional diversity in U.S. higher education is commonly described.'[8] Academic libraries identify themselves first by the Carnegie classification, their institution, and then, by the libraries status of being a member of Association of Research Libraries (ARL), '... organization comprising the leading research libraries in North America.'[9] Non-ARL libraries use ARL libraries as benchmarks towards their own achievement. The Carnegie Foundation classifies the University of Toledo as a Doctoral/Research-Extensive.[10] In addition to this identification, the University refers to itself as being a public metropolitan research university. This acknowledgment is part of the University's alignment with the Coalition of Urban and Metropolitan Universities (CUMU).[11]

> 'The Coalition began, in part, because some urban and metropolitan presidents became increasingly aware of the things their campuses had in common, and of shared frustrations. The mission and characteristics of their institutions were not well understood, and any system for ranking or describing universities and colleges was based on the traits of highly traditional, residential colleges serving full-time 18-21 year-old students.
>
> Systems such as Carnegie's classification scheme did not include measures for the significant applied research and service activities of urban and metropolitan universities. These presidents found themselves gathering on an ad hoc basis at the national meetings of major higher education associations, and eventually decided to organize their own affiliate group.'[12]

To know the community of incoming direct-from high school students, and meet the students where they are, in terms of their information literacy skills, it becomes necessary to examine the students the university recruits and retains. The National Resource Center for the First-Year Experience and Students in Transitions [FYE] has been researching the changing face of direct-from high school student who in years past came to college, lived in dorms on campus, and made college their life for four years. The Coalition is conducting similar research to identify the common characteristics of new direct-from high school students who attend metropolitan and urban research institutions. Noel-Levitz, a recognized name in

enrollment management for colleges and universities throughout North America, identifies 'only one of six students is a traditional age, undergraduate, residential student.'[13] The changing face of today's post secondary education student is real and here to stay. This changing portrait affects all facets of the university community. It especially affects academic librarians who are working to exert information literacy leadership roles in their respective university communities. Accepting and incorporating the changing picture of today's college student requires the academic librarian to step back and take an objective examination of the students arriving on campus. *The Changing Mosaic: Designing Successful Experiences for the New American College Student,* Teleconference #3, from the National Resource Center for the First-Year Experience and Students in Transition documents both how dramatically the American college student has changed and how institutions of higher education, in order to survive, will also need to change.[14] Lengthy discussions were presented during the video teleconference outlining the impact these "new students" will bring first to their university experience and then into the workforce.[15] College is only a part of their lives. The traits of these "changing faces" have to be factored into the design of information literacy instruction initiatives in academic libraries.

The impact K-12 education has on the design of information literacy instruction for students can be demonstrated by examining the student demographics for the University of Toledo. As of the Fall of 2001, 8,172 of 20,313 of the university's students came from Lucas County, which is the county where the university itself is located.[16] The K-12 educational picture for Lucas County shows eight public school districts with fifteen high schools and at least eight private high schools. [17] After Lucas County, the top five Ohio counties providing students to the University for Fall 2001 were:

Cuyahoga County (Cleveland area) 1310
Wood County (south border of Lucas County)776
Lorain County (east border of Cuyahoga County) 433
Fulton County (west border of Lucas County) 395
Erie County (southeast of Lucas County) 335

Since Wood, Erie, and Fulton are within an hour's drive of the university, their student contribution coupled with Lucas County's student contribution accounts for 40 percent of the student body. An additional 45 percent of the student body comes to the University of Toledo from other Ohio counties. Students from within the United States but outside of Ohio accounted for just fewer than 9 percent of the University's students. The international student body as of Fall 2001 was just under 6 percent for a total of 1176 international students.[18] If the number of international students for Fall 2001 is eliminated from the total student population [20,313 – 1176 = 19,137] based on the belief that this unique niche population with specific information literacy needs to be addressed,[19] the percentage of local students rises to 42.7 percent from Lucas County alone and 48 percent from other Ohio counties. The starting point for the design and implementation of ACRL information literacy initiatives at the University of Toledo must be the acknowledgment that 90.7 percent of the university's student body is from the state of Ohio. The impact of Ohio's K-12 educational experience on the university's students cannot be ignored.

The "changing face" of the today's college students is reflected in some additional student demographics for the university. Only 11,849 of the 16,754 undergraduate students are full-time as reported by the university in Ohio's required Fifteen Day Full time Head Count for Fall 2001. For this same time period, the university reported that 3217 new, direct-from high school students [full and part-time] were enrolled. This is about 15 percent of the total student population.[20] Reflective of the national level research reporting by the Center for the Study of First-Year Experience[21] the University has slightly more female students than male students with the largest minority group [11.2 percent of university students] being African American followed by Non-declared at 5 percent, Hispanic at 2.1 percent and Asian at 1.7 percent. White/non-Hispanic represents 73.2 percent of the university's population. Students over 25 years of age accounted for 20.54 percent of the Fall 2001 student population.[22] Approximately 30 percent of the full-time enrolled students live on campus in campus housing.

After an examination of the University of Toledo's student demographics, additional clues for the design of ACRL information literacy information are derived from, a return look at the 9th –12th grade curriculum from both the Lucas County school districts and the bordering counties with a focus on the presence and availability of computer technology in the schools and in the classrooms along with a better understanding of the resources offered by both the school and local public libraries. Site visits to the local high schools brings the myths of technology in the classroom into focus. In Northwest Ohio public schools, it is common for the classroom teacher to have a computer, but student access to computers is either in a computer lab for a scheduled elective or in the school library via a pass from a classroom teacher. And, although the Toledo-Lucas County Public Library has maintained a long and close working relationship with the school districts in Lucas County, and the Wood County public library recently underwent a major renovation to further its mission of better serving their community, the public libraries in the other surrounding counties work tirelessly to provide resources to their rural populations. OPLIN has provided the necessary Internet access and linked the rural public libraries with a multitude of Web-based resources but the number of public workstations is limited and requires "reserving a time." The after school hours fill the public library with middle and elementary grade children who live within walking distance of the public library and "play" on the computers. Most of the public libraries in the area offer basic computer training to their users on an ongoing basis with the two largest public libraries, Toledo-Lucas County Public Library and the Way Library in Perrysburg, providing computer labs and classroom space to their communities.

These clues provide a different direction than previously thought. The working premise for the creation of an information literacy curriculum for academic libraries is to start the information literacy curriculum with the incoming direct-from high school students. It is a common belief that direct-from high school students will arrive on college campuses with existing computer skills and some familiarity with Web-based resources. In Ohio, this working premise should be true. The state of Ohio funds three parallel but separate Web-based information systems for its population. OhioLINK is the oldest piece of Ohio's information troika. Started in 1988, OhioLINK represents the post-secondary 2-year and 4-year public and private institutions and the State Library of Ohio.[23] INFOhio, the Information Network For Ohio Schools, is a statewide cooperative project initiated in the late 1989 and officially adopted in the late 1990s to create an electronic network linking Ohio students, teachers, library/media specialists and others via computer to other state information resources. INFOhio automates and electronically links all 615 school districts in Ohio and their 3,500 library media centers.[24] OhioLINK and INFOhio were made possible because of the existence of two state-supported electronic networks, which link the universities (OARnet) and the schools (OECN).[25]

However, Ohio had a missing link. In 1995, under the guidance of a Blue Ribbon Commission, Ohio's Public Library Information Network or OPLIN was formed to link Ohio's 250 public libraries.[26]

'Ohio cannot remain in a position where the information and networking needs of schools and universities have been met, but where public libraries are not included in the solution. Ohio's public libraries serve everyone, including students and teachers after 3:00 p.m. and college students home for the weekend.

It is inconceivable that Ohio's public libraries are not a part of the information infrastructure already established in the state for schools and universities.'[27]

About the same time that OhioLINK, InfOHIO, and OPLIN, were gaining ground, Ohio's SchoolNet and SchoolNetPlus projects, funded through the state budget, and again implemented under the direction of OECN, gave every K-5 public school district classroom in Ohio, five networked computers to help integrate the curriculum with technology.[28]

Ohio, with a history of leading library technology, has created and is providing a true lifelong learning environment for its population. During the K-12 years, a student would access InfOHIO from the classroom, school library or from their home via remote access. After school, on weekends and in the summer, students would access OPLIN at their local public libraries or by remote access from their homes. Their library card serves as their user name and password for research databases with restricted access. OhioLINK offers Ohio's faculty and students desktop access to a multitude of Web-based resources. All three systems have union catalogs, offer inter-institutional borrowing, provide full-text documentation, link to multiple general and subject specific research databases, and access digital images, archival sources and government resources. Within Ohio, lifelong learning is not a cliché but a reality.

So it is a fair assumption by academic librarians, especially in Ohio, to feel that direct-from high school students are computer literate. It is also a fair assumption to expect that Ohio's direct-from high school incoming freshmen should have basic information literacy skills upon which to build their post-secondary information literacy skills. Yet, this will not be the reality until the Fall of 2008 when the "SchoolNet" generation of Ohio's students arrives at Ohio's post-secondary institutions. In these interim years, the pre-SchoolNet generation of high school students may need more basic levels of information literacy instructional support than previously thought. An examination of Ohio's Post-Secondary Education Option program (PSEOP) provides some insight into the level of support that needs to be incorporated into Ohio's academic information literacy instruction. This niche population is important because of its back and forth movement between secondary and post-secondary education.

Under Ohio's HB _____, a high school student in Ohio can take college level courses for credit during the 9-12 grade school years.[29] After being admitted to a post-secondary institution, 2-year or 4-year, the student takes college level classes for free or for minimal level costs. The student can take college level classes to complete the necessary requirements for high school graduation, called dual enrollment, or can begin to take college level classes towards an associate or bachelor's degree. Approximately 15 other states offer a similar program. The purpose of the Post Secondary Education Option Program is to encourage high school students to further their education. It is driven by state economic initiatives to attract business investments in the state. When the state began the Post-Secondary Education Option program in 1995, the University of Toledo had 50 students enrolled; for Fall 2001 the University had over 400 high school students participating. For this coming Fall 2002, the University is expecting a 25 percent increase. This is an important student group for the University since it will retain about 32 percent of the PSEOP students it admits.

Since the Post-Secondary Education Option population is already identified as "college bound" and has a 3.2 G.P.A. or above, this group should personify the computer and information literacy skills that academic librarians will be working with at the reference desk, in the required First-Year Experience orientation classes, in required College Composition classes, and in required general education classes. During May 2001, 300 PSEOP students were asked to volunteer with their parent's permission to take the survey. Of the 300 possible participants at the 20 different orientation sessions held during the month, 98 responses were received. The survey results confirmed the presence of home Internet access and plans to further their education by going to a 4-year institution but it came as a great surprise that the 87 percent of the participants had only written one research paper averaging 5–8 pages at this point in their high school careers. It also came as a surprise that 85 percent of the survey participants stated that they rarely used either a school or public library. The students admitted to doing their "research" on the Internet using search engines. The popular search engines being Yahoo, followed by AskJeeves and Google. Ninety-four percent had taken a keyboarding class as an elective and 50 percent had taken a word processing/spreadsheet class during high school. On the other hand, interestingly, 90 percent of the student did know how to get a book through an OPAC. This same percentage of respondents knew how to cite electronic resources when needed. The same survey is currently being given to the PSEOP students admitted for the Fall of 2002 and the initial 2002 survey results to date are almost identical to the Fall of 2001 results.[30]

How does the impact of K-12 educational experiences and the university's student demographics translate into the design of information literacy instruction for direct-from high school students? The first step is to meet the direct-from high school students

—MARCIA KING-BLANDFORD—

where they actually are. Prior to attaining the Association of School Librarians/Association for Educational Communications and Technology (AASL/AECT) first information literacy standard, and Association of College and Research Librarians' (ACRL) corresponding second information literacy standard, 'Information literate students access information efficiently and effectively,'[31] may require a computer competency test for all new direct-from high school students. Is it part of the academic instruction librarian's role in the university community to teach basic computer competencies and basic Internet access to students? Is this a necessary preliminary step to the evolution into learning 'efficient and effective searching' under the information literacy standards? Can academic instruction librarians lead the discussion with their university communities about the need for this baseline of computer competency before the introduction of the library's home page and academic level research? At the University of Toledo, for Fall 2002, the College of Business Administration has received approval through the Faculty Senate Program and Curriculum Committees to implement computer competencies for all incoming business students. The University's College of Engineering has incorporated computer competencies into their required freshmen Orientation course. Avenues for gaining or strengthening computer competencies for other majors have not been addressed. Computer competencies at the University are college-driven. Is this an aspect of the haves versus the have-nots within post-secondary education?

Since the University of Toledo is predominantly a commuter campus, where students are likely to work 20+ hours a week, and spend a minimal amount of time on campus to study, use computer labs, the library, etc., "getting the word" out about the library electronic resources via OhioLINK is a real challenge. How does the commuting student find the library's home page to start their information search? How does the library "market" its Web-based resources when Yahoo, AskJeeves, or Google are the first choice for starting? If Yahoo has worked successfully for high school assignment and research papers, it makes sense that the students would continue to use this resource for their academic work. Is it feasible to use the campus newspaper, or student radio station or even with the assistance of the university's public relations office, other channels of media resources, to "get the word" out to the students? Are displays, "rip-offs," flyers, etc., available and up-to-date at the most popular campus locations? Information literacy instruction as part of the academic, discipline specific curriculum is of paramount importance, but it is the critical first step of recognition that needs attention.

How do information literacy initiatives get the student to first recognize information as a resource and then to identify the library, or its home page, as first choice for searching for information?

Instructing college students to identify, select, evaluate, and utilize information are higher-level cognitive skills. With an amateur's interpretation of pedagogy, it makes sense that a student must move through various stages of learning, e.g. lower to higher-level cognition. This is where Bloom's taxonomy meets information literacy. Just as reading literacy starts with recognition and moves on, today's direct-from high school student has to first learn to recognize the library as synonymous with information. Perhaps marketing the academic library is counter to a fundamental belief in the role of the academic library but today's higher education environment requires academic librarians to rethink marketing within the context of an instructional strategy if the goal is truly to build an information literate student body.

The questions are part of the quest. With almost 30 years of instruction research, from Breivik Senn's early work in Colorado schools to Mary George's infamous "Wish List for College Freshmen"[32] to Kuthlau, Rader, Iannuzzi, and Jacobson, just to name a few, milestones exist to challenge continued movement forward as information literacy instruction goes to the core of lifelong learning. If the students are admitting that they have not used their school or public libraries when writing their one 5-8 page research paper and conduct their "research" by using a search engine, it makes the antidotal evidence at the reference desk and in library instruction classes about their lack of research skills more plausible. If high school students are not writing and researching on a regular basis, they really do not know how to write and research when they arrive on campus. If their computer use is directed at e-mail, searching Yahoo and they have had only limited experience using word processing/spreadsheet packages, or are in the 50 percent of students who have not had classes in keyboarding and word processing, how and when do they learn the computer basics? Does computer ownership translate into computer competencies? How do academic librarians move a student towards the higher levels of learning required to access, identify, select, evaluate and utilize information without a defined instructional role within the university's curriculum? Who meets today's direct form high school student where they are at and builds from that point on? Perhaps, the new college freshmen arriving on campus aren't where we want them to be in terms of computer or information literacy skills. So maybe this is the point where academic instruction librarians becomes the 'instructional leader'[33] within the university community to meet the students at their skill level so that real lifelong learning can begin. The quest continues.

NOTES

1. American Library Association, Association of School Librarians, and Association for Educational Communications and Technology, *Info*•*nation Power*, 2002 < http://www.ala.org/ aasl/ip_nine. html > (8 February 2002).

2. *"Quality Counts 2002." "Reports by State." Education Week on the Web*, 10 January 2002 < http://www.edweek.org/sreports/qc02/ > (1 May, 2002.) See also: National Center for Educational Statistics, *The Nation's Report Card*," May 2002 < http://nces.ed.gov/nationsreportcard/ > (1 May 2002).

3. Ohio Department of Education. *Strategic Plan*. 15 April 2002 < http://www.ode.state.oh. us/ centers/ strategic_plan.asp > (1 May 2002). See also: Ohio Department of Education, *Operating Standards for Ohio Schools*, 2002 < http://www.ode. state. oh.us/ school_improvement/Standards/ > (1 May 2002), Chapter 3301-35, Ohio Administrative Code.

4. Colorado Department of Education, *Information Literacy and Technology Checklist for Schools – Draft* < http://www.cde.state.co.us/cdetech/download/pdf/ et_TechPlanChecklist.pdf > (11 February 2002) See also: Colorado Department of Education, *Alignment of Information Literary Standards with the Colorado Information Literacy Guidelines* < http://www. cde.state.co.us/cdelib/download/pdf/slcoaaslinfolit.p df > (11 February 2002).

5. Ohio Department of Education, *Technology Academic Content Standards*, April 15, 2002 < http://www.ode.state.oh.us/academic_content_stan dards/acstechnology.asp > (1 May 2002).

6. American Library Association, Association of School Librarians, and Association for Educational Communications and Technology, *Information Power* < http://www.ala.org/aasl/ip_nine.html > (11February 2002).

7. Ohio Department of Education, *Standard Operating Procedures*,15 April 2002 < http://onlinedocs.andersonpublishing.com/revisedc ode/home.cfm > (1 May 2002) See also: State Library of Ohio, *State Library of Ohio's Five Year Plan* < http://winslo.state.oh.us/publib/lsta5yr.html > (1

May 2002).

8. Carnegie Foundation, *Public Institutions: Carnegie Foundation for the Classification of Institutions of Higher Education* < http://www.carnegiefoundation. org/Classification > (11 February 2002).

9. Association for Research Libraries, *Member Libraries,* April 23, 2002 < http://www.arl.org/ members.html > (1 May 2002).

10. Carnegie Foundation, *Public Institutions: Carnegie Foundation for the Classification of Institutions of Higher Education* < http://www.carnegiefoundation. org/Classification/ > (1 May, 2002).

11. Coalition of Urban and Metropolitan Universities, *Introduction of CUMU*, < http://www.metrou niversities.com/ > (1 May 2002)

12. The Coalition, *Introduction*, 2002.

13. Kathryn Karford, *Consultant's Response to the Research Report: What Are the Demographic Projections for Adult Students...* < http://www. noellevitz.com/library/ask_the_consultant/answers.as p#q129 >(1 May 2002).

14. National Center for the First Year Experience and Students in Transition, *The Changing Mosaic: Designing Successful Experiences for the New American College Student*, *Teleconference #3 of the 2002 Teleconference Series*. Thursday, 25 April 2002. See also: National Resource Center for the First Year Experience and Students in Transition, *2000 Survey of First Year Seminar Programming*. See also: National Center, < http://www.sc.edu/fye/ research/ surveys/ survey00.htm > (1 May 2002).

15. National Center for the First Year Experience, *Changing Mosaic*, 25 April 2002.

16. NCA Reaccreditation Committee. The University of Toledo. NCA Self Study, Appendix A: Demographic Data. April 2002. 1-3.

17. Yahoo! Real Estate – Schools, *School Information for Lucas County, Ohio,* < http://list.realestate.yahoo .com/re/schools/oh/lucas > (1 May 2002).

18. NCA Reaccreditation Committee. The University of Toledo. NCA Self Study, Appendix A: Demographic Data. April 2002. 1-3.

19. Sara Baron and Alexia Strout-Dapaz, "Communicating With And Empowering International Students With A Library Skills Set," *Reference Services Review* 29, no. 4 (2001): 314.

20. Institutional Research. The University of Toledo. *Fall 15ᵗʰ Day Headcount*, undated <http://fbs.utoledo.edu/insti_research/reports/data_book/undergraduate_headcount.html > (1 May 2002).

21. National Center for First Year, *The Changing Mosaic*, 25 April 2002.

22. NCA Reaccreditation Committee. The University of Toledo. NCA Self Study, Appendix A: Demographic Data. April 2002, 1-3.

23. OPLIN Position Paper. September 1994, <http://www.oplin.lib.oh.us> (1 May 2002), Background.

24. OPLIN. Position Paper, Introduction, 1994.

25. OPLIN. Position Paper, Background, 1994.

26. OPLIN. Position Paper, Introduction, 1994.

27. OPLIN. Position Paper, Need for OPLIN, 1994.

28. SchoolNET. c1998-2002 <http://www.ohio schoolnet.k12.oh.us/home/> (1 May 2002).

29. Marcia King-Blandford, *Post-Secondary Education Option Program* (The University of Toledo, Fall 2001 Survey, May 2001).

30. King-Blandford. Survey, 2002.

31. American Association College Libraries. "Information Literacy Standards for Higher Education" c2002 < http://www.ala/acrl/il/ toolkit/ standards.html > (1 May 2002). See also: American Library Association, Association of School Librarians and Association for Educational Communications and Technology, *Information Power*, 15 January 2002 < http://www.ala.org/ aasl/ip_nine.html > (8 February 2002).

32. Mary George, "What do College Librarians Want Freshmen to Know? My Wish List," *Research Strategies*, 6 (Fall 1988): 189.

33. Jennifer L. Branch and Dianne Obert, "The Teacher-Librarian in the 21ˢᵗ Century: The Teacher Librarian as Instructional Leader," *School Libraries in Canada* 21 (2001): 9.

SEARCHPATH, A NEW INFORMATION LITERACY TUTORIAL, OR HOW A GRANT, HARD WORK AND OPEN PUBLICATION LICENSING MADE IT POSSIBLE

Elaine Anderson Jayne and Maira Bundza

Introduction

Our story is all too familiar. The need to teach informationa literacy and critical thinking skills to students at our institution, Western Michigan University, has never been greater. As at many other universities, however, student enrollment continues to rise each year while the number of instructional librarians remains the same.[1] We can no longer provide instruction in person to all the students who need it, and we suffer burnout from teaching fifty-minute sessions in which we repeat the same basic information many times. Because this is such a universal problem, our experience in finding a solution may be helpful to others.

Background and Precursors

In 1993, we turned to computers for help when a colleague produced our first HyperCard tutorial for a one-credit university orientation class. When the tutorial needed to be updated, we replaced it in the Fall of 1998 with *Labyrinth*, a Web-based tutorial targeted for this class.[2] At the 1997 LOEX Conference we heard an impressive presentation on CLUE, the University of Wisconsin's multimedia tutorial, and inspired by its wider possibilities for use, we returned and began work on a Web-based

Jayne is the Instructional Services Librarian and *Bundza* the Web Resources Manager at Western Michigan University, Kalamazoo, MI.

information literacy tutorial for all undergraduates.[3] We called it *Searchpath* to reflect a process-based approach to research, proceeding from the initial idea to a student's final research paper. We completed much of the groundwork for *Searchpath*. We defined the skills and competencies this target group should possess, organized the tutorial's structure, and wrote part of the content. We even created a few Web pages for the tutorial, but for lack of time and competing demands, this project died on the vine.

In Spring 2001, in collaboration with faculty from the business writing program, we applied for funding from our university and received a Teaching and Learning with Technology grant that breathed new life into *Searchpath*.[4] Our goal continued to be the creation of a tutorial that would teach basic concepts and skills to a large undergraduate population, beginning with the business writing classes. We organized the content into six modules: (1) starting smart (about information sources); (2) choosing a topic and Boolean searching; (3) finding books; (4) finding articles; (5) using and evaluating the Web; and (6) citing sources, (which includes the topics of plagiarism and copyright). The grant money was used mostly to buy out one reference shift and to pay for technical help over the Spring and Summer semesters. Hardware was not needed; we possessed the needed skills and software. Then serendipity struck! Within the same week that we received grant funding, the University of Texas Information Literacy Tutorial (*TILT*) was released under an open publication license.[5] This collaborative act opened up many more possibilities for our tutorial.

We had looked at about 20 tutorials, and of these, we were most enthusiastic about *TILT*. It possessed many of the features that we were interested in creating and went beyond our technical expertise in providing others. Some features of *TILT* that we found appealing:

- It was on a Web platform, so it was widely accessible to anyone, anywhere with an Internet connection.
- It presented concepts and skills within the context of information literacy and promoted critical thinking.
- Learning objectives were stated at the beginning and end of each module.
- It was well-organized with links to its contents, a glossary, and a user feedback form.
- It provided interactivity to engage students in the learning process.
- It liberally used images and possessed a pleasing color scheme.
- Its informal language was accessible to students.
- It provided quizzes to assess learning, with printable quiz results.

Clearly, a lot of thought and talent had gone into *TILT*.

Starting Out

Unlike other *TILT* adapters who have either used it "as is" or who have made superficial modifications such as changing the title, we used *TILT* selectively and drew upon it for ideas, images, and content. We downloaded *TILT* and, since we planned substantial changes, set up our own files using *TILT*'s site structure as a pattern. We expanded the structure from three to six modules, each module having its own directory.

We also created a test site, so that we could view the pages "live" internally. For convenience, we printed out all of the *TILT* screens and placed them in a three-ringed binder, so we could refer to a hard copy reference. A second binder was started for *Searchpath* and a third for ideas from other outstanding tutorials.

Decisions

We still had decisions to make about *Searchpath*. For example, it seemed important to find the appropriate level of detail for our freshman audience and to strike a balance between telling them *everything* about a topic as opposed to presenting concepts, and then getting students started applying them. If the material were treated in depth, we feared it would make the tutorial too long, and students would lose interest. We tried to break down the content into smaller units and create short pages of text, since users are reluctant to scroll down to read text that is "below the fold." We wanted to adopt a tone that was informal and friendly without sounding cute. From a Web usability study conducted the previous year, we learned how important it was to avoid library jargon, but when it seemed essential that students learn certain terms, we followed *TILT*'s lead and used pop-up pages for definitions. Finally, we wanted to create visually interesting pages that were easy to read, so layout and the liberal use of images was important.

The Look and Feel

We retained the module choice page from our earlier version of *Searchpath*. Then we developed color-coded graphics for each module to create continuity in design and navigation, and the color-coding was used throughout the tutorial—on the introductory module page, table of contents, and on the navigation bars. We kept *TILT*'s main color scheme and the Verdana font. Because the *TILT* images sometimes pushed text below the screen border, we reduced the size of those we used, adding our own images and a number of clipart pieces along the way. As we added colors in buttons or table backgrounds, we tried to maintain a consistent color scheme.

Navigation

From the *Searchpath* home page students can select "First Time Users" and read a three-page introduction or they can choose "Return Users" to go directly to the module choice page. This page provides easy access to all the modules and to the contents of the complete tutorial. "Next" and "Back" arrows are used for page-by-page navigation in both *TILT* and *Searchpath*. In addition to this linear progression, users can easily jump to pages within a module or choose a different module by using the navigation bar. In *TILT*, navigation bars are set up in frames and appear on some pages but not on others. We eliminated the frames and used one navigation bar at the bottom of each page to provide consistency. We also changed the names of links on the navigation bar, for example, "Map" to "Contents," "Word" to "Terms" and removed the link to "Objectives," since these are stated at the beginning and end of each module.

—ELAINE ANDERSON JAYNE AND MAIRA BUNDZA—

When naming individual pages we included both a name and a number, so we could keep track of the order of our pages in the tutorial. Since *TILT* used a frames format and unnumbered pages, it was sometimes difficult to find a specific page quickly.

Interactive Searching

We all know that students learn better when they are shown how—for example, how to construct a search—and then given the opportunity to practice the skill themselves. One of the outstanding features of *TILT* is the amount of interactivity incorporated into it, and this was a high priority for us. We retained many of *TILT*'s interactive features and added a module to practice live searches in our catalog.

Another of *Searchpath*'s modules features live searching in an article index. A prior version of *TILT* had used a subset—an older year—of the *Periodical Abstracts* database for this purpose, and we spent many weeks trying to negotiate a similar arrangement with vendors. Predictable search results from a stable, unchanging database would have allowed us to construct better exercises, questions, and answers. In addition, a database that included both scholarly and popular sources, provided abstracts, and included a mixture of full-text sources as well as those with citations only would have been ideal to illustrate search return possibilities to students. However, we were unsuccessful in gaining permission, and in the end used the complete *Periodical Abstracts* database to which Western Michigan University (WMU) subscribes. Unfortunately, this means that non-WMU users cannot use this "live" search.

We wanted to lessen the chance that students would leave the tutorial. At first, we considered having a separate search window open for the live searching, but decided instead to use frames, in order to provide guidance and keep users on task. Search instructions appear in a narrow frame on the left and live searching is conducted in a window on the right.

Macromedia Flash Animations

Like *TILT*, *Searchpath*'s introduction includes a test animation so that users can tell if they have a Flash viewer installed and provides a link to download the viewer for those who need it. Flash software was used to create a number of the animations in *TILT*, but we retained only a few of these, most notably the "Think Fast" game. We added two short Flash sequences of our own: "Information Overload" to reinforce the message of the importance of information literacy and a sequence

that shows students how to locate indexes on our library Web site. These two pieces were created in collaboration with our IT department, since we have not yet learned to use Flash software ourselves.

Flash has great promise for instructional use, but it can present problems. If it is not set up properly, Flash pieces show up as a gray box, and, if navigation forward is dependent upon it, users cannot gain access to the rest of the tutorial. Flash applications can run excruciatingly slow on computers using a dial-up modem connection. Finally, if a Flash piece is too long and there is no independent navigation, users may begin to feel they are a captive audience. *TILT* offers users the option of a non-flash version of its site, *TILT*-Lite. Originally, we also began to set up a parallel site, but found managing a double site too time-consuming. Instead, we removed the non-Flash site and created short non-Flash go-arounds. Now if users become impatient with the load time or do not want to download the viewer, they can click on a "non-Flash version" link and are taken to either a single still image of the page or a series of individual pages that cover the same content as the Flash piece.

Quizzes and Games

At the end of each *Searchpath* module there is a quiz consisting of seven to ten multiple choice or true/false questions. After choosing an answer, students click on a submit button and receive feedback to the answer before proceeding on to the next question. This format and response originated with *TILT*. At the end of each quiz, students can type in their names to receive a printable summary of their quiz results, which they can submit to instructors as proof of completion. Students may retake the quiz as many times as they wish, but cannot go back to an earlier page once they are in the quiz. We used JavaScript to modify the *TILT* quizzes and, in order for students to be able to print their quiz results, we employed Cookies for the duration of the quiz.

We thought *TILT*'s use of games to reinforce learning was innovative and appealing. In addition to the Think Fast game, we had planned to add several games of our own—including a "Build a Bronco" game—but ran out of time. (The bronco is WMU's mascot.) This is a feature we would like to add later after mastering Flash software.

Use of *Searchpath*

The response by academic instructors to *Searchpath* has been excellent. Instructors are aware that their students lack basic skills and realize that a fifty-minute library session alone is not adequate. They like *Searchpath*'s self-instructional nature, which is convenient because they can assign it outside of class and give students extra points for completion. Some instructors are requiring that students pass the quizzes with a score of 85 percent, while others require students to retake the quizzes until their score is 100 percent.

It takes 15-20 minutes for a student to complete a module. Although this may seem like a major time commitment, students can complete one or two modules between classes, rather than work through the whole tutorial in one sitting. Now when students who have completed *Searchpath* attend our library instruction sessions, they are not as overwhelmed. *Searchpath* has given them a context for new information presented in the session, and as a result, they seem more receptive. We, in turn, can spend less time on reviewing basic skills and devote more time to critical thinking skills such as evaluating sources.

Over the Fall and Winter semesters of 2001-2002, we have been using *Searchpath* with pilot groups. The use of *Searchpath* will expand in Fall 2002, when we plan to make it a prerequisite for library instruction. In addition, we will promote its use widely with students and faculty as a self-instructional resource for students. Groups such as distance learners, transfer students, and international students may find it especially useful. Ultimately, if the disparity between the number of librarians and student enrollment continues to widen, we may need to replace library instruction for freshman classes with *Searchpath*.

Assessment and Evaluation

As each of its modules was written and uploaded to our test site, reference librarians and student employees critiqued and tested *Searchpath*. We have been able to analyze a sizeable number of students' quiz results, supplied by instructors after recording them. Mainly, these have been helpful in identifying problems in the presentation of concepts or with the wording of a quiz question, and we make the necessary revisions. We will soon add a survey from the exit page for students and instructors in order to obtain more information about users' response to the tutorial. Finally, we plan to conduct small focus group testing.

Conclusion

In a recent children's book, Jane Goodall retells an old fable regarding a quarrel among the birds about who could fly the highest.[6] Lark, dove, vulture, and eagle each claim they can surpass the others. But a tiny wren secretly hides herself among the eagles' feathers and when he soars above all the others, she flies higher for a look around. Back on Earth, the wren concedes victory to the eagle who made her flight possible. Like the wren, we built upon the innovative work of the *TILT* team. And like them, we plan to release *Searchpath* under an open publication license so that other librarians may build upon our work and customize it to meet the needs of their own students and faculty.

NOTES

1. Nine librarians provide the bulk of instruction to over 23,000 undergraduates at Western Michigan University. Last Fall semester 2,400 of them were in freshman writing classes.

2. Patricia Fravel Vander Meer, "Welcome to the University Libraries," a HyperCard tutorial, 1993. The *Labyrinth* tutorial, still in use, can be found at http://www.wmich.edu/library/Labyrinth/Labyrinth.html.

3. *CLUE*, originally a multimedia tutorial developed with Macromedia's Authorware, was featured in a presentation by Abbie Loomis and Lee Konrad at the 1997 LOEX Conference.

4. *Searchpath* is at http://www.wmich.edu/library/*Searchpath*/.

5. *TILT* was released under open publication license on 20 March 2001. Its principle creators are Elizabeth Dupuis, Clara Fowler, and Brent Simpson. *TILT* is at http://*TILT*.lib.utsystem.edu/.

6. Jane Goodall, *The Eagle and the Wren* (New York: North-South Books, 2000).

Helpful Resources

Adaptations of yourTILT
http://*TILT*.lib.utsystem.edu/your*TILT*/docs/adaptations.html
A list of the institutions that have adapted *TILT* are available here.

Bare Bones 101
University of South Carolina, Beaufort Library
http://www.sc.edu/beaufort/library/bones.html
This is a rather long but excellent tutorial on searching the Web.

—ELAINE ANDERSON JAYNE AND MAIRA BUNDZA—

CartoonBank
http://cartoonbank.com/
Individual New Yorker cartoons may be purchased for educational use at a reasonable price.

CLUE: A Multimedia Tutorial for the University of Wisconsin Libraries University of Wisconsin
http://clue.library.wisc.edu/main-menu.html
CLUE uses individual students' problems to present concepts. This and their concept of "scaffolding" in teaching are two of many interesting ideas.

CORE: Comprehensive Online Research Education
Purdue University Libraries
http://core.lib.purdue.edu/
CORE presents its content in a comprehensive way, as its title indicates.

Information Literacy Competency Standards for Higher Education
Association of College & Research Libraries
http://www.ala.org/acrl/ilcomstan.html
This is a touchstone site for formulating your outcomes and objectives.

Internet Guides
University of California, Berkeley
http://www.lib.berkeley.edu/TeachingLib/Guides/Internet/
The Teaching Library offers some excellent material here.

Labyrinth: University 101 Tutorial
Western Michigan University
http://www.wmich.edu/library/*Labyrinth*/*Labyrinth*.html
This tutorial was created for WMU's introduction to the university class.

Patrick Lynch and Sarah Horton, *Web Style Guide: Basic Design Principles for Creating Web Sites*, (New Haven, CT: Yale University Press, 1999). Also on the Web at http://info.med.yale.edu/caim/manual/

The *Web Style Guide* is superb. If you are interested in creating pages that are readable and visually pleasing, read this for basic principles.

net.TUTOR
Ohio State University Libraries
http://gateway.lib.ohio-state.edu/tutor/
Ohio offers a collection of tutorials that have a straightforward clear presentation style. They include suggested exercises and quick quizzes.

OASIS: Online Advancement of Student Information Skills
San Francisco State University
http://oasis.sfsu.edu/
OASIS makes liberal use of images, states learning objectives for units, and has extensive content.

OWL: Online Writing Lab
Purdue University
http://owl.english.purdue.edu/
This is a site worth exploring. It does have a tutorial on Internet searching but offers much more. Also excellent is the Writing Center at the University of Richmond at:
http://www.urich.edu/~writing/wweb.html

Searchpath
Western Michigan University
http://www.wmich.edu/library/*Searchpath*/
Based on *TILT*, this is WMU's information literacy tutorial.

TILT: Texas Information Literacy Tutorial
The University of Texas System Digital Library
http://*TILT*.lib.utsystem.edu/
TILT offers many ideas. Our favorite feature is probably its use of various kinds of interactivity to break through the limitations of the Web.

Tips for Developing Effective Web-Based Library Instruction
ACRL/IS Teaching Methods Committee
http://www.lib.vt.edu/istm/WebTutorialsTips.html
Although this list is short, it does highlight the most important components for good instruction on the Web.

INFORMATION LITERACY FOR COLLEGE STUDENTS WHO ARE BLIND OR VISUALLY IMPAIRED: A TEAM APPROACH INVOLVING STUDENTS WHO ARE BLIND

Galen E. Rike

Origins of the Project

This project grew out of the author's longstanding interest in library service to physically disabled users. Currently the author serves as Western Michigan University Libraries' Ombudsman for Physically Disabled Users. In this capacity the author conducts ten or more one-on-one instructional sessions per semester to help blind and visually impaired students. The immediate impetus to move forward on this project came from three sources. Marcie Brink, a graduate student in blind rehabilitation, suggested that WMU Libraries provide instructional sessions for blind and visually impaired students. Albert Walker, another graduate student, offered his assistance. The Office of Disabled Student Services agreed to transfer a modest amount of money to the University Libraries to get the project started.

Goals of the Project

The goals of the project are: (1) to provide blind and visually impaired students with the information skills to make them more independent users of University Libraries, and (2) to provide blind and visually impaired users with the same level of information literacy instruction as is currently provided to sighted students.

Rike is a librarian at Western Michigan University, Kalamazoo, MI.

Status of the Project

Instructional materials are being developed and tested. This testing includes testing the Western Michigan University (WMU) Libraries' online tutorial *Searchpath* to determine what changes need to be made to make it accessible to blind students. Regular instructional sessions will be offered starting Fall Semester, 2002. This instruction will be offered in cooperation with the Office of Disabled Student Services.

Context of the Project

Some description of the context at WMU is necessary to understand the project.

WMU has an internationally recognized Blind Rehabilitation Program. This program offers master's degrees in several areas, and plans to offer the doctorate starting next Fall. The existence of these programs brings an additional number of blind graduate students to campus. Currently about forty blind and visually impaired students attend WMU. This number includes both undergraduate and graduate students. The size of the blind and visually impaired enrollment has remained relatively constant for the last several years.

The Office of Disabled Student Services coordinates campus-wide services to students with a variety of disabilities. For blind and visually impaired students textbooks and readings are scanned to disk, which enables the students to access them via voice synthesizers. A pool of volunteer readers is also maintained to provide these students accessibility to information in print.

The Multipurpose Enabling Technology Laboratory (METL) is located in the Computer Center, now called the Office of Information Technology. METL contains the largest collection of enabling technology hardware and software on campus. It is designed to meet the needs of disabled students as well as serving as a classroom laboratory. Some Blind Rehabilitation and Special Education courses include sessions in METL. This author has conducted several instructional sessions in METL and plans to hold additional sessions this next academic year.

In terms of hardware, METL currently has twenty-one IBM compatible and four Mac workstations, two Braille embossers, two networked laser printers, and several closed circuit displays for enlarging printed materials. In terms of software, METL currently provides *Jaws v. 3.7* (a widely-used screen reader for blind users); *Zoomtext*, Level 2 (provides screen enlargement for visually impaired users); *Atlas Speaks* (for maps); *Winvik* (an onscreen keyboard); *PhotoShop*, micro edition; *OmniPage Pro v.10* (OCR scanning); *Kurzweil 1000*, *Dragon Dictate*; *Dragon Natural Speaking*; *Easy Keys*; and *Duxbury* (translates language for Braille embosser). All software currently operates on a Windows 95 platform.

The enabling technology in WMU Libraries is part of METL, and supplied with the same software. This helps to ensure consistency as blind and visually impaired students move to different locations. Waldo Library, the main library, provides a suite of three rooms for blind and visually impaired students. One room contains two workstations with METL software, scanners, and connected to a Braille embosser and laser printer. The second room contains Braille dictionaries and a print enlarger, called a Telesensory closed circuit display. The third room contains a table and chairs and is used by blind students when working with readers or studying in groups. An additional workstation with scanner, Braille embosser and large-print printer is made available in the Education Library, which is located in the same building as the Department of Blind Rehabilitation.

Review of the Literature

The literature relating to library services to users with disabilities is voluminous. However, the number of articles relating to library instruction for blind and visually impaired students is very small. The following review is selective and focuses on sources that illustrate major themes.

Mainstreaming and Physical Barriers

Significant legislation was passed in the 1970s that helped to improve access to education, public facilities, and services for persons with disabilities. (Velleman 1990, 101-102) The literature of the 1970s and 1980s indicated a growing awareness of the special needs and problems of users with disabilities. Attention seemed to focus primarily on physical access. See Vasi (1976). For the blind and visually impaired, sighted readers and a growing array of enabling technologies provided this access. See, Needham (1977), Lovejoy (1978), Needham and Jahoda (1983), and Jahoda and Johnson (1987).

Comprehensive Legislative Mandate

Legislative efforts to improve the quality of life for Americans with disabilities culminated in the passage of the Americans with Disabilities Act (ADA) in 1990. This landmark legislation has generated a large body of literature. For guides and review articles, see Foos and Pack (1990), Crispen (1993), Mayo and O'Donnell (1996).

Academic Library Services

The literature shows that academic libraries responded quickly to comply with the ADA. For examples, see Jones (1991), Jax and Muraski (1993), McNulty (1993), and Mendle (1995). For an insightful perspective on the ADA and academic library services by a librarian who is blind, see Wilhelmus (1996).

Web Accessibility

By the early to mid-1990's concerns began to surface about Internet access for print disabled users. These concerns focused primarily upon the ability of existing enabling technology for the print disabled to keep abreast of the rapid growth of graphical user interfaces. See Lazzaro (1994), Wilson (1994), Dixon (1996), *Guidance* (1996), and Reagan (1997) for an overview of the access issues.

A number of positive steps were taken during this period to improve Web accessibility by disabled users. Perhaps most notable was the formation of the World Wide Web Consortium (W3C) in 1994, and its Web Accessibility Initiative (WAI) in 1996. The WAI guidelines and checklists provide authoritative help to web designers who want to make their sites universally accessible. Coombs (2000) provides a recent summary of guidelines to enhance accessibility including a list of quick tips, as well as readily available Web resources.

Several other organizations active in promoting universal accessibility include the Trace R&D Center and the University of Wisconsin, Equal Access to Software and Information (EASI), and the Center for Applied Special Technology (CAST). The latter has prepared Bobby, a software package available on the Web, which tests the extent to which a Web site meets WAI Guidelines for accessibility. For librarians wanting to make their Web sites accessible to blind users, EASI provides an online courses culminating in a certificate.

In past few years the American Library Association (ALA) has published materials to assist libraries make their Web sites universally accessible. The most recent is Barbara Mates (2001) "Accessibility Guidelines for Electronic Resources " which appeared in *Library Technology Reports,* July/August, 2001. This helpful and current report includes a seven-page listing of Assistive Technology Web Sites. Other helpful ALA publications include McNulty (1999) and Mates (2000).

A closely related body of literature reports empirical tests of the accessibility of Web sites. Axel Schmetzke is an active proponent of studies of this type. For a research example, see Schmetzke (2001); for an overview of this research, see Schmetzke's Web Survey Homepage.

Academic Library Instruction to Blind and Visually Impaired Users

This author could find few reports of instruction for blind and visually impaired users in academic libraries. Several reports are so dated that they are of limited usefulness, for example, Broadway (1983) and Huang (1983). An article by Graubart (1996) describes a diversity project at the University of Missouri at Kansas City that included library users with disabilities. This project included an instructional session for blind and visually impaired users, but attendance was a problem. Although not library instruction, an article by Cleaver and Shorey (1992) reports how a class on media skills was modified to accommodate blind students. Information of this type can be useful to those planning instruction for blind students.

What Can Academic Libraries Do?

It seems appropriate to make a few general observations concerning what academic libraries can do to improve services to blind and visually impaired users.

Designate a Contact Person

It would be helpful if all academic libraries would designate one or more staff members to specialize in serving users with disabilities. This designated person or persons need to keep abreast of campus-wide needs, monitor developments in enabling technologies, develop programs and procedures as needed to assist users with disabilities, and maintain communication with other campus units that assist users with disabilities.

Provide a Locked Enabling Technology Room

Libraries are open longer hours and are often more centrally located that other service points on campus. It is usually more convenient to use library materials in the library rather than taking them to other locations. Therefore large academic libraries should take the initiative by providing a locked room with the enabling technology needed by special needs groups on campus. This room should be kept locked to restrict availability to students who are blind or otherwise qualified. If these facilities are made available to all students, sighted users may try to re-configure screens and disable software without realizing the problems this will cause for users who are blind.

Establish Uniform Policies and Procedures

Academic libraries should develop standardized policies and procedures so that users with disabilities receive consistently appropriate service. Step-by-step procedures for public service points help assure service consistency. In-service training sessions, and perhaps sensitivity training, are needed to prepare the entire public services staff to serve students who are disabled.

Obtain Systematic Feedback

Academic library services should be evaluated systematically for ways to improve. Campus units concerned with planning, assessment, or disabled student services often conduct surveys to obtain feedback from students. Libraries should try to get these agencies to include library-related questions in these surveys.

The Need for Customized Instruction

This author's experience suggests that most blind and many visually impaired students cannot learn effectively by attending instructional sessions designed for sighted students. A good rule of thumb is to assign students to instructional sessions on the basis of the software they use for searching. The screen reader of choice for blind students at WMU is *JAWS* (Job Access with Speech), and the screen enlarger of choice is *Zoomtext*. In addition, some students prefer handouts and practice questions in Braille; others prefer to receive this information on a disk.

Perhaps the strongest evidence that blind and visually impaired students need customized instruction was uncovered while doing usability testing at WMU Libraries. The original study, which tested about fifty sighted subjects, was reported by Jayne and Cockrell (2000), and an article based on this data will appear later this year as Cockrell and Jayne (2002). All of the sighted subjects tested were able to complete the usability test within one hour. This author conducted usability tests, using the same questions and procedure, on ten students with disabilities. Three participants were blind and two were visually impaired. None of the blind or visually impaired students were able to complete the usability test. Even if two or three hours had been allowed, it is doubtful that the blind participants would have been able to complete the test.

What Has Been Learned?

A number of things have been learned from this project that can improve library instruction to blind and visually impaired students in academic libraries.

Team Approach Works

Teaming up with blind students to present information literacy instruction began as a common sense idea. However, this author has become convinced that instruction provided by this approach is superior to instruction provided solely by a sighted librarian. In a word, the team approach is the most efficient and effective way to provide instruction to this special needs group.

Blind Users Need 2-3 Times Longer

Be sure to allow sufficient time when working with blind students. Under the best of circumstances it will probably take blind students twice as long to search library databases with commonly used screen readers. If the sites searched contain pages with complex graphics, then additional time will be required.

Active Learning is Essential

Active learning was made for working with blind and visually impaired students. This author's experience suggests that blind students, and to a somewhat lesser extent visually impaired students, need active learning exercises for best results.

Step-By-Step Instructions Needed

Step-by-step instructions should be prepared for each instructional module. In addition, students participating in the instruction should be given their choice of Braille or digital handouts and practice exercises.

Small Homogeneous Groups are Best

One session of providing instruction to a group which contained both blind students who used the *JAWS* screen reading software and visually impaired students who used *Zoomtext* screen enlarging software convinced this author that homogeneous groups are best. Future instructional sessions will divide JAWS users and *Zoomtext* users into two separate groups.

In addition, this author's experience suggests that the ideal class size is four to six students. It might be possible to work with slightly larger groups of *Zoomtext* users, but it would be very difficult to work with larger groups of *JAWS* users.

Multiple Short Sessions are Better

Instructional sessions of about one hour in length seem to work best with blind or visually impaired students. In no case should a session of longer than two hours be attempted. The longest session this author has conducted was two hours in length. Some of the participants in this two-hour session were getting tired. Although many visually impaired students prefer to read screens with *Zoomtext*, some of these students may experience significant eyestrain when reading for long periods of time.

Need to Keep Software Up-To-Date

It is important to keep enabling technology software up-to-date for several reasons. Software improvements are being made continually as developers attempt to keep abreast of the rapid development of graphic user interfaces. The protocols taught in information literacy instructional sessions should be as close as possible to those used by blind or visually impaired students when working at their personal workstations.

Characteristics of the Model

The model used to develop the information literacy instructional program described herein focused on networking with providers of related campus facilities and services and teaming up with blind students to develop instructional materials and present training sessions. In terms of sequential steps, this involved: (1) identifying and establishing communication with campus providers (in this case the Office of Disabled Student Services, the Department of Blind Rehabilitation, and METL); (2) determining the size of the population to be served and their needs with the assistance of the Office of Disabled Student Services; (3) identifying possible team members (one volunteered and another was suggested by Disabled Student Services); (4) building on existing strengths and modifying existing instructional materials where possible (WMU has a well developed library instruction program with materials which could be modified); (5) working closely with blind students when preparing instructional modules (this serves as a built-in field test); (6) advertising and scheduling instructional sessions in cooperation with the Office of Disabled Student Services and METL; (7) conducting instructional sessions with the assistance of at least one blind student; and (8) evaluating and modifying the instructional program.

Can the Model be Generalized?

Although this project was designed to teach information literacy skills to students at WMU who are blind or visually impaired, the general approach and many of the procedures used herein could be used to develop information literacy instruction for other special needs groups at WMU and elsewhere. Key questions to be answered at the outset include: (1) what groups on campus need customized information literacy instruction, and (2) are enough students enrolled to hold special instructional sessions? Individual instruction may be a better approach if the number of special needs students enrolled is not sufficient to justify group instruction.

REFERENCES

Americans with Disabilities Act of 1990, Pub. L. No. 101-336, 104 Stat. 328.

Broadway, Marsha, *Bibliographic Instruction for Disabled Students*, ERIC, ED 240757 (1983).

Center for Applied Technology (CAST), *Created Bobby* < http://www.cast.org/Bobby/About Bobby313.cfm >

Cleaver, Betty and Mary Shorey, "Teaching Media Skills to Visually Impaired Students," *Ohio Media Spectrum* 44, no. 3 (1992): 22-27.

Cockrell, Barbara and Elaine Jayne, "How Do I Find an Article? Insights from a Web Usability Study" *Journal of Academic Librarianship*, [at press].

Coombs, Norman, "Untangling Your Web." *Library Hi Tech* 18, no. 1 (2000): 93-96.

Crispen, Joanne, ed. *The Americans with Disabilities Act: Its Impact on Libraries, the Library's Responses in "Doable" Steps.* (Chicago, IL: Association of Specialized and Cooperative Library Agencies, 1993).

Dixon, Judith, "Levelling the Road Ahead: Guidelines for the Creation of WWW Pages Accessible to Blind and Visually Handicapped Users," *Library HiTech* 14, no. 1 (1996): 65-68.

Equal Access to Software and Information (EASI). < http://www.rit.edu/~easi >

Foos, Donald and Nancy Pack, *How Libraries Must Comply with the Americans with Disabilities Act (ADA)* (Phoenix, AZ: Orynx Press, 1992).

Graubart, Marilyn, "Serving the Needs of Students with Physical Disabilities," *Library Hi Tech* 14, no. 1 (1996): 37-40.

Guidance from the Graphical User Interface (GUI) Experience: What GUI Teaches about Technology Access, ERIC, ED 399757 (1996).

Huang, Samuel, *Library Services for the Physically Impaired at Northern Illinois University in DeKalb, Illinois*, ERIC, ED 234587 (1983).

Jayne, Elaine and Barbara Cockrell, *An Evaluation of Western Michigan University Libraries' Web Usability Study* (Kalamazoo, MI: Western Michigan University, 2000).

Jax, John and Theresa Muraski, "Library Services for Students with Disabilities at University of Wisconsin—Stout,"*Journal of Academic Librarianship* 19, no. 3 (1993):166-168.

Jones, Dorothy, "Ask So You Can Give: Reference/Research Services for the Disabled in an Academic Library," *RQ* 30, no. 4 (1991):479-485.

Lazzaro, Joseph, "Opinion: Adaptive Computing and the Internet: One Step Forward, Two Steps Back?" *Internet Research* 4, no. 4 (1994): 2-8.

Mates, Barbara, "Accessibility Guidelines for Electronic Resources: Making the Internet Accessible for People with Disabilities," *Library Technology Reports* 37, no. 4 (2001): 1-81.

Mates, Barbara, *Adaptive Technology for the Internet: Making Electronic Resources Accessible to All* (Chicago, IL: American Library Association, 2000).

McNulty, Tom, ed., *Accessible Libraries on Campus: A Practical Guide for the Creation of Disability-Friendly Libraries* (Chicago, IL: American Library Association, 1999).

McNulty, Tom, "Reference Services for Students with Disabilities: Desktop Braille Publishing in an Academic Library," *Reference Services Review* 21, no. 1 (1993): 37-43.

Mayo, Kathleen and Ruth O'Donnell, eds., *The ADA Library Kit: Sample ADA-Related Documents to Help You Implement the Law* (Chicago, IL: Association of Specialized and Cooperative Library Agencies,
American Library Association, 1996).

Mendle, Jill, "Library Services for Persons with Disabilities," *Reference Librarian* 49-50 (1995): 105-121.

Reagan, Michael, "An Accent on Access: Writing HTML for the Widest Possible Audience." ERIC, ED 412905 (1997).

Schmetzke, Axel, "Web Accessibility at University Libraries and Library Schools," *Library Hi Tech* 19, no. 1 (2001): 35-49.

_____, *Web Accessibility Survey Homepage* < http://www.library.uwsp.edu/aschmetz/Assessible/websurveys.htm >

W3C's Web Accessibility Initiative (WAI), < http://www.w3c.org/WAI >.

Wilhelmus, David, "Perspectives on the Americans with Disabilities Act: Accessibility of Academic Libraries to Visually Impaired Patrons," *Journal of Academic Librarianship,* 22, no. 5 (1996): 366-370.

Wilson, David, "Assuring Access for the Disabled," *Chronicle of Higher Education* 40, no. 35 (4 May 1994): A25,28.

—GALEN E. RIKE—

LIBRARY SERVICES AND INSTRUCTION FOR ONLINE DISTANCE LEARNERS

Frances A. May

Abstract

All students, whether they are taking classes on campus or through a distance-learning program, need to develop research skills in order to encourage life-long learning. Research skills the students need are: the ability to locate information, evaluate it, arrive at a synthesis, solve problems, and make decisions based on the information. Additionally, students need to form the habit of reading journals and publications in their fields. This training is normally accomplished by bringing the students to the library, so another way of accommodating this need must be developed when the class is taught online and the students never set foot on campus.

This paper describes the development of a model for providing library and information literacy instruction to distance learning students who are taking classes online. Two library liaisons, a distance learning and a subject specialist, collaborated with a professor from the School of Merchandising and Hospitality Management to develop a strategy that would help the faculty member's graduate class find information about their subject.

Background at the University of North Texas Libraries

Several years ago, the decision was made by the Libraries to consider each student as a potential distance learner. This altered the focus of acquiring resources to include and emphasize electronically available indexes and journals, and electronic books. Many of the indexes contain full-text articles, and, among the electronic books ordered, some duplicate

---

May is the Coordinator of User Education and Outreach at the University of North Texas Libraries, Denton, TX.

titles the Libraries already owned in hard copy, most notably books used in the School of Library and Information Science and the Department of Computer Science.

Additionally, numerous services geared toward distance learners have been implemented, including e-mail reference service, an online reference help desk chat service,[1] and a toll-free telephone number that is nationwide in scope. Campus-based students also use these services. Other services that were already in place were interlibrary loan and a service called Reference by Appointment, for students who are close enough to come to campus occasionally. There is a form for requesting materials on interlibrary loan specifically for distance learning students. On the Library Home Page (http://www.library.unt.edu) is a link labeled "Library Services for UNT Off-Campus Users" to connects users to a page where there are several help pages for distance learners and students who want to access the library remotely.

Description and Background of the Class

Taught by Dr. Joan Clay, the class was entitled "Issues and Trends in Merchandising and Hospitality Management," (SMHM 5350) and was intended to familiarize the students with the literature in their field, and help them build the habit of keeping up with reading journals and trade publications. The students were graduate students working on a Masters' Degree in hospitality management or merchandising. Many already worked in the industry, some were managers, and were going back to school for their Master's in order to move up in the industry. For many, it was the first class in the program they had taken, and for others it was their first class taken entirely online. For all of them, research had changed drastically since they were in college. It was also the first time the teacher had taught an online class. She had offered it in a face-to-face environment several times, and was teaching another section at the same time that met on campus. She believed that her students needed to develop critical skills, including fact-finding, analysis, and evaluation skills.

Dr. Clay's objectives for the class included: discover the myriad ways students can find information on issues and trends in the field; use sources to examine trends impacting the field; evaluate the findings of others; stay on the cutting edge of gathering information important to their profession; and adapt to changes in information gathering.

Their assignments were to identify ten sources they could use for information, including trade or practitioner publications, academic journals, and Web sites. This dictated the format of the class page that was developed for them, as will be shown below.

A further concern developed as Dr. Clay was reading papers that were turned in to her in conjunction with a section of this class taught in an earlier semester. The students were using information from spurious Web sites. She found herself asking, "Where did you get this information? Who was the author of the Web site?" Most of the students had never even thought to ask. If it was on the Internet, they thought, it was factual. So this added another dimension to the library assistance we gave her.

The class was taught entirely online, and there was no textbook, so the need was even greater for the students to find articles in their fields online, since the class entailed learning about the literature in the field, and finding out how to utilize it in their work.

On the Way to a Solution!

A three-faceted approach was devised to meet the needs of Distance Learning students who are taking classes across the Internet to receive library instruction, with the further condition that everything had to be accessible through WebCT, the software that the University of North Texas uses for its online courses. (No matter what software an institution uses, an adaptation of these approaches will provide a starting point for library services for online distance learners.) A tutorial in basic use of the library answered the need for information literacy for the students. To meet the needs for evaluating Web sites, a more detailed tutorial was devised, focusing solely on that topic. The use of Subject Guides, for more subject-specific direction was used, and, for specific classes, Class Pages were developed in collaboration with the teacher, and dealt with specific class needs and assignments.

The Tutorials

The University of Texas at Austin has developed an excellent information literacy tutorial called TILT: Texas Information Literacy Tutorial, and has made it available to other schools. Its URL is http://tilt.lib.utsystem.edu/. This was used as the basis of the UNT tutorial. TILT consists of three modules and an introduction. The introduction gives a definition of information literacy, discusses the impact of technological advances, and addresses common misconceptions about the Internet. Module 1 discusses different information sources, where to find them, and how to choose the best ones for research. The second module focuses on skills for searching databases and the Web. It includes choosing keywords and combining terms. The third module covers criteria for assessing the credibility of sources, and how to cite print and online information. The modules were moved into a WebCT class called Libtutorial. The students in the SMHM WebCT class were added to the Libtutorial class, and the quizzes for the TILT modules were loaded into the SMHM WebCT class, so the quiz results would go to the teacher.

Since Module 3 in TILT included evaluation of all types of information formats, from book to Web, another module was designed that focused exclusively on the evaluation of Web sites. At present, there is no quiz to go with it, but one is under development. When the quiz is completed, it will be loaded into the SMHM class as well. As time goes by, other tutorials will be added, some for specific tools, like PsycInfo or MLA Bibliography, which can also be used by WebCT classes in those subjects.

On the home page in WebCT for the class SMHM 5350, a link was placed entitled "Library Resources." This opened to a page that linked the students to the Library Tutorial, the Library Tutorial Quizzes, the Library's Home Page, the class page developed for SMHM 5350, and a page that directs the students to the different help services the Library offers.

Subject Guides

Subject Guides are developed by the library liaisons to the various departments. They are general, covering the entire subject discipline. They include books, periodical indexes, handbooks, manuals, directories, etc., and may include bibliographic and biographical sources and some Web sites—all the things found on the more traditional paper pathfinders. These are recommended to the teachers of online classes as useful to the students, and it is suggested that they make a link to the pages from their WebCT class home page. The Subject Guides are also pointed out to students who are on campus as good starting places for them, during bibliographic instruction sessions or one-on-one instruction. (2)

Class Pages

Class pages are much more detailed. While they may duplicate some of the information on the Subject Guides, they often reflect specific class assignments. There is a general listing of class pages available from the Library Web site (3), but there are direct links from within the WebCT class to the class page.

The page developed by Martha Tarlton, the library liaison to the School of Merchandising and Hospitality Management, very specifically reflects the assignment Joan made to her students. First, it has a link to a page giving instructions on connecting to online library resources from off-campus. Then follows a section on resources that is broken down into Periodicals, Electronic Databases & Indexes, and Style Guides, with links to internal anchors within the page. The Periodicals section includes Periodicals for the Practitioner, Academic Periodicals, and General Business Periodicals. This reflects the assignment where the student is to become familiar with the trade publications and the academic periodicals. The General Business Periodicals section was included because many times these publications will include articles on the different fields of interest to the students. Where possible, direct links to the electronic journal are included. When the journal was a part of a large package, such as EbscoHost's Business Premier or ABI Inform, it was somewhat complex, since the Library's LAN department had to assign direct links to the periodicals otherwise the IP address validation would not work. Titles available in hard copy at the Library that were applicable to the different fields of interest to the students, but which were not available electronically, were also included, since students might be able to locate those titles at local college or university libraries near their home.

Next follows a section with links to annotated electronic indexes specifically recommended for the class. When the student clicks on any of these links, a pop-up box asks for their individual ID and password, which are automatically generated by one of the university computers. There is a link for finding the ID from the page giving instructions on connecting to online library resources from Off-Campus. In addition, there is an annotation for a paper index specific to the hospitality industry, again, so the student can try to locate a copy at a college or university library near them. Another section follows that gives the students access to online style guides for APA style.

Finally, there is a help section, which gives them links to the online reference help desk, the e-mail reference form, and contact information for the librarian, Martha Tarlton, including e-mail and telephone, in case the student wants to set up a consulting session by appointment, or just ask her a question directly.

Other WebCT Courses Incorporating Class Pages

From small beginnings... At present, some other WebCT classes incorporating class pages are:

- SLIS 5420 and 5430: Literature for Youth / Information Services for Youth
- SLIS 5000: Introduction to the Library Professions
- MGMT 5710: Management Strategies for Public Issues

Comments from the professors:

- Literature for Youth, etc: (refers to presentation given during the students' only on-site visit)

> *Frances, this is to thank you for all your assistance with our online classes. First, we appreciate you coming...to the orientation for new masters students where you demonstrate how to access the UNT Library online. This session and your handouts are invaluable to the program. The library is beginning to make resources relevant to our program available online, but without your introduction, it would not be utilized the same. Second, the Web pages you are working on specific to my courses...means a great deal to the students and to the vitality of the course. Your willingness to come to my office and work with me on what needs to be added to that page and to help conceptualize how to convey this information has proven most useful. I look forward to continuing to work with you on this project. –Dr. Barbara Stein*

Results

Comments from students:

- This is my first master's degree class. I have been out of school for a while. Research has really changed during that time. The library tutorial enabled me to feel more comfortable.

- This was my first class at UNT. Library tutorial helped me know what resources were available at UNT and how to use them.
- Tutorial was good because it was a structured required way for me to learn. Probably wouldn't have done it on my own.
- I found two instruments to be extremely useful. The first is the link to the list of periodicals that the UNT library actually possesses at their facility. This link also provides a listing of those periodicals that are accessible via the Internet. Second is the ability to contact a reference librarian Monday through Friday from 10-5 via the Internet and chat in real time and have my reference questions answered immediately.

Comments on the on-site Web page evaluation class:

Dr. Clay asked the students, "What was the best thing you learned tonight?"
- Meaning of domain designations and which were more likely to be reliable
- Most said they'd never paid much attention to the author of the site
- Students were more cautious, less ready to use the information on Web sites
- More critical thinking

One problem surfaced, though. One of the Web sites included as part of the exercise was entitled "Feline Reaction to Bearded Men" (http://www.improb.com/airchives/classical/cat/cat.html). One of the students thought it was an excellent example of a scholarly paper, pointing out the description of the methodology, the findings, the bibliography, etc. Therefore, it is necessary to make certain the students understand it is a hoax. (4)

Conclusion

In many cases, it is relatively easy to provide access to library resources for distance learning classes. Even if it is not possible initially to put up a tutorial within the Web-based class program, it is still possible to provide Web pages that guide the student to the appropriate indexes and research tools, and help them navigate through some of the difficulties of using them.

I would like to thank Martha Tarlton, Head of Reference and Information Services at the University of North Texas Libraries, and Dr. Joan Clay, Associate Professor in the School of Merchandising and Hospitality Management, for working with me on this project. Your professionalism and cooperation have made it possible for us to extend the scope of library services.

1. For a description of the chat service, see Monika Antonelli and Martha Tarlton, "The University of North Texas Libraries' Online Reference Help Desk," in *Digital Reference Service in the New Millennium: Planning, Management and Evaluation*, ed. R. David Lankes and John William Collins (New York: Neal-Schuman, 2000), 197-206.

2. For examples of UNT's Subject Guides, visit this URL: http://www.library.unt.edu/subjects/default.htm

3. UNT's Class pages are located at http://www.library.unt.edu/classes/default.htm.

4. There is a Web page that describes the evaluation criteria at http://www.library.unt.edu/genref/internet/evaluate.htm.

REAL-WORLD SOLUTIONS FOR REAL-WORLD COLLABORATION PROBLEMS

Alexius Macklin and Michael Fosmire

Introduction

What do information retrieval skills and problem-based learning (PBL) have in common? All too often, in this age of instant answers, data collection begins before the information need is really identified. Technology savvy students consult their favorite search engines for details about a particular interest or problem by entering in a few key words and clicking on the search button. For these students, information retrieval is based solely on dumb luck and finding a smart search engine that returns something useful back to them.

PBL, on the other hand, promotes critical and analytical thinking skills by applying the learner's own expertise and experience to the initial problem solving and data collection—a much more effective way to begin the information retrieval process! In most PBL activities, the students should be prepared to gather facts based on what is known, identify and ask questions about what is not known, formulate a problem statement and hypothesize about the solutions, locate information to support those ideas, and evaluate the materials they find—skills librarians refer to as information literacy.

This workshop introduces ways for librarians and faculty to collaborate using information literacy skills as the foundation for developing effective problem-based learning experiences. Participants will engage in hands-on activities to identify where information literacy skills fit into particular courses, incorporate these skills into real-world problem solving activities,

and strategize ways to collaborate with faculty by integrating these activities directly into the course projects and assignments.

What Exactly is PBL?

Problem-based learning (PBL) started at McMaster University in 1969[1] as a component of curriculum reform for medical schools. It is now one of the most advanced teaching approaches being used across many disciplines. This strategy creates learning opportunities out of everyday situations, turning otherwise boring lectures into dynamic experiences.

PBL is based on real-life simulations. The problems are deliberately ill-structured and designed for thoughtful and careful analysis to help improve students' critical thinking skills. The open-ended nature of these problems allows the students to explore areas of interest, thus establishing ownership of the learning experience.[2]

PBL is a challenging but rewarding teaching strategy. It involves a significant change in the way we teach and learn. As the role of the instructor changes from leader to facilitator or coach, the role of the students becomes very active as they take control of the problem.[3] This approach requires a certain amount of willingness to try (and fail) before you get it "right." Using PBL to advance information literacy training calls for buy-in and good, solid partnerships with subject-area faculty.

Forming Collaborations

PBL exercises for building information literacy skills are created in the context of a course's syllabus. Unlike the situations where a faculty member just asks

---

Macklin is the User Instruction Librarian and *Fosmire* is the Science Librarian at Purdue University, West Lafayette, IN.

for 'a how-to-use-the-library' 50 minute one-shot, you will be working with a faculty partner to jointly develop problems that both meet the needs of the curriculum and can be accomplished with the information resources available to the students.

When looking for potential faculty collaborators, investigate the local "excellence in teaching" unit on campus. Purdue University, for example, has the Center for Instructional Excellence (CIE), which uses permanent staff as well as regular faculty to provide instruction on improving teaching. We found that by faculty's attendance at CIE-sponsored events, they demonstrate an interest in innovations or otherwise improving their teaching, and thus are disposed for creating potential partnerships.

In addition to networking, making connections with influential instructors and leaders within CIE means that, if instructors go to the leaders with a problem-based learning question, we can be referred to as people to talk to about it. Indeed, we can even influence those leaders to increase the visibility of information skills at the institutional level. By actually giving a CIE seminar, you can increase your visibility across campus even more so. In other words —become involved!

All the usual methods of finding potential collaborators apply in this situation. Observing students using the library for assignments, checking course syllabi, and networking with faculty all will help to determine which professors are giving research projects to their students. Creating problem-based learning exercises is time consuming. Look for faculty who are interested enough in improving student learning outcomes to devote the extra time to successfully implement PBL.

The instructional design process: start with a needs assessment:

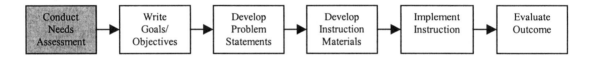

Once you establish a collaborative arrangement to work with faculty, then the real work starts. You will want to begin with information literacy needs assessments of the faculty members with whom you will be collaborating. At this point in the relationship, it is critical to listen and build trust. Try not to interject your ideas yet. Ask questions and take notes about their immediate information needs and concerns. Using a good reference interviewing technique will help you to elicit information about what they really want from you. This is the first step in a very thorough needs assessment. Some of the questions we found helpful in evaluating how to begin developing partnerships are:

- What are the goals and objectives for the course?

- On what kinds of projects will students be working?

- How will they use information sources to help them complete these projects?

- What problems did you observe in students' overall performance on these projects in past semesters?

- Do students need to know how to evaluate and cite information sources as a part of this course?

Another critical step in exploring information needs is to carefully review the syllabus with your faculty partner. If there is a textbook required for the course, or other assigned readings, ask to see those as well. The more information you can obtain about the course, the more effective the needs assessment—hence the better integration of useful information literacy skills. At times, when the content area is beyond your expertise, you may need to ask the faculty member to recommend some primer readings to help you understand the course materials better.

After you are confident that you understand what the faculty partner wants, reiterate those needs back to him or her. Try not to do this all in one day. Give yourself about 2 hours to conduct the initial interview. Another four to six hours to familiarize yourself with the literature and course materials. And another two to three hours to synthesize . . . (did we say this was an easy process?) When you have completed these tasks, your needs assessment is finished and you can start to pull some ideas together about how you will work information literacy skills into the course content.

The needs assessment will also tell you what direction the faculty member wants to take the

—ALEXIUS MACKLIN AND MICHAEL FOSMIRE—

information skill building experience. Knowing this up-front will clarify your role in the development and delivery of the instruction. You may take a more active role in the classroom, or you may be more of an instructional designer working on the development of various information seeking problems and problem solving activities behind the scene.

Is PBL the right approach?

Whatever role you play, there are some key requirements for a problem-based learning approach. Before you start to develop an instructional plan, consider if PBL is the best approach for your collaboration with the faculty member. If it is the right approach, the following profile will fit the course:

- *Problem-based learning is built on ill-structured problems.* These are basically problems or situations that simulate real life. Unlike structured problems that are designed to have right and wrong answers, ill-structured problems are open ended. Often there is information missing that the learner needs to address before solving the given problem. Does this course lend itself to an ill-structured problem? Are there real-life scenarios that can be adapted for instruction?

We used a variety of real-life scenarios—trying to incorporate current issues when possible. Some came from the field, such as the problems written for a policy course in forestry. These scenarios were taken from court cases and newspaper articles. Other courses required a more global approach. These broader problems came from sources such as newspapers, National Public Radio stories, magazines, and Web sites.

- *Problem-based learning requires teamwork.* The problems are complex enough to provide a role for every member (for teams of 4—5 people). Is there enough time to devote to problem solving—either in or outside of the regular class meeting? Establishing a good learning environment means adjusting class schedules to accommodate the needs of group activities. Sometimes this means giving up class time to do hands-on work. Is the faculty partner open to this?

- *Problem-based learning activities end with a project or product to show resolution to a problem scenario.* In our PBL experiences, we required the students to present an electronic poster session. These posters were "peer reviewed" on content and style. Having them available electronically meant no one had to try to pay attention to 15 presentations—one right after the other. They could look at the posters—taking as much or as little time as needed—to offer a complete review.

These three statements provide a quick overview of what a PBL experience might look like. Once you determine if this approach is right for your collaboration, start writing the instructional goals and objectives you want to achieve with your faculty partner. Knowing what you want the learner to accomplish in solving the problems will ensure that the information competencies you set out to integrate really do become a part of the course content.

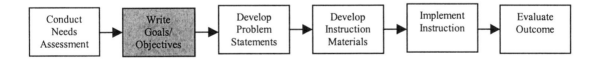

Planning the instructional goals and objectives:

You might start the instructional goal setting by showing the faculty partner an abbreviated list of the *Information Literacy Competency Standards for Higher Education.*[4] This Web site provides a comprehensive view of what information literacy is and how these skills will help improve students' overall learning outcomes. (We have yet to have a faculty member turn down an opportunity to work with us after reading the information found there.)

The trick to setting goals (especially after reviewing the competencies) is knowing how much you can cover in the time allotted for instruction. Typically, three goals are more than enough for one PBL activity. You might want to start small with the basics. For example, we started our first PBL sessions by having the students read the scenario and identify what they already knew about the problem. Second, they wrote a problem statement (hypothesis) and finally, they identified what they did not know and listed their information needs. At this point, they were ready to start constructing search strategies to find information to solve the given problem.

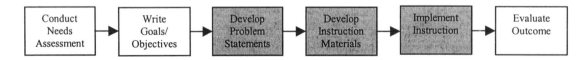

When the instructional goals are set, writing the problem scenarios should follow easily. Good problems will unfold like the telling of a story. The scenarios simply provide the scaffolding to entice the learner to add the middle and ending parts by building a plot. To start the story, try using the following five steps as a foundation.

Five steps (and hints) to writing problems for PBL:

1. Find a situation that has a set of phenomena or data in need of an explanation. Try to stay current and keep the situation relevant to the students' real-life experience. This will help to keep the motivation going and the problem solving experience interesting.

Hint: Try using newspapers, popular magazines like *Time* and *Newsweek*, websites, and television—especially the news or talk shows—to find sources for developing problem statements.

2. Identify 4—5 learning outcomes that you expect will result from completing the problem solving activities. Always ask yourself the question, "What do I want the learner to know—or be able to do— after solving the problem?"

Hint: Use *Bloom's Taxonomy*[5] as a guide to help you identify specific learning behaviors you want to see as the students are working through the problem solving experience.

3. Re-write the problem as a problem statement for the learning experience. One way to do this is to create a hypothetical situation in which the students must solve the problem.

Hint: Medical schools put the students in the role of the doctor, or a team of doctors, working with a

patient. You might want to take the same approach, giving students various roles appropriate to the problem statement.

4. List the skills or life experiences you expect students already have to solve the problem. This existing knowledge is the building block for new knowledge—the KEY to PBL.

Hint: Use the Information Literacy Competency Standards as a guide and ask the faculty partner to help identify some skills the students may already have. You might also want to administer a pretest, if time allows.

5. Test the problem statement to ensure it requires critical thought and explanation. Avoid being subjective in your questions. The best way to do this is to require the solution to be a product of some kind.

Hint: A bad question looks like this, "Nuclear power is an alternative energy source supported by the Bush Administration. Do you feel this is a good decision? Support your answer." This is OK for an essay exam —but there is no real problem solving accomplished in answering this question.

A better way of writing the problem statement would be: "Nuclear power is an alternative energy source supported by the Bush Administration. Your team is a group of lobbyists either in support of or against the Administration's decision to put more federal funding into research for nuclear power. Your constituents at home are seeking action on Vice President Cheney's announcement of $1.5 million dollars to three California universities conducting research on nuclear and alternative power sources as possible solutions to the recent shortage of electricity. *Write a letter to the editor explaining your group's position.*

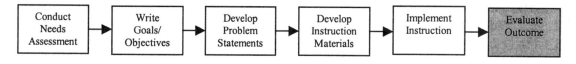

—ALEXIUS MACKLIN AND MICHAEL FOSMIRE—

Evaluating the problem-based instruction:

Since, most likely, you and the subject faculty are new to problem-based learning, it is important to get feedback from the students to see what you are doing well and what can be improved. Writing effective and engaging problems is difficult, and there will be the inevitable skinning of knees as you learn how to do it well.

Even if a problem scenario does not go well, the subject faculty are usually forgiving, as they have certainly had situations in their own teaching careers where they have run into trouble. The key to maintaining faculty collaborations in this situation is to have plans for making the instruction better "next time." To do that, and, in general just to help improve your instructional performance, it helps to have data. Especially when developing new techniques for teaching it is important to get both summative and formative data. The former gives you some idea of how students feel about the actual instruction, while the latter helps to determine whether course objectives have been met.

To obtain summative information, for our problem scenarios we gave students evaluation forms to determine what their self-identified learning outcomes were. For example, do they agree with the following statements: "my search skills improved," "I can apply skills to my final project," "I am able to find and evaluate information". To determine what the students actually learned, we examined the problem solutions, feedback from the instructors, and our own evaluation of students' work on assignments and final projects.

For the formative information, we get a feel for the student attitudes during the class session. Are students engaged, are they staring off into space, are they working as a group or ignoring each other and doing their own thing? We also ask formative questions on our student evaluations. Did they like the way the problem was introduced? Was it interesting? Was working in groups valuable? Were the problem solving steps logical? Did the students find workable solutions? These kinds of questions can help you determine how your teaching or facilitating of the problem can be improved, and what activities within the problem scenario were done well.

Conclusion:

We have sketched out the framework for implementing problem-based learning techniques to advance the information literacy curriculum. First, you need to find a subject faculty member motivated to improve student-learning outcomes. Second, you

must conduct a complete needs assessment to determine what information literacy skills are most important to your faculty partner. Don't skimp on the time spent in doing this assessment. It is the most essential tool in developing a successful collaboration. Once you accomplish these steps, implementing a new teaching approach will be less daunting and much more rewarding.

We are keeping a list of the challenges and benefits of using PBL to integrate information literacy skills into the curriculum. We hope that if you try this approach with your faculty, you will contact us with questions and comments. Good luck!

Challenges:

- A PBL curriculum takes an enormous amount of time to create and maintain.

- Not every student learns well in this environment. Equally notable, not every instructor can adapt to the PBL approach.

- The initial experiences can be difficult until the faculty and students adapt to the change in learning and teaching methods.

Benefits:

- Students are highly engaged in the learning process and there are improved learning outcomes as a result.

- Information literacy skills are learned and used at point-of-need.

- Librarians are equal partners with subject faculty in the development and implementation of curriculum.

NOTES

1. Vic R. Neufeld, Christel A. Woodward, and Stuart M. McLeod, "The McMaster MD Program: A Case Study of Renewal in Medical Education," *Academic Medicine* 64, no. 8: 285-94.

2. Barbara J. Duch, Susan E. Groh, and Deborah E. Allen, 2001. *The Power of Problem-based Learning: A Practical "How to" for Teaching Undergraduate Courses in Any Discipline* (Stirling, Vir.: Stylus, 2001); and Robin Fogarty, *Problem-Based Learning and Other Curriculum Models for the Multiple Intelligences Classroom* (Arlington Heights, IL: I/RI, 1997).

3.   Alexius E. Smith and Joeseph M. La Lopa, "Teaching Students to Think: How Problem-Based Learning is Revolutionizing the Classroom," *Chef Educator Today* 1, no. 1: 25- 27.

4.   Association of College and Research Libraries. 2000. *Information Literacy Competency Standards for Higher Education* [Online].   Available :http://www.ala.org/acrl/ilcomstan.html [8 April 2002].

5.   Samuel Benjamin Bloom, *Taxonomy of Educational Objectives: The Classification of Educational Goals, by a Committee of College and University Examiners* (New York, Longmans, Green, 1956-64).

TAKE A RIDE ON THE DESIGN CYCLE: INSTRUCTIONAL DESIGN FOR LIBRARIANS

Jerilyn Veldof

This paper covers an instructional design process used at the University of Minnesota to create innovative and effective library workshops. The first part of the process helps librarians determine what content to cover and how to immediately assess whether students are learning that content. The second part of the process focuses on choosing appropriate instructional methods to spice up teaching and affect learning. The last part of the process pulls together the design into a coherent lesson plan and script that can be used by multiple instructors.

The lesson plan and worksheets for the workshop discussed in this paper is available at: http://staff.lib.umn.edu/rcs/usered/depository.html/# unravel.

Most instruction librarians have never had training in effective instructional design. They develop their workshops intuitively, use another colleague's teaching outlines, or just fly by the seat of their pants. Whether or not these kinds of approaches are effective or efficient is usually left up to the individual librarian to decide. Many, lacking methods to assess student learning, have a vaguely uneasy sense that perhaps this is not working as well as it could. This unease, coupled with extreme staffing shortages and many more instructional requests on campus then could be handled, raised University of Minnesota Library staff interest in discovering ways to use their instructional time more wisely.

This paper outlines an instructional design process that improves library staff effectiveness in the classroom by maximizing student learning in the one-shot session. The U of MN Libraries has used this process to design three classes thus far, with plans to develop a fourth during Summer 2002. Although the process is very time-intensive (with teams of 6-8 librarians and staff spending three to five months developing the workshops), the outcome is a workshop design that is multi functional:

1. It provides an effective in-depth lesson plan that is used by over 14 instructors delivering more than 30 sessions a semester.
2. It provides modules (or chunks) that instructors can insert into their own subject specific classes. Handouts and worksheets are already created and can be easily customized.
3. It provides training that enables librarians and staff to individually design their own classes.
4. It allows a group of self-identified library stakeholders to take part in deciding what content will or will not be covered in the freshmen level library curriculum.

The particular class discussed is called "Unravel 2: The Research Process." Although it is offered through an open registration system, the class is marketed directly to English Composition instructors who send their students either as a requirement, or for extra credit. The sessions are usually full and students are given a certificate of completion as proof of attendance.

Veldof is the User Education Coordinator at the University of Minnesota Libraries, Twin Cities, Minneapolis, MN.

As demand has increased, the Libraries have added additional Unravel 2 classes over each of the four semesters it has been offered. For the fall 2002 semester we anticipate offering about 30 classes, with additional instructor-scheduled classes also using the Unravel 2 lesson plans.

The Unravel sessions are taught by a myriad of staff and librarians who go through a standardized training process and who are given an elaborate lesson plan as well as all their handouts and worksheets. The class was designed and is continuously improved by a team of six to eight librarians and library staff. This team met initially over a four-month period to design the class and pilot it. A year later, the design team reconvened to redesign several sections and refine others.

The Design Process

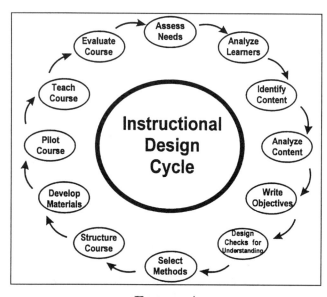

FIGURE A

The Process Step By Step

1. Review learner needs

The Unravel 2 class was explicitly created to address the needs of students in the first-year English Composition courses *who are required to attend* the library class. Their overall need is to find several scholarly books and articles on their topic.

2. Brainstorm content

Brainstorming the content that would meet these needs is perhaps the easiest step in this cycle. There is no shortage of tips, instructions, or detail that a student would need to know in order to find scholarly books and articles on their topic. The design team brain stormed enough content for what could be several

weeks of training. Examples of the lists we generated are available in Appendix A. The broader the session, the longer and more unwieldy the list. Next, it is time to get selective.

3. Filter the Nice-to-Knows from the Need-to-Knows and the Really-Want-to-Knows

Early in the process members of the design team went through a three-day training where they learned, among other things, the perils of cognitive overload and the importance of active and cooperative learning.[1] One of the goals of the design team, therefore, was to reduce cognitive overload and to experiment with active and cooperative learning techniques. It was clear that in order to do this we needed to follow the "less is more" strategy. "Less is more" in practice meant that the list of items we felt students vitally needed to know in order to successfully complete the research for their English Composition paper needed to be very lean.

The need-to-know list was reduced to:

- What an article index is and when to use one
- How to find and pick an article index from
- Research QuickStart
- Distinguishing between popular vs. scholarly materials
- Keyword vs. subject searching
- Finding good subject headings from a keywordsearch
- Distinguishing between book and article citations
- Searching MNCAT (the OPAC) to find if thelibrary owns a journal/book/newspaper
- Where to go for help

[Note: MNCAT is the name of the University of Minnesota's library catalog]

The really-want-to-know list was reduced to just one item:
- Identifying full-text indexes

4. Group the need-to-knows and the really-want-to-knows into major tasks or content area chunks

The team grouped the Need and Want lists into five content area chunks that reflect tasks the students need to identify books and articles for their topic. The team arranged these tasks to somewhat reflect a sequential process a student might take:

1. Finding Articles: Choosing an Article Index
2. Finding Articles: Searching for Articles
3. MNCAT Searching for KNOWN Items

—JERILYN VELDOF—

4. MNCAT Searching for UNKNOWN Items
5. Scholarly Vs. Popular

5. Create a task analysis for each content area chunk

Next, the team created a task analysis for each of the tasks above. A task analysis is a very vigorous process that challenged members to identify the discrete steps necessary to complete each task. It brings what is often an unconscious process to the conscious level.

Analyzing the task of distinguishing between a scholarly verses popular source, for example, forced each member of the team to greatly simplify a rather complex process. This exercise helped the team identify what were the most important components of the process of distinguishing between scholarly verses popular sources. See Appendix B for the complete task analysis. The steps later informed the key points we emphasized in the lesson plan.

6. Write objectives for content area chunk

Once the team clarified among ourselves the Needs and Wants lists in #4 as well as the critical steps involved in each task, we were ready to identify learning objectives. Learning objectives are action oriented, focusing on what the student would be able to do at the end of the session (as opposed to what they would know).

EXAMPLE: Objectives for Chunk 1—Finding Articles:

- Choosing an Article Index
- Define an article index
- Locate three appropriate article indexes for a particular topic
- Access and choose an article index from QuickStart for a particular topic

7. Create a "criterion test"

In previous semesters, a "reaction" evaluation was used to help the design team shape a workshop that met expectations and kept the interest of the students. In contrast to a reaction evaluation, a criterion test checks that actual learning has taken place. In an ideal situation, with much more time than a one-shot session permits, the criterion test would allow students to pull together all they had learned from the workshop and apply it to an actual situation—in this case finding books and articles for their paper topic. The reality of the one hour and fifteen minute workshop, however, necessitated that the design team create a multiple-choice test given to the students at the end of the class

and exchanged upon completion for a workshop certificate.

The results of this test are extremely helpful in assessing the effectiveness of both the instructor and the lesson plan. If a student, for example, answers this question incorrectly:

In MNCAT, I need to search by the _____ to find out if the U of MN Libraries own the article I want.
a. title of the article
b. title of the journal/magazine/newspaper
c. author of the article
d. any of these

We know we did something wrong in our workshop - we are not meeting one of our learning objectives and this section of the workshop would need to be redesigned. In this way, we test that our "need to knows" are actually getting known.

8. Create "checks for understanding"—or do this during steps 9 & 10

This step ensures that we build in ways to check that students are understanding what we are trying to teach at incremental steps during the class so that we still have time for the instructor and an assistant to give needed feedback and corrective assistance when necessary. In this way, we can help to ensure that each student is fulfilling the learning objectives and will be successful in the criterion test. It is not enough to check that one or two or three students in the class have an understanding of the content B the lesson plan should provide avenues for each student to give you that assurance.

Each chunk of the lesson plan includes worksheets where the students have a structured task and a place to write down evidence that they are completing the task. Most of the class content is learned during these segments of the class B and not when the instructor is lecturing or demonstrating. Each class gets both an instructor and assistant (called a "rover") and their job during these application segments of the class are to be actively engaged with each student in the class.

9. Revisit the Need-to-Knows and the Really-Want-to-Knows and narrow down the list even further if necessary.

When one is building a class around learning objectives that must be learned by the end of the workshop, the Needs and Wants lists must be very lean and very pointed. Often the design team will need to go back to their lists at this point and whittle them down even more—and then eliminate the corresponding objectives.

10. Brainstorm teaching methods and narrow the list down

It is only at this point in the design process that the team is ready to identify the best ways to deliver the content they have so painstakingly narrowed down. Diverging from the old "lecture, demo, practice" mode necessitates that the team draw on a wide-ranging toolkit of teaching methods (e.g. games, coaching, think-pair-shares, reading, and of course, the "lecturette"). Working chunk by chunk, the team brainstorms a variety of teaching methods they think might work, preferring cooperative and active learning methods to the instructor-driven methods we usually use in our library classes.

11. Choose teaching methods

From this list of possibilities, the team balances time constraints with variety and effectiveness, and then pulls in the "checks for understanding" from Step 8 to round out the teaching methods for each chunk. The overall lesson plan reflects various teaching methods including: think-pair-shares, reading, brainstorming, critique, laboratory, mini-case, lecturette, and simulation. Note that the vast majority of the teaching methods are not about the librarian being the "Sage on the Stage," but rather the "Guide on the Side."

12. Structure the workshop (including introduction)

Next, the team pulls the workshop together. The introduction includes the welcome, the benefits of taking the class, and the overall objectives and agenda. Each chunk of the lesson plan includes notes to the instructor, as well as an outline of what to cover and how to facilitate the class. To see the lesson plan for this class go to: http://staff.lib.umn.edu/rcs/ usered/depository.html/#unravel

13. Develop materials

The worksheets and handouts are provided to the student in a packet, with each sheet a different color for easy referral in the class. Only those materials directly related to the class are included—supplementary information is available, but not handed out to each student.

14. Pilot workshop

Each new workshop is an experiment. There are often glitches, pieces of the lesson plan that fall flat, and some oversights in each of the class designs we have created so far. Piloting the class before truly going live with it will help ensure that you're putting out a solid, effective product to your faculty, library instructors and students. New student staff are often a good pool for pilot subjects. Having as many of the design team there as possible is also useful.

15. Change class as needed

There were several adjustments in both the lesson plan, worksheets and flipcharts.

16. Deliver class

During the time the class is offered, remind library instructors, assistants and design team members to take notes about problems and improvements they would like to see in the next iteration of classes.

17. Evaluate

As soon after the criterion tests (and/or reaction evaluations) are tabulated, the team and the library instructors and assistants meet to discuss how well the design met the learning objectives. We look for patterns in the tests. What are the questions consistently answered incorrectly? What about those answered correctly? What comments do the library instructors have about delivery of the class? Did any of the teaching methods flop? Were the worksheets clear? What could be done to improve the class?

18. Change class as needed

Based on the evaluation the design team reconvenes to make changes to the class for the next semester. The Unravel 2 class has undergone changes after each semester that it was taught. Most recently, two chunks were changed based on both criterion test responses and library instructors' input and several of the worksheets were improved. A small segment of a Powerpoint presentation was added as well as flipcharts that included directions for each activity and a summary of the key points for each chunk.

NOTE

1. This workshop was called, "Instructional Techniques for New Instructors," given by Langevin Learning Services.

—JERILYN VELDOF—

Appendix A

Abbreviated Brain stormed Content List

What article index is-When to use one; What a catalog is—When to use one; Distinguishing indexes vs. web search engines; WorldCat; What we pay for-what don't; Distinguishing between popular vs. scholarly materials; How to find and pick an article index from LUMINA; What don't get if "full text"; Boolean (AND/OR); Subject searching—Controlled vocabulary; Keyword-"uncontrolled" vocab.; Natural language problems (e.g."What is my opinion?" in Yahoo!); Truncations; Limiting by date; Limiting by format; Mix author and title keyword, etc.; Using advanced search screen in MNCAT; Finding e-journals through MNCAT; Finding e-journals from e-journals list; Using e-journals; Output options (E-mailing citation) and full-text; Can't find articles in MNCAT; Finding if own journals—MNCAT and Holding; Distinguish between a book and article citations *(Ultimate benefit is to have correct citation info.)*; Where to go for help; What article is— in a journal which is not a book— in pop. Vs. school? ; Abbreviations for journal titles ; Capturing correct citation info; Why everything isn't full-text; Narrowing and defining topic (Using subheadings in Expanded Academic Index); Field Searching (Author, Title); All indexes are different. (Who publishes them?)

Appendix B

"Scholarly vs. Popular" Task Analysis

Task	Subtask	Step
1. Identify whether my citation is scholarly or popular	1.1. Identify if scholarly	1.1.1. Check to see if the title of the article uses specialized language of the discipline 1.1.2. Check to see if the journal title is not something you'd see on the newsstand 1.1.3. Check to see if the length of article is lengthy
	1.2. Identify if popular	1.1.4. Check to see if the title of the article uses language for a general audience 1.1.5. Check to see if the journal/magazine title is something you'd see on the newsstand 1.2.1. Check to see if the length of article is on the brief side
	1.3. To achieve clarity of distinctions, go to task 2	See below, task 2
2. Identify whether my article is scholarly or popular	2.1. Identify if scholarly	2.1.1 Check to see if the article has a bibliography 2.1.2 Check the expertise of the author (use handout) 2.1.3. Check to see if the article has an abstract at the beginning
	2.2. Identify if popular	2.2.1. Check to see if the article does not have a bibliography 2.2.2. Check the expertise of the author (use handout) 2.2.3. Check to see if the article does not have an abstract in the beginning

—JERILYN VELDOF—

Appendix C

Example of Row 1's "check for understanding" for the AMNCAT Searching for Known Items@ chunk

Students are to look up the item in the bibliography in the library OPAC (called MNCAT) and write down the library location and call number.

Bibliography	Library location and Call number
Byrne, John M., Schulz, David A., and Sussman, Marvin B.,eds. *Families and the energy transition.* New York: Haworth Press, 1985.	
Purdum, Todd S. "Keeping the lights on." *The New York Times* Feb 4, 2001 pWK2(N) pWK2(L).	
Joskow, Paul L. California's energy crisis. *Oxford Review of Economic Policy* Autumn 2001 v17 i3 p365.	
Anderson, Teresa. *Rural energy services: A handbook for sustainable energy development.* London: IT Publications, 1999.	
Roaf, "Ecohouse." 2001.	

TEACHING INFORMATION LITERACY SKILLS TO UNDERGRADUATES: THE ELECTRONIC RESEARCH LOG MODEL

Elizabeth Mulherrin

Introduction

The University of Maryland University College (UMUC) is one of the eleven degree-granting institutions of the University System of Maryland, serving over 70,000 students worldwide and an online student population of approximately 30,000. In the Fall of 2001, UMUC instituted several significant changes for the undergraduate curriculum, including a comprehensive, systematic information literacy program. An important element in the implementation of the program was the development of a required, one-credit Web-based course on information literacy skills for all undergraduate students, Information Literacy and Research Methods, or LIBS 150, was to be taken in a student's first 15 credit hours. The course was piloted in Fall 2001 with full implementation scheduled for Spring semester, 2002.

LIBS 150 Course Development Process

The new requirement, and an ambitious timeline from UMUC's School of Undergraduate Studies (SUS), presented many challenges to Information and Library Services (ILS) staff. A course development team was quickly formed that included five ILS librarians: a curriculum specialist, three co-authors, and a peer reviewer. Instructional designers from SUS were also members of the design team.

Mulherrin is a librarian at the University of Maryland University College Libraries, Adelphi, MD.

Course development began in March 2001. A course outline was developed and possible textbooks identified. Previously, UMUC offered undergraduates a one-credit elective, Introduction to Library Research, or LIBS 100, offered both online and face-to-face. The staff of ILS developed the online LIBS 100 course and it served as a model for LIBS 150, but substantial changes were necessitated by the difference in class size. LIBS 100 had never enrolled more than thirty-five students in a section with one faculty member. For LIBS 150, SUS desired to permit enrollment of one hundred students per section.

LIBS 150, like LIBS 100, is a seven-week Web-based class. LIBS 100 consisted of six modules covering the main topics of the course:

1. Libraries and the Research Process
2. Basic Search Techniques for Electronic Resources
3. Web/Internet Resources
4. Library Catalogs
5. Reference Sources
6. Periodical Literature

The final project for LIBS 100 was a pathfinder of annotated resources in either MLA or APA citation style on a topic of the student's choosing. The required learning activities for the course gave students the opportunity to search for information in various sources on their chosen topic and receive feedback from the instructor before turning in the final pathfinder project.

The projected enrollment for LIBS 150 challenged the course writers to devise a new model that would retain the iterative process of the pathfinder project at its core. As the course modules were written, the team condensed them from six to four and reordered them. Team members were responsible for writing individual modules with editorial review by the group as a whole.

The instructional design team members were responsible for the final edits before publication after sign-off from the authors. The instructional design and production team also created interactive pop-ups and animations, with input from the course authors, designed icons, and did the programming for the course.

Snapshot of LIBS 150 Course Modules

Emily Thiroux's, *The Critical Edge: Thinking and Researching in a Virtual Society* (Upper Saddle River, NJ: Prentice Hall, 1999), inspired the team to think about adapting the pathfinder model from LIBS 100 to an electronic research log format for LIBS 150. A research log project needed to be standardized for the large number of students and weighed heavily enough toward the final grade that students would be motivated to complete it. By asking students to record the steps they took in searching, evaluating and citing resources on a particular topic instructors could evaluate their approach to the research process.

Research Log Development

The challenge faced by the team was how to automate the research log project given the large number of students in each course section while retaining the iterative aspects of the assignment.

The log was designed in five steps:

    Step 1 - Select a Topic
    Step 2 - Enter Your Thesis Statement
    Step 3 - Web - Search Statements

    Step 4 - Evaluate Your Results
    Step 5 - Cite Your Materials

In Step 1, students select from three topics in a drop-down menu: communication in the workplace, global warming, and computer security. Step 2 is a thesis statement on their chosen topic. Search statements are recorded in Step 3 Web for three different search tools: Web, library database, and online catalog. Drop-down menus allow Boolean operators to join search terms. More sophisticated searching strategies, such as truncation or nesting, can be recorded in the search box provided for each search tool. Step 4 consists of radio button questions to evaluate the three types of sources retrieved. For book sources, the option "Unable to be determined" was added since not all students learning in an online environment would be able to view book sources first hand. Step 5 asks students to cite sources in APA style and annotate the selected sources. Students are not required to annotate a book source in Step 5.

A team member designed a research log form template in steps using html form templates. Very few programming changes were required for this original template to be operative in the classroom. The log form does not currently support the ability to italicize

—ELIZABETH MULHERRIN—

or indent the APA citations in Step 5, a functional enhancement that we are working to incorporate.

To simplify the log for grading purposes several decisions needed to be made. The team had originally thought the research log steps would be submitted to the instructor for feedback and grading as students moved through the course. However, the team soon realized the difficulties this would present in terms of grading multiple submissions, and the log was revised so it would be submitted only once for grading at the end of the course.

The log form is designed to permit drafts of each step to be saved, allowing students to make revisions before submitting their work for final grading. The learning activities are designed to mirror some of the steps of the log and students are given feedback on those activities before submitting the final draft.

The log form implemented in the pilot sent completed logs to the instructor as a text file in an email message. The placement of the log in the course content area of the Web classroom grouped together instructions about the log, a template of a log to be printed or saved for future use, a completed model log, and the log form to submit for the course.

LIBS 150 Pilot

Course development began in early March 2001, and the target date for a pilot of the course was the second term of the Fall 2001 semester beginning in mid-October. Two sections of the course were offered for the seven-week term and 50 students enrolled in each section. Two of the course co-authors were instructors for the pilot. Based on experiences with the pilot, several changes were made to the learning activities content and format of submission. However, there were very few technical problems overall with the course and the research log format worked well for both the students and faculty.

LIBS 150, Spring 2002

Nine sections of the course were offered in Term 1 of the Spring semester with an enrollment of 900 students. The technical staff immediately identified a problem with the research log form location when the larger number of students enrolled in the course. There was a concern that saving the draft logs on a single University server might overburden the system and that students might lose drafts of their work if the server went down. The log form was moved to a different location where it could then be replicated to multiple servers. This move

occurred just a few days before the course began and created some confusion for the instructors. While the research log was now in a more prominent location in the classroom menu, it was separated from the model log and the blank log form. The design team will now need to address how to best accommodate this change.

The log relocation also changed how the log form would be submitted to the instructor. The research log could now be accessed in its html form from within the online classroom rather than receiving it as a text file in an e-mail; this change allowed the instructor to readily check the URLs recorded by the student. The instructional design and production team also proposed and implemented a text box format for grading the logs to allow an instructor to comment using text boxes at each step of the log as well as providing a text box for comments and a final grade. A planned future development is the capability to save a draft of the corrected log before releasing it to the student.

Student Feedback

Student comments about the research log model have generally been positive. Some students complained that being asked to do the learning activities and then recording steps in the log was duplicative work. The design team is again considering the possibility of the log being submitted in steps, replacing some of the learning activities, in a planned revision of the course. Several students volunteered that they plan to use the blank log template to help them prepare for research projects in other courses.

This was a very rewarding class...I particularly like the step-by-step process that was employed to walk us through the entire process using the research log. It made it easy to understand and apply. Thanks for the opportunity to learn something that not only can be applied here, but elsewhere as well.

This class was indeed helpful...I will definitely utilize the research log approach from now on.

Faculty Feedback

Most of the LIBS 150 faculty found the research log to be an effective tool for teaching students research skills in an online teaching environment. There were some frustrations for instructors due to some of the technical changes made to the log by the production team while the course was running, at both the beginning and the end of the course. Some instructors felt there should be more emphasis on the evaluation steps of the log and additional preparation for the students to cite resources in APA style. Other suggestions included allowing students to select their own topics and not restricting students to the use of only one citation style.

I liked the overall idea and think it will work well in the long run. I liked this better than the design for LIBS 100. Student comments indicated that they like it as well. Several students said they were using the process to help them write papers for other classes.

Summary

The electronic research log model is designed to give students the opportunity to test search strategies, identify, and evaluate resources on their chosen topic as they move through the content of the course. The tasks they perform with the learning activities and the log steps reinforce the major concepts of the course: searching, evaluating, and documenting sources effectively. The standardized format accommodates the large number of students per section and helps to balance faculty workload. It provides students with a useful tool for understanding the steps of the research process. The log model is intended to be the foundation of an expanded information literacy initiative at the University. The skills taught by the process of devising search and thesis statements, recording search tools, evaluating results, and annotating and citing resources are reinforced as students move through the curriculum.

—ELIZABETH MULHERRIN—

FROM 50 MINUTES TO 15 WEEKS: TEACHING A SEMESTER-LONG INFORMATION LITERACY COURSE WITHIN A FRESHMAN LEARNING COMMUNITY

Tammy S. Sugarman and Laura G. Burtle

Our experience teaching a 15-week class came because of the opportunities provided by the Freshmen Learning Community (FLC) program at Georgia State University (GSU).

Freshmen Learning Communities at Georgia State University

Freshmen Learning Communities consist of 14-16 credit hours from the core curriculum. All FLCs include English 1101 (English composition) and GSU 1010 (New Student Orientation). The communities are centered on a broad theme, and the remainder of the courses in the community supports the theme. A deliberate effort is made to integrate two or more courses around the theme. Incoming freshmen register for the community as a whole, rather than class by class. FLCs are limited to 25 students, and the English 1101 and GSU 1010 classes are made up of only those students.

The learning community program at GSU has been quite successful, and has grown from 11 communities in 1999, to 22 in 2000, 25 in 2001, and 33 FLCs are planned for Fall 2002.

All GSU colleges with undergraduate programs, as well as the Library and the Counseling Center, now offer learning communities.

Sugarman and *Burtle* are librarians at Georgia State University, Atlanta, GA.

History of Library Involvement

Before 1999, the university's Counseling Center faculty taught "college success skills" classes for Learning Support students—usually students on academic probation. These courses have always included a library instruction section, and the professors who taught these classes believed the ability to use the library was vital to the success of these students.

As part of the development of learning communities, a 3-credit New Student Orientation course was developed (GSU 1010). The Counseling Center was the major unit responsible for designing the curriculum for this new course. Because a library component had always been included in the learning support classes, it was natural that the GSU 1010 courses would also include a library module.

Along with the GSU 1010 courses that were part of FLCs, a number of "generic" sections of GSU 1010 for non-FLC freshmen were taught by Counseling Center faculty. As demand for these classes grew, the Freshmen Studies Office, responsible for the FLC/GSU1010 program, asked if any librarians would be interested in teaching some GSU 1010 sections. Librarians now teach generic sections, as well as the GSU 1010 in some of the learning communities.

Participating in this program led to more widespread recognition of librarians as faculty by the other faculty teaching in FLCs. Teaching faculty now recognize that librarians have much to offer to the program beyond 50-minute library instruction sessions.

Librarians express interest in developing own FLC

After teaching GSU 1010, we decided that we were interested in leading a FLC of our own. After getting approval for the idea from the library administration, we approached the Director of Freshmen Studies with the idea. Given the prior involvement of the librarians with this program, the director knew our work and respected what we already contributed. The response to our initiative was positive, and we were encouraged to submit a proposal.

In order to create our FLC we had to develop two proposals. One was for a "Perspectives" course. These courses are special topic courses taught on a wide variety of topics, and are a required component of the undergraduate core curriculum. Rather than being approved by a particular college, the proposals are considered by a college-wide committee. We submitted a proposal for a course called "Citizen in the Information Age," a 2-credit hour, semester–long course that would meet once a week.

We also submitted a proposal to create the complement of classes that would make up the learning community. In addition to the Perspectives class, these were GSU 1010, English Composition, Introduction to Political Science, and a course on Media, Culture, and Society. We proposed team-teaching the Perspectives and the GSU 1010 courses. Our proposals for the Perspectives course and the FLC were approved.

Development of "Citizen in the Information Age" *(Handout 1)*

The focus of the Perspectives courses is to provide students with a better understanding and global view of the contemporary world. Using these parameters, we brain stormed to come up with a list of topics that we could use to explore some of the key issues in today's "information society." We wanted to select issues that students would face in school and everyday life and give students a foundation for understanding global information-related issues. Although we decided not to develop a library research course per se, we felt it was vitally important to include several components of the research process into our course. In addition, we believed this was a great opportunity for us to try to incorporate at least some of the ACRL "Information Literacy Competency Standards for Higher Education."[1] We focused on selected sections of standards three, four and five. After researching and reading syllabi, books, and articles in the areas of business, sociology, technology, history, information and library sciences, we selected topics and determined goals and learning outcomes

based on competencies we wanted students to be able to demonstrate by the end of the course. These included showing an ability to analyze Web and print materials for credibility and accuracy, evaluating information critically, and understanding ethical and legal issues surrounding the production and use of information. Recognizing that some topics would be discussed over more than one class period, and allowing for a review session and exams, we developed a curriculum that included the following topics:

- Computer Mediated Communication
- Global village vs. Fragmented society
- Ethics/legality (intellectual property)
- Censorship/content control and regulation
- Research methods and search engine bias
- Digital Divide
- "Free" Internet?
- Privacy
- E-commerce

Originally, our syllabus also included class periods for discussions about how government documents are disseminated (or not, as in the case of "fugitive" documents) as well as issues of archiving and long-term storage of information. By the midpoint of the semester, we realized we would have to cut out these two topics due to a lack of time.

Between the two of us, we divided the weekly topics, and each took responsibility for an equal number of topics. We tried to alternate weeks so that one of us would not be lecturing or leading the class discussion two weeks in a row (we thought the students might enjoy that, and hoped it would make preparation easier for us), although our other library commitments sometimes made that impossible. Whoever was responsible for that week selected the assigned readings, including chapters in a textbook we adopted and any additional magazine or journal articles, prepared Microsoft Powerpoint ® slides for the topic, and developed the in-class writing assignment for that day. We used WebCT to manage the course online, and *tried* to place the Powerpoint slides in WebCT no later than twenty-four hours before class (we did manage to get them in WebCT before the start of class, although we have to admit sometimes it was the morning of class!). Whoever was responsible for a particular topic also developed questions for that material to use on the midterm and final examinations.

Assignments *(Handout 2)*

We decided to assign one large group project that would provide students the opportunity to demonstrate

—TAMMY S. SUGARMAN AND LAURA G. BURTLE—

competencies in our stated learning objectives. The group project would also allow students the benefit of working together and learning collaboratively, and give them the opportunity to demonstrate written, oral and presentation skills. In groups of 3-4 (we had a total of 37 students), students were required to select, compare, and critique two Web sites on the same topic, one "authoritative" and one of "questionable authority." The group project grade was based on the choice of Web sites selected, thoroughness of the evaluation, quality of the written report (including appropriate supporting documentation), and the quality of the oral presentation. Before handing out the assignment, we spent several class periods discussing criteria useful in the evaluation of Web sites, the nature and use of search engines and directories, and library research methods. Students were encouraged to turn in a "rough draft" of the project two weeks before the due date in order to receive comments and suggestions to improve the final product. The project counted for forty percent of the final grade.

Students' final course grades were also made up of weekly in-class writing assignments on a question relating to either the reading assigned for that week or an opinion about an issue covered in the class discussion, and multiple-choice/short-answer mid-term and final examinations.

Positive Outcomes

Students willingly participated and shared relevant experiences during class lectures and discussions, and in particular, were enthusiastic about several topics including copyright infringement issues surrounding Napster, how communication methods have changed over time, and search engine bias.

The group project assignment was an effective way to test student competencies on the stated learning outcomes on the syllabus. Unfortunately, most students did not choose to turn in a rough draft (which was optional) and were unpleasantly surprised when they did not receive maximum points for the assignment. Overall, the oral presentations were very good and the written reports were average. While we felt we spelled out very clearly the assignment and our expectations, we may revise our assignment and make a rough draft mandatory, or perhaps develop a smaller assignment that would give students a "practice run" before doing the group project assignment.

Throughout the course, the library was a significant component of our discussions and the group project assignment. The students knew we were librarians and that they were expected to take advantage of the library's physical and virtual offerings. Students came into the library to see us during office hours and to drop off assignments, and we feel this made the library seem less of an intimidating place to them. Since the end of the course, several students have dropped by the reference desk to say hello and seek assistance with their assignments.

We created a bibliography assignment for the GSU 1010 course within our FLC, and were very pleased to see that the students were able to integrate the information they learned in the Perspectives course about searching for and evaluating sources into this capstone assignment.

Room for Improvement

We both felt that there was too much lecture and not enough active learning. We plan to develop in-class activities and limit the amount of lecturing we do as instructors. We discovered that the attention spans of the students were no more than one hour, and in effect, the last forty minutes of class was not very productive. In light of this, in Fall 2002, we are offering the course twice a week for fifty-minute sessions.

It was very difficult for us to find a textbook that addressed the issues we wanted to cover during the course. Library research textbooks focused too much on the process and mechanics of doing research and writing, while textbooks in areas such as business and sociology were too narrowly focused. We have decided to forgo using a textbook and instead will put together a course package of readings from journals, magazines, and Internet sources. The articles and Web sites we used last Fall were available to the students via WebCT, however many students—to our surprise—were not very "Net savvy" and had trouble accessing this material. Therefore, we plan to devote a class period or two for students to have hands-on practice in accessing materials available to them in WebCT. We realize that putting together our own course package will be more time consuming for us (selecting, getting copyright permissions, etc.) but believe the students will benefit from having one place in which to find assigned readings that are directly relevant to the topics discussed in class.

Students complete a course evaluation at the end of the semester. However, we feel it would benefit the instructors and the students to have students complete an evaluation midway through the course so that problems and concerns can be addressed before the completion of the course.

The enrollment in our FLC was only 15 students (25 is the maximum for the course), so we have revised the description of the FLC to try to interest more students. We included phrases that emphasize how the FLC will help students succeed in college and keep their scholarships. The course description now speaks directly to the students by using phrases such as "essential to your academic success" and "the Internet's impact on your life as a student at GSU will be pervasive!" We decided to replace one course and add a math class to the complement of courses within the FLC in the hopes of attracting more students interested in computer science and business. *(Handout 3)*

Recommendations

Overall, we enjoyed the experience, and are offering our community again this Fall. If you have the opportunity to teach a full course, it is vital to be prepared for the amount of time it will take, in terms of both preparation and actual teaching and grading. We spent about 15 hours a week each on the two courses, and there are two of us! The first year is the hardest, since the curriculum must be developed from scratch, but time to work on teaching responsibilities is vital. Given this reality, administrative support is essential, especially when negotiating release time. There is no way to simply add this to your regular duties and do a good job.

When possible, team-teaching with another librarian (or other faculty member) provides important support, both in the development of the curriculum, and with trepidation regarding teaching a full semester class.

When proposing librarian-taught classes, use existing contacts to get your foot in the door. Many of us have worked with numerous faculty on campus, on everything from library instruction for their classes, to collection development, to research assistance. Find out how they can help you. What committees are they on that influence the curriculum?

It is also important to make new contacts. Does your campus have a freshmen or undergraduate studies office? Who administers learning communities? Send an e-mail or stop by the office and tell them what you can do to advance the program.

Finally, if you want to teach a class, you have to ask. Don't wait for someone to come to you. It won't hurt to ask. Even if the response is negative, the knowledge that you are interested is planted, and a more positive response may be down the road.

1. Association of College and Research Libraries, "Information Literacy Competency Standards for Higher Education: Standards, Performance Indicators, and Outcomes," 28 November 2000, <http://www.ala.org/acrl/ilstandardlo.html>. Accessed 9 April 2002.

PERS 2001I "The Citizen in the Information Age"
Fall 2001 Tuesdays, 1:00 – 2:40 pm

The course website is on WebCT (http://webct.gsu.edu)

The Internet and World Wide Web are influencing nearly all aspects of personal and public life. They are changing interpersonal and public communication, commerce, civic activity, and how people participate in society. What are the implications of this change for those who do not have access to the Internet, or do not have as convenient or unrestricted access as do others? What impact has the Internet had on the questions of censorship, privacy, intellectual property, authority, and ethics? Knowledge about and a degree of mastery over these and other information related issues are essential for students to become educated information-age citizens.

This class will explore these issues through readings, lectures, and a collaborative research project. The class will provide students the opportunity to discuss and debate these topics, and to explore what it means to be a participant in, and help shape, the Information Age.

The general goals of this class are to:
- ✓ Expose students to key controversial issues in the Information Age
- ✓ Encourage students to think critically about those issues
- ✓ Understand the social issues surrounding the use of information
- ✓ Understand how information is formally and informally produced, organized, and disseminated
- ✓ Provide the opportunity for verbal and written communication of well researched ideas
- ✓ Access needed information effectively and efficiently
- ✓ Evaluate information critically

Faculty:

Tammy Sugarman, M.A., M.S.I.
Pullen Library
Library North
Voice 404-463-9944
Email: tsugarman@gsu.edu
Office hours: Thurs. 10-11 or by appointment

Laura G. Burtle, M.S.L.S.
Pullen Library
Library North
Voice: 404.463-9945
E-mail: lburtle@gsu.edu
Office hours: Wed. 4-5 or by appointment

Date	Topic	Read for Class
Aug 21	What is the "Information Age"	
Aug 28	Communication Cybercultures	Text, Chapter 1, 2, 11
Sep 4	Global village vs. Fragmented Society	Text, Chapter 8, 10 Weiner, Eric. "Cell Phone Rally." Morning Edition. National Public Radio, 29 November 2000 <http://www.npr.org/> *Go to Morning Edition, Archives, Wednesday, 11-29-00*
Sep 11	Class canceled	

Sep 18	Ethics/Legality (Intellectual Property)	Text, Chapter 7 p. 148-164 only Mann, Charles. "Who Will Own Your Next Good Idea?" The Atlantic. September 1998 <http://www.theatlantic.com/issues/98sep/copy.htm>
Sept 25	Censorship/Content control/Regulation	Text, Chapter 9 Jost, Kenneth. "Libraries and the Internet." CQ Researcher 01 June 2001 <libraries_internet.pdf>
Oct 2	**Midterm** **Group Assigment** Research Methods Search Engine Bias	Lasica, J.D. "Search Engines and Editorial Integrity Is the jig up for honest search results?" Online Journalism Review 23 July 2001 <http://ojr.usc.edu/content/story.cfm?request=611> Sherman, Chris. "The Almost Invisible Web, Part I." <http://websearch.about.com/library/weekly/aa091800a.htm> Sherman, Chris. "The Almost Invisible Web, Part II." <http://websearch.about.com/library/weekly/aa091800b.htm> Mieszkowski, Katherine. "Google a go-go." Salon. 21 June 2001. <http://www.salon.com/tech/feature/2001/06/21/google_henziger/index.html>
Oct 9	Research Methods (continued) Digital Divide	U.S. Dept. of Commerce. National Telecommunications and Information Administration. "Americans in the Information Age Falling Through the Net: Executive Summary." October 2000. <http://www.ntia.doc.gov/ntiahome/digitaldivide/execsumfttn00.htm>
Oct 12		**Last day to withdraw with a possible grade of W except for hardship withdrawal**
Oct 16	The "Free" Internet	Ebert, Roger. "My 2 Cents about Paying for Content." Yahoo! Internet Life. October 2000. Retrieved from MasterFile Premier via GALILEO <http://search.epnet.com/direct.asp?AN=3707441&db=aph&>
Oct 23	Privacy **First draft of group assignment due**	
Oct 30	Privacy	Chapter 7 p. 135-148 Peralte, C. Paul. "Private info exposed on Net; HOPE scholars' personal data discovered in routine search." Atlanta Journal and Constitution. 25 July 2001, pg. 1A. Online. Lexis-Nexis Academic Universe
Nov 6	E-commerce	Text, Chapter 4

—TAMMY S. SUGARMAN AND LAURA G. BURTLE—

Nov 13	Group Presentation **Group assignment due**	
Nov 20	Group Presentation	
Nov 27	Review	

Final Exam Tuesday, December 11; 12:30pm

Required Text:

Albarran, Alan B. and David H. Goff. *Understanding the Web: Social, Political, and Economic Dimensions of the Internet.* Ames, IA: Iowa State University Press, 2000.

Additional readings as assigned.

Grading Policy and Scale:

Course grade components are:		The grade scale is:	
Midterm:	200 points	900-1000 points	=A
In-class assignments:	100 points	800-899 points	=B
Class Participation	50 points	700-799 points	=C
Group Project:	400 points	600-699 points	=D
Final examination:	250 points	0-599 points	=F

Attendance Policy:
Regular attendance is expected. Students are responsible for all assignments and information covered in classroom discussion and in reading materials, including those distributed during the class whether they are present or not. All examinations and classroom activities are cumulative. There will be no opportunities to make-up classroom activities. *Students who miss more than 3 class sessions may be withdrawn by the instructors*. If you cannot attend a class session you are expected to contact one of the instructors to inform them that you will be absent.

Make-up examinations:
Permission to make-up an examination must be granted in advance of the assigned administration of the examination. Permission will be granted in the event of illness or extreme hardship. To receive permission, e-mail one of the course instructors. Make-up examinations may or may not be the same as the original examination.

Academic Honesty:
This course is governed by the University Policy on Academic Honesty, which is described in *On Campus: The Undergraduate Co-Curricular Affairs Handbook* available at http://www.gsu.edu/~wwwcam/code/academichonesty.htm

The course syllabus provides a general plan for the course; deviations may be necessary.

Perspectives 2001: Citizen in the Information Age
Group Project

Date Due: November 13
Presentations: November 13 and November 20

Evaluating and Comparing World Wide Web Sites

The goal of this assignment is to compare and critique 2 web sites on the same topic. To effectively use the WWW for personal and academic research, skills in evaluating the credibility, authority and point of view of websites are crucial.

Your project will be submitted as a written report, and will be presented to the class on one of the two dates listed above. The report must be written in a clear, logical format. Be sure to address the criteria listed below, but do not submit the report in a "list" format. The oral presentation should be approximately 15 minutes long.

Topics: Your group should identify two websites on the same topic. One of the websites should be authoritative and appropriate for use in research. The other should be of questionable authority. Your group should decide on the selection of a topic. In order to find websites of varying quality and authority, try to find a topic where people have strong opinions or agendas. If you are looking for ideas, you may want to look at Issues and Controversies on File. You can access it via the Index of Databases link on the Pullen Library homepage http://www.library.gsu.edu.

Your grade will be based on the following:

- Choice of Websites selected
- Thoroughness of evaluation
- Quality of the written report: free from grammatical and spelling errors; organized and logical format; appropriate conclusion; appropriate documentation
- Quality of oral presentation

Criteria: A good summary of what to look for when evaluating an Internet site can be found at http://milton.mse.jhu.edu:8001/research/education/net.html. Below are items that should be included in your written report:

- Complete URLs of both websites (MLA style)
- How you found the site (search engine? Which one – keywords used to search)
- What information is covered on the sites? (a summary)
- Who is the intended audience?
- What are the main links included on the sites? How do they relate to the main themes of the sites?
- Type of graphics on the sites. Do the graphics enhance or detract from the information provided on the sites?
- Accuracy (a main portion of your report). Is the information provided reliable and error-free? Does the information seem credible? Is there supporting documentation to back up any claims made on the sites? Are there many spelling or grammatical errors? Is there an editor or "fact-

—TAMMY S. SUGARMAN AND LAURA G. BURTLE—

checker" to verify the information provided on the site? Has the site been "rated" by another web service or library?

- Authority (a main portion of your report). Who is responsible for the site? Is the site "signed"? What are the qualifications/credentials of the authors of the site? Are they experts on the topic? **For any author or organization responsible for the websites you select, you must provide information about that person or organization. That information should come from a source external to the website, and must be documented in your report (MLA style).**

- Objectivity (a main portion of your report). Do the sites have particular social or political agendas? Is that made clear? Do the sites have a particular bias? Is there advertising? What type? Does the advertising present a conflict of interest?

- Currency: is the information contained on the sites up to date? Updated regularly? Do the links on the site work or are they "dead" links?

- What did you learn about the topic you selected from these web sites? What did you learn about using the web as a research tool or source of information?

Perspectives 2001: Citizen in the Information Age
Group Project
Date Due: November 13
Presentations: November 13 and November 20

Evaluating and Comparing World Wide Web Sites

400 points

Your grade will be based on the following:

Choice of sites – is one more authoritative than the other? Are they on the same topic?	15 points
Complete URL? Can I get to it using the URL you entered? Does it point to the site, or to a root directory from which I have to look for the site? Are there typos in the URL?	10
How you found the site - What search engines did you use? Provide the name and URL. The search methods may be different for the 2 sites. What did you type into the search box to find the site? I should be able to duplicate your search and locate the site.	15
What information is covered? Should be a good summary – not just "it covered the topic." Include the specifics on the different pieces of information, but don't just duplicate the site. Give an informative abstract.	15
Audience – how do you know – is it explicitly stated on the site, or did you have to derive it from the content? What led you to your conclusion about the intended audience?	15
Links – not just a list, but a discussion of how they are related to the site. Are they closely related, or tangential? Do they lend authority to the site? Are they "good" sites?	15
Graphics – do they provide information or are they just decorative? Do they interfere with the readability or accessibility of the site?	15
Accuracy (a main portion of your report). How did you determine its accuracy? Provide a properly formatted list of resources you consulted to determine credibility. If you found supporting documentation where did you find it? Provide full references.	50
Authority (a main portion of your report) Is external evidence of authority provided and documented? If no external evidence was found, is there a record of what was searched while looking for information about the author, including search engines, databases, keywords used?	50
Objectivity – why did you determine that there was or was not a bias – what did you look for? Why or why not did the advertising present a potential conflict of interest? Where you able to identify an example of an advertiser's effect on the content of the site?	50
Currency - if there is no date, did you look for more current information on the same topic to judge your site's currency? Where did you look?	50
What did you learn about the topic you selected from these web sites? What did you learn about using the web as a research tool or source of information?	25
Quality of the written report: free from grammatical and spelling errors; organized	25

—TAMMY S. SUGARMAN AND LAURA G. BURTLE—

and logical format; appropriate conclusion; appropriate documentation	
Quality of oral presentation – was it well organized? Were visual aids appropriate and useful? Did it cover the major points of the project?	50

Brochure Description

Freshmen Learning Community:
The Internet and the Information Age

In today's global environment, the ability to recognize the need for, be able to access, and critically evaluate information is <u>essential to your academic success</u>! The Internet and the World Wide Web influence nearly all aspects of your life, and are changing the way you communicate, spend your money, and participate in society. The Internet's impact on your life as a student at GSU will be pervasive! This FLC will introduce you to issues surrounding information and information technology in today's society. It will teach you to be aware of the structure and impact of information and information technology in your life, and how to make wise decisions about the information you will use to succeed in college. This FLC is relevant to all areas of study and careers, and is a good choice for those students interested in majoring in business, computer science, or communications, and students with undecided majors.

—TAMMY S. SUGARMAN AND LAURA G. BURTLE—

INSTRUCTOR COLLEGE: PROMOTING DEVELOPMENT OF LIBRARY INSTRUCTORS

Patricia Yocum, Doreen Bradley, and Amanda Forrester

Instructor College, an initiative of the University of Michigan Library, was launched in Winter 2001 as a specially focused staff development effort to promote the growth of instructional skills of the Library staff. With strong support from Library administration and senior library managers, Instructor College embarked on an ambitious program during its first year. It has continued along the same lines during its second year, enjoying many achievements. Still a pilot program, Instructor College continues to consider how best to achieve a sustainable model in order to help library instructors develop their capabilities as effective teachers in a specialized setting.

Organizational Issues and Challenges

Instructor College is open to all Library staff involved in instruction. Two categories of membership are available:

- General Members are staff who are interested in improving their instructional skills and who plan to attend one or more of the sessions sponsored by the College during the year.

- Contributing Members are staff who wish to contribute at least one special effort during the year. They may conduct a workshop, serve on a task force, lead a discussion group, or help the College in some other capacity.

Yocum is the Coordinator for Collections at the University of Michigan's Shapiro Science Library; *Bradley* is the Head of Instruction Services at the University of Michigan's Taubman Medical Library; *Forrester* is a Public Services Librarian at the University of Michigan's Shapiro Undergraduate Library.

Enrollment via an online form provides information on members' interests, the category of membership, and any special contributions members are willing to make. Although plans called for members to renew their enrollment each year as a way to convey their continuing interest, it was subsequently decided to forego this step as unproductive busy work. Instead, continuing interest was assumed and renewal was made automatic. Membership now terminates only when a person leaves the Library, as did several during the year or asks to be removed from the roster, which no one has yet done.

As of 15 April 2002, the College has forty-nine members, a number that has remained constant for nearly twelve months and represents over seventy-five percent of front-line instructors. Twenty-two are General Members and twenty-seven are Contributing Members. The fact that more staff enrolled as Contributing Members indicates a willingness to devote time and effort to a unique initiative. This trend also speaks to the perceived importance and need by individual staff members to improve their own instruction skills. Members represent almost all units within the library that are involved with user instruction, plus several from outside the University Library system such as the Population Studies Center and the Kresge Business Administration Library. College members have a wide range of instruction experience, from brand new librarians to several staff with two decades or more of experience. Because enrollment in the College is voluntary, the number and distribution of members are particularly heartening.

Oversight as well as management of Instructor College is the primary responsibility of the Instructor College Steering Committee (ICSC), a group appointed by the Associate Director for Public Services and consisting of five members from units throughout the Library system. Each member serves a two-year term. Because members represent different units, the Steering Committee has a broad understanding of the varying needs of library instructors. In the current organizational structure, the ICSC functions as an operating committee, envisioning and delivering College programs. It is important to note in this ongoing experiment that none of the members of the Steering Committee has any formal training in staff development or human resources. All however, have been able to draw liberally on their experiences as managers, supervisors, and especially participants in professional organizations to contribute to the College.

Since it was appointed in Fall 2000, the Steering Committee has gained valuable experience in leading a staff development effort. The Committee has been able to identify skills needing improvement, present informative programs which speak to those needs, and provide resources for further development. It has been rewarded with consistently positive feedback and often explicit "thanks" from participating colleagues. The Committee has also come to see some limitations in its capacity. Consisting of volunteers with strong interest but other full time responsibilities, the Steering Committee is sometimes challenged to maintain programmatic momentum because of the logistical details involved. For the College's first year, the Chair of the Steering Committee was formally able to devote up to 50 percent of her time as needed to launch the College, a helpful arrangement that has since expired. One of the central challenges for the coming year will be to consider adjustments to the organizational structure. Priorities will be to better accommodate logistical demands in programming while promoting the sustainability of the College and retaining its strengths as demonstrated to date.

Development of a Curriculum

Terming the staff development effort a "college" implicitly committed modeling it like a college insofar as possible. No feature was more critical in this regard than the development of a curriculum. Webster's defines curriculum as "a set of courses constituting an area of specialization." [1] In a conventional college, courses typically meet weekly or more often. Such a sustained commitment was beyond the capacity of Instructor College. The critical notions "curriculum" connotes, however, were readily recognized as applicable. These included the ideas of purpose, commonality, coherence, and prospective outcome.

Translating these notions into specifics for Instructor College was a major challenge. Practicality–the urgent need to present program sessions–shaped early curricular development as material prepared for "Opening Day," 1 February 2001 illustrates:

"Building the Instructor College curriculum is an iterative process. Topics as well as content evolve to meet the changing needs of IC members....After surveying the instructional environment in the University Library, the Instructor College Steering Committee (ICSC) selected two modes for developing the initial curriculum. These are:
1) **Foundation Sessions** organized by the ICSC
2) **Thematic Sessions** designed by task forces comprised of IC members and a liaison from the ICSC." [2]

As reported previously [3] "Foundation Sessions are designed to provide the core skills and knowledge that all U of M Library instructors need to possess." The first four such sessions in Spring 2001 covered orientation to instruction at the U of M, marketing, working with faculty, and planning an instructional session. Although the intention was to offer such topical sessions annually, the Steering Committee subsequently revised the plan to a two-year cycle. Reasons for the change included scheduling competition with other Instructor College sessions as well as other library events, the need to explore additional topics germane to instructor training, and a shortfall in the discretionary time of Steering Committee members to plan and produce events.

Session planning and aspects of curricular development for Academic Year 2001-02 took a somewhat different route. Working from internal survey data previously collected, the Steering Committee during Winter 2001 selected five areas for the potential focus of near-term programming. These were learning theory and design, assessment, technology, presentation skills and instructional content. Five task forces consisting of Contributing Members of the College plus liaisons from the Steering Committee were appointed and asked to examine each topic. Further, each task force was asked in its brief written report to recommend goals for its area and, if possible, to propose sessions that could achieve them. The five reports submitted in early Summer 2001 proved very useful, listing key concepts, outlining preferred outcomes and offering creative ideas based on thoughtful considerations.

The reports also furnished guidance to the Steering Committee regarding thematic directions to pursue in the near-term. Well aware that not all needs can be addressed at once, the Steering Committee carefully considered which thematic areas were of

—PATRICIA YOCUM, DOREEN BRADLEY, AND AMANDA FORRESTER—

greatest interest. The topics of assessment and presentation skills quickly emerged as prime candidates. Interest in assessment has been long-standing in the Library where it is often viewed as fundamental to teaching. In relation to library instruction, assessment includes determining user needs, evaluating instructional methods, and measuring instructional impact. Presentation skills, especially public speaking skills, were also seen as having priority while technology and its role in instruction would be given attention as opportunities appeared. These selections were further encouraged by the task force reports that identified specific U of M people as potential speakers, three of whom were subsequently invited to give presentations. In addition, four librarians, all members of Instructor College, served as featured speakers at various sessions.

Theme Sessions Presented

During Academic Year 2001-2002, Instructor College presented eight sessions. Actual planning and scheduling for most sessions fell to the Steering Committee with the exception of two sessions that were organized by the task force members who had proposed them. In addition to topics and speakers, the Steering Committee experimented with program format. For example, three of the fall sessions were presented in a formal manner. Sessions were two hours long, included pre-printed feedback forms, and attendees were asked to register in advance. Two sessions were held elsewhere on campus and generally there was a great deal of preparation involved. During Winter term, a brownbag format was adopted for all four sessions. These more relaxed events were one hour long, took place in a library classroom, busy attendees were encouraged to bring lunches, and there was no pre-registration, thus allowing for last minute decisions to attend. No formal feedback was requested.

A brief review of the sessions suggests the development of the themes the Steering Committee selected for focus and the variety of interpretations offered.

- "Outward Bound: Developing Web-based Training for a Global Community of Students" was a brownbag session offered by a member of Instructor College reporting on her experiment in developing an online tutorial using the latest software.

- "Instructional Presentations: Speaking with Style" was the first formal session offered in Fall 2001. The session featured practical techniques for giving effective instructional presentations and showed how these techniques can be applied using four different styles of communication.

- "Introduction to Assessment and Evaluation" was the next session and featured a specialist in instructional evaluation from the U of M Center for Research on Learning and Teaching who covered the fundamentals of the topic. A panel of librarians then provided practical examples of assessment activities undertaken at the U of M Library and discussed lessons they learned from the work.

- "Writing Effective Assessment Items" was the final Fall session. Led by a specialist from the U of M Medical School Office of Educational Resources and Research attendees explored the characteristics of "good" evaluation questions and learned what to avoid when designing assessment questions.

- "Easing into Assessment: Help for Early Steps", was the first Winter brownbag. Again featuring the evaluation specialist from CRLT, the session focused on the practical aspects of assessment and especially the construction of formative questions.

- "Snapping the Big Picture: Handling a Large-Scale Survey". Led by the Director of Advanced Academic Technology, Information Technology Campus Initiatives, U of M, the brownbag dealt with the user survey administered annually to either students or faculty at the U of M.

- "Designing Instructional Web Sites and Tutorials" featured a specialist from the Media Union Usability Lab who evaluated Web pages and tutorials volunteered by several Library instructors. Attendees could see real examples of what works well and what could be improved for Web pages that have been used in instruction sessions.

- "You and Your Research: Protecting Human Subjects", with a speaker from the Human Subjects Protection Office at the U of M, was the final brownbag of the academic year. The interactive discussion, covering University and Federal policies, explained the need for Institutional Review Board review and extended the exploration of user surveys in a critical area.

Full descriptions of the sessions as well as extensive presentation material are available on the Instructor College Web site.

The final event of the academic year will be an open meeting in early June 2002 with all members of the Instructor College in order to get feedback about the past year's events. The Steering Committee hopes to obtain constructive criticism in order to improve offerings and to gain insight into possible future activities for Instructor College.

Observations

Overall, it appears that Instructor College programming was quite successful. Organizers were able to tap many local experts, such as assessment specialists and education faculty, as session speakers. This was a very positive aspect for the College for a number of reasons. First, the sessions were of exceptionally high quality. Local experts were very willing to partake in our activities and expressed enthusiasm at the concept of an "instructor college." Additionally, College members could easily contact the speakers for individualized assistance subsequent to the sessions as several did, including members of the Steering Committee. Use of local experts also resulted in lower programming costs. Only one speaker charged a fee and that was significantly reduced from her standard fee. The College, of course, cannot rely solely on local experts working gratis to meet the needs of instructional staff, but on an experimental basis and as enrichment, the arrangement worked well.

Sessions typically were fairly well attended with participation averaging twenty-two for the more formal sessions and nineteen for the brownbags. Attendance was voluntary. With the exception of one highly specialized brownbag focused on survey research involving human subjects, almost half of the College members were present for each session throughout the year. Attendance of staff from several units such as those in the health sciences and basic sciences was consistently high. Staff turnout overall was encouraging for the Steering Committee, indicating that programming was accurately targeting staff needs. Feedback on session evaluation forms was also gratifying. College members rated all the sessions and presenters quite highly, with frequent requests that sessions be longer than two hours and some requests suggesting that sessions be repeated for staff whose scheduling conflicts made attending impossible.

One of the most significant, and perhaps unexpected, benefits to come from the College programming is the enthusiasm for networking which sessions provided. As evidenced from comments made to Steering Committee members as well as from feedback noted on evaluation forms, contact with Library colleagues is highly valued by instructional staff. Instructor College sessions provide a focused environment in which staff can exchange ideas, learn from each other, and share expertise. In this vein, the College appears to be fulfilling an important need for instructional staff.

Additional Activities

Program sessions were clearly the centerpiece of Instructor College activity but were not the only efforts undertaken. During the year, Instructor College added new features to its Website in an effort to add to the growing record of College events and to maintain a repository of helpful information for members. The Website includes links to information about the Instructor College curriculum, an explanation of membership and enrollment, a section on upcoming events, another section on past events, and a link to collections of print and electronic resources. Handouts and PowerPoint slides from generous program presenters have been added wherever possible. Including this material makes the information accessible to staff who are unable to attend a particular session, and for those who have attended a session but would like to go back and review content. [See http://www.lib.umich.edu/staff/icollege/]

Instructor College has also made print and electronic resources available through University Reserves (available only to U of M staff). Additionally, to further aid staff development the Library created an Instructor College Resource Center (ICRC) housing various instructional technology such as a TV, VCR, and video camera. The ICRC also included a PC with printer and network connection. It was hoped that this physical space within the Library would serve as a meeting place for instructors as well as a place for group work. The space, however, was not used extensively. It served primarily as a meeting place for the Steering Committee and as a workspace for a graduate student affiliate of Instructor College. Its low use answered an early question and suggests that in a heavily networked environment a physical meeting place is probably unnecessary. Indeed, when another Library unit needed office space, the ICRC was identified as a possibility and was dismantled in Spring 2002 after one year of service.

A more enduring contribution to Instructor College was that made to curricular development through the work of a student in the U of M School of Information who affiliated with the College for four months on a field placement. Certified to teach grades 7-12 social studies, the student drew upon her previous professional training and experience and applied the

—PATRICIA YOCUM, DOREEN BRADLEY, AND AMANDA FORRESTER—

perspective to the Instructor College setting. In addition to other contributions, she compiled highly selected reading lists tailored to the needs of working librarians and rich with curricular ideas.

Development Characterized

Instructor College opened with excitement and enthusiasm, not unlike the start of an academic year. Its second year has more closely resembled classes as they actually unfold, filled with content, opportunity to learn and try new things, and the realization of how much work is really needed. By focusing its resources, Instructor College in its second year has been able to explore in greater detail the themes selected, confirming that they are indeed core to a curriculum. If development of the College has been slower than some might have wished, it is also clear that the facets that have been developed have been of high quality and valued by the intended audience. Consistent feedback from session attendees and College members attest to the many successes and to the clear desire for Instructor College to continue.

Still an experiment and without a model to copy, the College looks forward to a third year filled with opportunities. Work at hand includes exploring matters such as programming (what to offer, how, and when), organizational structure (role of the Steering Committee, program planning and delivery, purpose and timing of college convocations), policy matters (the role of instruction in the library, curricular development, instructor proficiencies) and, finally, practical concerns (how to find time to study, learn and apply new knowledge). Precisely how Instructor College will proceed has yet to be determined. The evidence of the last two years suggests there is strong incentive to "to work out the details." The College continues to enjoy support from Library Administration and senior managers. Further, through their sustained expression of interest in Instructor College activities, Library instructors are voicing awareness of their need to develop their instructional skills and their willingness–indeed eagerness–to do so. Such strong grass-roots commitment augurs especially well for the future.

NOTES

1. *Webster's New Collegiate Dictionary*, 1977, s.v. "curriculum."

2. University of Michigan, "University Library Instructor College," brochure [undated].

3. Patricia Yocum, Laurie Alexander, Doreen Bradley, Laurie Sutch, and Robert Tolliver, "Instructor College: Staff Development For Library Instructors," in *Managing Instruction Programs in Academic Libraries, Proceedings of the 29th National LOEX Conference, Ypsilanti, Michigan, May 4 & 5, 2001* Pierian Press, Ann Arbor, MI, 2003.

PROMOTING COLLABORATION WITH FACULTY

Margaret Fain, Peggy Bates, and Robert Stevens

Introduction

How many librarians have said, "If I could just get with the professor before the assignment is made, then the students wouldn't be having these problems." At Coastal Carolina University, a state supported school of 4,500 students; this has been a recurring issue. To address this, collaboration has been established as the foundation of the library instruction program. This has lead to instruction librarians actively reaching out to faculty and working with them to create research components for their classes. Working with faculty has had many positive results. For librarians, it ensures that projects have been thought through and can be completed with the resources of the library. Class-tailored instruction sessions expose all students in the class to both the resources and the skills needed to complete projects. For faculty, the resulting papers or projects are more successful both in content and in citations. Faculty also use this opportunity to learn more about new resources and services in their discipline for their personal research. For students, it provides projects that can feasibly be accomplished. With librarians working so closely with professors, students now have an additional resource person who understands their assignment and the objectives of the professor and the class. The key is successful collaboration between faculty and librarians.

Fain, *Bates*, and *Stevens* are librarians at Coastal Carolina University, Conway, SC.

Objectives

This presentation will be covering successful and unsuccessful strategies for collaborating with faculty. Using the TRUST formula (Tact, Respect, Understanding, Support and Tenacity) and case studies, proactive strategies will be presented for developing trust, marketing services, engaging faculty, developing projects, negating resistance, and evaluating and revising projects. The end result of these efforts are research projects that meet the teaching needs of the class and engage students in meaningful research to develop their information literacy skills. These projects also foster an atmosphere of mutual respect and cooperation between faculty and librarians.

Collaboration

Collaboration is essential. It is the state where participants recognize common goals and work together achieving those goals. Collaborators must share the "give-and-take-listening that creates the bond of belonging to a learning community." [1] But in developing collaboration, there are misunderstandings on both sides. Faculty want research projects that meet the objectives of their class. Librarians are interested in research projects that develop information literate students. Faculty look at the needs of one particular class. Librarians look at developing skills and strategies that will enable students to succeed in all their classes. Many professors are not accustomed to sharing their classes. Librarians on the other hand, are quite good at sharing. Faculty know their disciplines and librarians know theirs. At the same time, students want interesting assignments that can be done with available resources. How do we reconcile the various outlooks?

The first step is to create conversation with faculty. Librarians must be pro-active, taking every opportunity to market themselves and their services to faculty. Rosemary Young and Stephena Harmony offer ten suggestions for faculty education that librarians should do to "become involved and highly visible campuswide." [2] These include:

- Meet new faculty one-on-one.
- Present library services at department or school meetings.
- Offer workshops for faculty or presentations at faculty retreats.
- Participate in brown-bag lunches or discussion groups.
- Get involved in centers for teaching excellence or with similar groups.
- Create research components for workshops.
- Write articles for journals that are not library-oriented publications.
- Attend cultural, athletic, and social events with faculty.
- Offer an on-campus "information literacy summer institute."

All of these ideas share a common theme—making librarians visible in the broader context of the institution and thus seen as active and involved partners in the many learning experiences and initiatives both inside and outside the classroom. Many of the best contacts and opportunities for "conversation" come from these casual interactions. Being involved in the academic life of the campus makes it easier to initiate the types of partnerships that are "necessary if students are to become effective independent learners." [3]

The second step is matching perceived needs with services and solutions. By creating conversation, breaking the ice so to speak, librarians open the door to a valuable exchange of ideas concerning the goals of the faculty member and how librarians can help them meet these goals. Discovering the needs and objectives of individual faculty up front is vital. Since librarians tend to see the larger picture on campus, they provide faculty with an awareness of how their research goals relate to the overall development of students as researchers and how their class assignments fit into the larger goals of the department or school. This allows librarians to make suggestions about ways to incorporate research skills in a class that build on the students' pre-existing knowledge.

The third step is to recognize the three distinct types of research assignments librarians encounter: reactive, cooperative, and collaborative. Reactive assignments do not exhibit any signs of collaboration

between faculty and librarians and are, unfortunately, very common. In a reactive assignment, the professor develops the assignment and the students are sent off to do it, often with no library instruction. The assignments can range from carefully thought out research projects to assignments that demonstrate a lack of familiarity with current resources and services. Librarians react to these assignments, interpreting them to students without knowing the objectives of the class or professor while attempting to determine which resources are best suited for the needs of the class and the student.

When librarians and faculty begin to talk, cooperative assignments result. The librarian may approach the professor or vice versa. Often the class syllabus is already set, but the research assignment is yet to be determined. Working together, they develop a project that satisfies the needs of the class within a cognitive framework that students can carry with them to other classes. In this spirit of cooperation, the librarian can offer suggestions for revising or developing assignments that will assist in obtaining the student outcomes desired for the class. With this type of cooperative assignment, course integrated instruction becomes a reality.

Collaborative assignments most often take place before the class is set. The librarian and the professor are engaged in a dialog before the objectives are set out. With the research needs of the students foremost, they design research projects that are directly related to the course and incorporate library instruction within the syllabus of the class. This allows the instruction to be timed to the work required of the class and may allow for working sessions to be set up in the library. Collaboration of this nature also increases feedback between the instructor and the librarian. The ability to discuss the progress of students in relation to the desired outcomes is an excellent assessment tool. The professor and librarian then have the ability to modify the project or outcomes based on student performance and then use that information to improve in the future.

Case study:

The professor teaching "Introduction to the Study of Language" wanted to re-design the course to make it more interesting and relevant to students. Inspired by a quote about learning everything from one thing, she thought that if each student took one word that meant something to them and researched that word through the course of the semester, applying the different linguistic approaches they would be studying to the word, the students might retain the principles better. The professor asked one of the librarians if this idea might be feasible. The librarian took the idea, tried it

—MARGARET FAIN, PEGGY BATES AND ROBERT STEVENS—

out, and then made additional suggestions to the professor. After this "trial run" the professor and librarian worked together using the class text and the resources of the library to design the "Word Study" project that, became an integral part of the class and has been successfully used for six years.

TRUST:

What does it take to create a library instruction program that fosters collaboration, which is beneficial to all involved? TRUST. TRUST is a formula that describes the necessary elements for creating and fostering a campus environment that allows collaboration to take place. The five elements of TRUST are Tact, Respect, Understanding, Support, and Tenacity. Using this formula, librarians can begin building a library instruction program that is responsive to the needs of its various constituencies and continually builds bridges to faculty and students alike.

TACT:

Tact is the art of diplomacy, the ability to make your point without belittling or challenging others. It is one of the most effective tools a librarian has when dealing with re-active assignments that are failing the student. Tact enables the librarian to suggest additional resources for an assignment or to suggest alternatives that might accomplish the goal with greater ease. Tact helps a librarian begin a dialog with a professor. Sometimes the dialog is repeated each semester with no change in the script. At other times, the dialog continues and the result is a cooperative assignment the next semester.

Tact is most often employed in approaching professors. The method of communication and language used will depend on several factors: the situation at hand, the discipline, the professor, the librarian involved and the pre-existing level of interpersonal contact. Every library and institution has its own culture. Understanding this culture assists in determining who needs to be contacted, who does the contacting, what medium (phone, e-mail, in person) and what approaches work best. In an informal atmosphere where the librarians know the faculty, a phone call might work best. In other situations, it might be an e-mail, combined with a follow-up call.[4]

Decide what works best for the library instruction department. Does just the library instruction coordinator initiate contact or can anyone do so who perceives the need? Keep in-house communication open to meet any problems head on and to ensure that a professor isn't deluged by "helpful" calls from the entire library instruction department. While experienced instruction librarians may not be daunted in dealing with faculty, new librarians often need coaching and assistance. The Library Instruction Coordinator should make sure that new librarians are given opportunities to develop effective methods and techniques for contacting faculty.

Case study:

Every semester it happens, the librarians begin talking about what went on at the desk the day and evening before and then realization hits, everyone has been dealing with the same troublesome assignment. Notes are made, a copy of the "problem" assignment is obtained if possible, and one person is delegated to make the call. There is no script, but it usually goes something like this "Prof. X, this is ....in the library, do you have a minute? Great, we have been helping some students from your class and aren't sure we are helping them find the right things, could you tell me what their assignment is? The students say they need to know what Coastal will be like in 50 years. What types of things are you looking for?" The conversation progresses from there. We'll offer suggestions if it's appropriate and usually offer an instruction session, if it's too late for this semester then next semester, and we make sure we follow up. Several ongoing instruction sessions have been established from these calls, especially with new faculty. They are usually stunned that someone else cares what happens to their students. Even if all it accomplishes is to give the professor a heads up on potential problems, the response to these calls has been positive.

With tact, librarians can use every misdirected assignment as an education opportunity. Be diplomatic and helpful. Let the faculty member know about new databases that can be incorporated into the assignment. Ask them to consider using specific sources in addition to the ones suggested. Phrase conversations with remarks about "new" services, even if they are three years old. Inquire about their desired outcome, what is it that they want the students to learn from the assignment. Constantly stress the desire to help their students succeed. Let the faculty know what you can do for them. Call faculty and then follow up with an e-mail. Begin building the dialog as soon as possible by solving, as best as possible, the problem at hand. At the end of the semester, ask how it turned out. Were the faculty's expectations met? What can the library do to help meet those expectations next semester?

RESPECT:

Respect and tact are mutually reaffirming. Librarians and faculty need to respect each other as colleagues and respect each other's areas of expertise in order to develop successful collaborations. Librarians must keep in mind that while it is "their" library, it is not "their" class. Ultimately, faculty make the final choice about whether or not to utilize the library for their students. Mutual respect, developed over time means getting to know faculty on a professional and personal level.

In instruction sessions, respect the faculty member's authority over the content of the class. Ask direct questions to the professor during the session regarding the topic, the assignment or to clarify the subject. Before the session, encourage the professor to reinforce what the librarian is saying. The most successful sessions occur when the librarian and the professor feel comfortable adding to each other's statements or comments. At the same time, the librarian is demonstrating their knowledge about library resources in the context of the class topic. When respect is present, the librarian and professor work as a team to get students fired up about research.

Case study:

Forty percent of library instruction sessions taught at Coastal Carolina University are for the first year English sequence, where composition is taught in the Fall and literature in the Spring. Several years ago, text requirements were dropped, so each professor designs his or her own unique assignments and class requirements, ranging from popular fiction to media studies. Consequently, instruction sessions had to change as well. Each session covers the same library resources, but in a manner tailored to the specific needs of the class. Because of this, the key to a great session is the participation of the professor in the instruction session. To get faculty to take a more active role in the sessions, they had to be encouraged and supported. We began asking them more questions about their assignment, their required sources, and what evidence of research they were looking for. As they got used to this, the more enthusiastic began to interject comments when they were excited about something the librarian said. Rather than upsetting the librarian, this was seen as reinforcement for the students. After a few sessions, faculty stopped apologizing for interrupting once they realized that this give and take was both expected and accepted. This in-class interaction has lead to increased communication and collaboration on research

assignments for these classes and the sessions are just more fun for everyone.

Librarians also need to respect students. If viewed as partners in research rather than passive recipients, students rise to the challenge. Make sure students know that librarians are there to help them succeed, to assist them in being the best that they can or want to be. Respect for the student allows the librarian to really listen to what the student is saying, not jumping ahead to what we think the student is saying. Students know what they want, but often they just cannot articulate it. Asking leading questions that encourage the student to re-state their needs enables them to see the issues more clearly.

UNDERSTANDING:

From respect comes understanding. Faculty, students, and librarians, are all in this together. Try to establish common ground with faculty. Don't they dislike reading the same essays year in and year out? So, do we. Librarians must let faculty know what drives them to create instruction programs and what the expected outcomes are. In turn, librarians need to understand faculty better: what are their teaching objectives, what passions drive them. Librarians need to take or create opportunities to get to know faculty better. In turn, these opportunities let faculty know us better.

Inform faculty about the goals and objectives of your library instruction program. What are the outcomes the librarians are striving toward? Use assessment to demonstrate how these goals fit in with their goals and with campus wide student outcomes. When discussing timing of sessions or the need for follow-up, draw on research for your supporting arguments. If we don't inform faculty about what we are trying to accomplish, no one will.

Understanding the objectives for a class makes it much easier to make constructive suggestions. The instruction sessions can be personalized for the class and the professor, increasing the relevance for students. The language of the instruction session can incorporate the class objectives creating a more coherent whole.

Knowing what faculty expect from their students is another key to understanding. What is their perception of what students can accomplish in research? What level of effort or skill is the professor expecting from the class? Are faculty expectations evolving as student abilities evolve? What will the students be doing next in their academic careers, what skills should they be bringing to upper level courses? Some of the most productive conversations about instruction have come from asking these questions to faculty.

—MARGARET FAIN, PEGGY BATES AND ROBERT STEVENS—

Case Study:

The professor teaching the senior level capstone research class in a small department was frustrated. The students weren't producing the papers they should have been, their citations were poor, and their research was minimal. Before the class began, he had talked with several librarians about structuring the research component of the class. They had offered suggestions and provided models based on what was working in other disciplines. They had read over his assignment, made a few more suggestions and then had done a library instruction session early in the semester and provided support to the few students who had come back in and asked for help. What happened? It took a casual question to identify the problem, "what research projects have students done before they take this class?" The answer was none. It was a new major, recreation, with many part-time faculty, and no one had ever asked the students to do any type of library related research before they were seniors. The students had so much to learn in their final year that they could not do it. After this conversation, more ensued. The librarians began working with the professor to help design research assignments for the lower level classes that would teach them the basic skills they would then expand on in the upper level classes. The results of this collaboration are not yet apparent as it was recently implemented, but informal feedback from all the teaching staff involved is being gathered to see where revisions will need to be made. The impetus for this collaboration was several years in the making, starting with just one class, but if it is successful, students in this major will be developing the information literacy skills they will need to use after graduation.

SUPPORT:

Support comes on many levels. To have a successful library instruction program, support is needed from administration, participating librarians, as well as faculty who use the program. Faculty who are happy with the results of instruction sessions continue to include instruction in their classes and recommend the same to colleagues. Support should also be present in a broader sense. Reach out to faculty who have been uninterested in discussing instruction through their research needs. Talk with them about their research, inquire into their progress, and be genuinely interested. Offer to track down obscure citations or verify references. Through department liaison activities, notify faculty of new materials or alert them to articles or publications in their area. Talk to faculty about their classes. If there is a class

that has been having problems with it's research assignments, ask the professor if they are satisfied with the results. If the professor isn't happy with student performance, discuss ways to improve the assignment so it meets the professor's objectives. Don't dwell on the problem, present possible solutions. It is easier to 'sell' classes and services if the professor already has a favorable impression.

Always be prepared. Have alternative research suggestions ready. Give faculty some general ideas to think about while you are pulling together something more concrete. Offering a variety of ideas enables the librarian to see which ones are most appealing to the professor. Ask if there are, things they'd like to do with their class, but haven't had time to investigate further. Offer to try out the assignment. Listen to their comments and build on their interests. Never be shy about offering alternatives to current assignments, especially if you can show that it worked elsewhere.

Support for faculty can also come from letting them know what other faculty in their discipline are doing with student research projects. In some situations, librarians may have a better idea of what is being done in regards to research in a discipline than the faculty do. Let them know what students should have experienced by the time they reach their class and what their class is preparing students to do next.

Case Study:

The English Professor was concerned. The students in his upper level English class weren't using the scholarly journals in the field and were relying too heavily on the Internet. Passing through the Reference Office, he asked what was wrong with his students. The librarians pointed out a very simple fact; the students did not know what the journals were. In all probability, few of the students previously had any library related instruction in searching for scholarly resources because very few English faculty were using library instruction with their upper level classes. Without knowing about the journal literature in the field or knowing the indexes to use to find the journals, the students were obviously using what they knew best. A passing remark lead to a half-hour discussion of what the library and librarians could do to help the professor the next time the course was taught. Knowing what was and was not being done in other classes, knowing the expectations of the professor, and knowing how students conduct research, enabled the librarians present to offer solutions that would work for the class.

Support faculty by keeping them up-to-date with what is going on with technology and access developments in their discipline. Keep up continuing education for faculty, both formal and informal. Offer workshops, one-on-one training, send out updates and solicit response. Go to faculty. Demonstrate new databases or services in their offices on their computers. Let faculty know that you are there to assist them and to assist their students. Begin to develop a history of collaboration.

TENACITY:

Tenacity is persistence—never giving up. Tenacity is taking advantage of every opportunity that presents itself. It is approaching faculty openly regarding instruction opportunities. When they say no, tenacity is approaching them when the assignment doesn't work and the students are frustrated and offering suggestions. When they still say no, tenacity is following up when the assignment is turned in and asking about the quality of the papers and if the desired result was achieved, offering again to do instruction next semester, just to see if it might help. Tenacity takes the final yes and keeps following up to make sure that the instruction did help, to see what could be improved further.

Case Study:

We thought the first, second and third student had misheard the professor. It made no sense, to us, to require that students only use paper, bound, or microfilmed journals. It's a small library and full-text databases had enabled us to expand our journal holdings in all disciplines. Yet, according to the students, the professor would not accept any electronic format journals. A call was made to clarify the assignment with the professor. The students were correct, no electronic journals. We explained the situation in the library and encouraged the professor to amend the requirements and offered an instruction session to help the students make sure they were locating "real" journals. He'd think about it.

The next semester we offered an instruction session and it was accepted. The librarian teaching the session made sure to go over how to find paper and electronic journal issues and the differences between the Internet and databases. Verbally, the professor agreed that electronic journals were okay, but the language on the assignment sheet stayed the same. More calls were made and the situation became sneaky, students discovered that if they printed out journal articles in PDF formats; the professor never said anything because the printouts looked like the "real" thing. This went on for three years. The professor never changed the language, but accepted electronic journal articles if they didn't look like computer print. Every semester the librarian doing

the instruction session for the class went over the same information about the different formats of journals and we continued to have to call to verify that indeed the electronic format was okay for journals he challenged. We never succeeded in changing his mind, but we succeeded in getting him to allow students to use the materials they needed through personal intervention and librarian authentication of their sources. In the fourth year, the class was restructured and the new professor has no problems with journal articles in any format, as long as the students were finding them. Instruction sessions for the class continued, but the many personal phone calls did not.

Tenacity is trying every approach imaginable, in subtle and unsubtle ways. It is promoting instruction services at committee meetings, lunches, social gatherings, classes, anywhere it fits into the conversation. Instruction librarians will use every casual remark as a teaching opportunity. Informal conversations often reap great rewards. You never know what you will hear, if you just listen. Librarians may need to approach faculty from different angles, using two or three librarians to make the point.

Once an instruction session has been agreed on or an assignment has been revised, librarians need to follow up and ask questions. Formal or informal assessment is essential. Did the students do better? Is the professor pleased with the results? What can be done to improve the session next semester? Feedback from professors and from students will enable the librarian to correct weaknesses and improve on strengths of the instruction session. Don't be afraid to work with the assignment and the professor to change things around. Keep trying new approaches and experiment until the desired outcome is reached.

Tenacity is optimism in the face of recalcitrant faculty. There are some faculty for whom library instruction will never be a priority for their students. Librarians need to adjust to faculty who will not change and do everything possible to assist their students without belittling the instructor. This goes back to TACT and brings the formula full circle.

Conclusion:

Initiating, developing, and sustaining a collaborative-based instruction program is too big for one person. The entire instruction team has to be involved. Every librarian involved in instruction should be willing to work with faculty to develop collaborative projects. They need to initiate and develop collaborative relationships that carry over into the design and creation of library instruction sessions. Librarians also need the support of the Library Instruction Coordinator or area head to have the time to

—MARGARET FAIN, PEGGY BATES AND ROBERT STEVENS—

develop both the relationships and the ensuing sessions. A supportive atmosphere, on all levels, within and without the library is essential for a collaborative instruction program to thrive.

With TRUST as a central focus of the library instruction program, librarians can begin to develop better collaboration opportunities with faculty and students. Collaboration doesn't happen overnight. It is developed through a series of small steps, one faculty at a time, each interaction building on the next. Faculty, who are happy with the results of their collaborative efforts, talk with colleagues and spread the word. Librarians who are visible on campus and are active participants in the academic community reinforce the positive message. Librarians who take the initiative will find that collaboration is both achievable and desirable.

NOTES

1. Dick Raspa and Dane Ward, "Listening for Collaboration: Faculty and Librarians Working Together," in *The Collaborative Imperative: Librarians and Faculty Working Together in the Information Universe* (Chicago: Association of College and Research Libraries, 2000), 5

2. Rosemary Young and Stephana Harmony, *Working with Faculty to Design Undergraduate Information Literacy Programs: A How-to-do-it Manual for Librarians* (New York: Neal-Schuman, 1999), 21-25.

3. Lynn Mullins, "Partnerships in Information Teaching and Learning: Building a Collaborative Culture in the University Community," *New Jersey Libraries* 26, no. 1 (1993): 19.

4. Shellie Jeffries, "The Librarian as Networker: Setting the Standard of Higher Education," in *The Collaborative Imperative: Librarians and Faculty Working Together in the Information Universe,* ed. Dick Raspa and Dane Ward (Chicago: Association of College and Research Libraries, 2000), 118-119.

TALKING WITH FACULTY AND ADMINISTRATORS: USING NUMBERS TO DEMONSTRATE THE VALUE OF BIBLIOGRAPHIC INSTRUCTION

Barbara J. Cockrell

Introduction

Many faculty and administrators do not consciously recognize the importance of teaching the intricacies of the information research process at the college level.[1] Many assume that students bring expertise with them from high school and that anything not already learned can be easily mastered. The notion that everything is now readily accessible on the Web, and the fact that many faculty received no formal instruction themselves in online information retrieval contribute to this view. Most take their own research skills for granted and overlook the advantages that experience and maturity lend to the task. Furthermore many can afford to shortcut the research process in their own field because of their knowledge of significant issues and players. Coupled with this is a tendency of administrators, faculty and students to equate the library with a building, books and a dated perspective on how research *was* done, rather than fully appreciating its continuing role within the online information environment. The standards, performance indicators, and outcomes presented in the ACRL's *Information Literacy Competency Standards for Higher Education*[2] address these issues, but librarians still need to sell these ideas on their own campuses.

A part of educating faculty and administrators about information literacy includes demonstrating the need for teaching these skills and measuring and communicating the resulting outcomes.[3] Documenting

Cockrell is the Science Reference Librarian at Western Michigan University, Kalamazoo, MI.

the library research skills of incoming engineering students, together with post-BI evaluations and assessments produced data that provided opportunities to engage in informed dialog about the role of information literacy with faculty and administrators in the University community.

Background

Western Michigan University (WMU) is a Doctoral/Research—Extensive University with an expanding Engineering College. Technical Communications is a required introductory writing class for all Engineering majors and is the recommended writing class for all science students in the honors college. Each academic year approximately 675 freshman-engineering students are enrolled in 25-30 sections of a Technical Communications class that is taught by approximately eight instructors. Approximately two-thirds of the students take this class in the Fall semester and the rest in Winter. It is the libraries' major contact with engineering and science freshmen and for many of these students is the only formalized library instruction they receive as undergraduates at WMU. The course has several library-related components that include investigating the technical literature, researching companies and careers, evaluating periodicals and Web sites, abstracting an article, preparing a bibliography and writing a research paper.

When I became responsible for the library component of this class in 1999, the students came to the library for a single 50-minute or 75-minute session referred to as the 'library tour.' I was keen to introduce information literacy concepts and employ active learning in the library's electronic classroom. I called a group meeting with the class coordinator and instructors, which confirmed that their primary concern was that I teach their students how to research for scholarly articles. In addition, they wanted an overview of the library's organization, and direction to some specific resources and indexes for particular assignments.

Turning Class Evaluations into BI Modifications

Student evaluations of these single sessions revealed enthusiastic endorsement of the hands-on elements, with 25 of 117 students (21%) writing this in as the most helpful part of the session even though there was often very little time available for it. At the same time "too fast" was the most frequent comment (8%) about what was most confusing. This feedback enabled me to return to the instructors with a list of learning objectives that drew from our previous meeting (Appendix 1), plus a prospective hands-on class assignment, and a request to meet for two library sessions per section. The first session would introduce the library and discuss its online and print resources in the context of the peer review process and the Web in general, while the second session would be almost entirely given to hands-on experimentation and research in article indexes. Most of the instructors agreed to this new format and over the next two years I continued to use the student evaluations to modify and improve the sessions. This included developing an online class guide[4] to consolidate materials and free up more class time for discussion, learning activities and hands-on experimentation. I also revised the class worksheet to better break down the process of article searching into its component parts. While the students worked through this, the class instructor and I would rove around the electronic classroom providing one-on-one input about topic suitability and searching strategies, drawing one another into the conversation as necessary or helpful.

Class evaluations of the two-session format indicated high success in accomplishing the objectives for the class with student performance and confidence generally improving over the single BI session. More than one-third of the class specifically cited the hands-on time or individual help as the most useful component of the sessions and the class instructors also greeted the new format with enthusiasm.

Need for Pre-BI Data

Despite this, during Winter 2001 there was some pressure to return to a single BI session. The library

electronic classroom was in high demand and tying it up for two sessions caused scheduling difficulties for other classes requesting library sessions. Some of the Technical Communications instructors felt they could not devote two sessions to the library as they had a lot of additional material to cover. Some questioned if it was necessary to spend time comparing the peer review process with the Internet in the first session or to devote almost the entire second session to hands-on time. Was it possible to combine all this into a single session (return to where we started)?

Faced with these issues I realized that I needed to know more about the experience and knowledge that these freshmen students brought to this class from high school. Interactions with students at the reference desk and in class had led me to think they would find it useful to spend time considering why the instructor wanted them to utilize article indexes rather than other information sources for their paper; and that aspiring engineers would learn a lot from actually experimenting with how the indexes functioned. Perhaps these were unnecessary extras or merely self-evident. Although the post-BI class evaluations were high, maybe the students came to my sessions already familiar with these ideas and did not need to spend more time on them. If I knew more about the mind set of students coming into the sessions, I could collaborate more constructively both with them and their class instructors.

The Pre-BI Questionnaire

I received approval from the Human Subjects Institutional Review Board and the instructors to administer two forms of a pre-BI questionnaire to 75-minute sections of the Technical Communications classes in Fall and Winter 2001. Both forms had ten questions, nine of which were identical multiple-choice alternatives concerning demographics, the number of previous library instruction sessions students had experienced and their feelings about researching for the class paper (Appendix 2). Question 10 of Form A asked students which of several specific library information skills they had been taught. Question 10 of Form B was open-ended, asking the student "How do you typically gather information for a class paper? Include any specific sources, interfaces or strategies". Form B did not prompt the students by presenting options. Students completed either Form A or Form B during the first ten minutes of the first class BI session. Many students in Fall 2001 took the questionnaire within the first month of coming to WMU during their first work-related visit to the University library.

—BARBARA J. COCKRELL—

Summarizing the Results

I was able to illustrate the main results using simple bar charts, some of which are included below. While the Fall class was composed entirely of incoming freshmen from the U.S. (94% from Michigan) the Winter class was much more variable. This contained 28% upper classmen, 15% repeat students and 11% international students, primarily from Malaysia, India and the Middle East. Whereas 90% of the Fall students had never used WMU libraries before, 69% of the Winter class had. These differences between Fall and Winter reflect the way the classes are filled and are quite usual from year to year. Clearly these different constituencies have different needs. The extended hands-on session provides one way of meeting them.

Fewer than 10% of all the freshmen felt "very confident" about the prospect of finding information for their paper. Overall the U.S. freshmen were more confident than their international counterparts but even so approximately one-third of the U.S. freshmen, and half the international freshmen were "somewhat apprehensive/concerned." More international students were overwhelmed/worried (19%) than their U.S. counterparts (4%). Responses to this question are important because of the documented impact that library anxiety has on procrastination and its negative feedback on performance[5]. One of the main reasons I value working with this class is the opportunity to help students starting in college to avoid these problems.

For some, library anxiety related to lack of previous BI (Figure 1). More than half (54%) the international students reported they had received no library instruction at the high school level although one quarter of them had received some instruction at WMU (generally from an instructor in an English language skills course). In comparison, all but 15 of the 271 U.S. students reported having library instruction in high school, most (40%) had experienced between three and five sessions while 10% had more than five sessions.

In general high numbers of the U.S. students indicated they had been taught many of the skills listed in Question 10, Form A (Figure 2). Notable exceptions were searching print and online article indexes both of which had been taught to fewer than 50% of the U.S. Fall and Winter classes. Even lower was 'Use of Boolean Operators' although in this case I suspect that if I had asked about using AND or OR in searches more would have responded in the affirmative. Fewer than 50% U.S. Winter students indicated they had been taught how to select appropriate materials following a search.

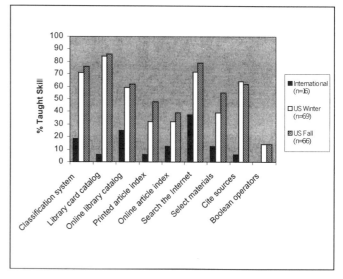

FIGURE 2: PERCENT OF STUDENTS IN TECHNICAL COMMUNICATIONS WHO HAD PREVIOUSLY BEEN TAUGHT SPECIFIC LIBRARY SKILLS.

The international students had received little instruction in any of the listed skills. The highest response was that 39% had been taught to search the Internet. More than 70% of the U.S. Fall and Winter students also indicated they had been taught to search the Internet, each semester this was second only to the number of students who had been taught to search the library catalog.

Even when library skills were taught, they may remain unfamiliar or unused. The results of Question 10, Form B that asked students to name the sources or strategies they typically used to gather information for a class paper suggested heavy reliance on the Internet. Only three international students filled out this question but all three cited the Internet, one together with books, one together with encyclopedias and one with journals. More than 50% of the U.S. students listed the Internet in their response to this question, approximately double

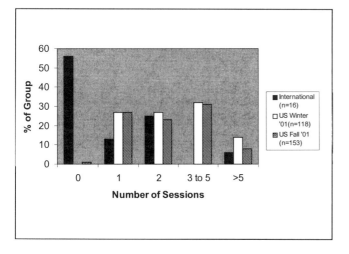

FIGURE 1: PREVIOUS HIGH SCHOOL AND COLLEGE-LEVEL LIBRARY INSTRUCTION SESSIONS OF FRESHMAN STUDENTS IN TECHNICAL COMMUNICATIONS CLASSES.

the number of students that listed any other single source (Figure 3).

Only 5% of these incoming fall freshmen indicated that the type of information source they would use would depend on the assignment and only 2% of all the students specifically mentioned credibility with respect to Internet sites. One fifth of those who indicated the Internet in response to this question in both Fall and Winter did not mention any other sources (Figure 3) while approximately the same percentages coupled it with either encyclopedias or books. Comparatively few students (7%) mentioned the Internet together with articles only, although more than one-third of the fall students indicated they used a combination of the Internet, books, and articles. (These were largely the individuals who had received multiple high school BI sessions). Considerably fewer of the winter freshmen (17%) indicated this combination.

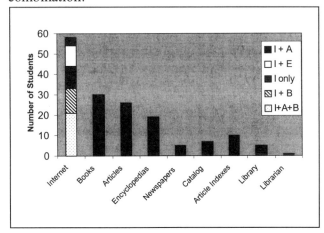

FIGURE 3: RESOURCES THAT 87 TECHNICAL COMMUNICATIONS STUDENTS INDICATED THEY TYPICALLY USED FOR INFORMATION FOR A CLASS PAPER. THE INTERNET CATEGORY IS BROKEN INTO CONSTITUENT PARTS ACCORDING TO OTHER RESOURCES THAT WERE MENTIONED TOGETHER WITH IT.
(I = INTERNET, A = ARTICLES OR ARTICLE INDEXES, E = ENCYCLOPEDIAS, B = BOOKS).

Fewer than 10% of students responded to the questions with anything that resembled a search strategy. Some responses included: "Usually I start with the Internet then wander around the library and hope I can find some books." "I do not have any strategies but I usually somehow end up on the Internet." "I normally use an encyclopedia and a Web site or two. The rest I write from my own knowledge of the subject." The response "I fly by the seat of my pants," though maybe written in jest seemed a accurate description for many.

Using the Results

These kinds of results are not especially surprising to librarians.[6] Through interacting with students we already know much of this and more. However, the focus of this presentation is not so much on these particular results but on the need to gather this kind of information. To maintain or hopefully increase our instructional role in the academic community we need to clearly document students needs, what we can do to enhance student learning, and the outcomes we can facilitate (e.g. Figure 4). We need to share this information with faculty and administrators who do not work in our field and who may not be familiar with the term "information literacy," many of whom will be more concerned with specialized areas of higher education than about skills that directly translate into enhanced learning across all areas.

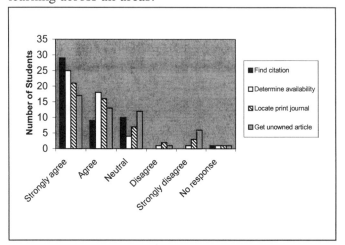

FIGURE 4: SELF-ASSESSMENT SKILLS BY 50 TECHNICAL COMMUNICATIONS STUDENTS FOLLOWING LIBRARY INSTRUCTION.

At a time when academic institutions are universally concerned about outcomes assessment we have an opportunity to provide evidence that supports what we do and recognizes its integral role in higher education. Academic institutions are charged with demonstrating that their programs are effective, that the education they offer is transferable into the workforce and into lifelong learning[7]. The concepts and skills that we teach are fundamental to this. We can demonstrate that many students lack the information-gathering skills and knowledge that many faculty assume they possess. We can show that library sessions can result in enhanced skills and confidence that feed back into academic success and are directly transferable to the workplace and beyond.[8]

—BARBARA J. COCKRELL—

Sharing Findings to Influence Change

Change can occur from the bottom up through collaborations with individual faculty and from the top down at the programmatic and institutional levels. Sharing these particular results with the Technical Communications instructors had unforeseen outcomes that were valuable in both these directions. Although I had routinely conducted class evaluations throughout our collaboration, previously I had viewed them as personal, a measure of my own teaching performance rather than as evaluating the effectiveness of what the instructor and I had agreed to try to achieve. Communicating the outcomes completed the collaborative process by allowing the instructors back into the picture. They were very interested in the results that demonstrated what I was trying to achieve and most of the instructors readily acknowledged the value of continuing with two class sessions.

The dialog also helped me understand more about their program and led me to share some of these findings with the faculty member responsible for accreditation in the Engineering College. This has opened channels of discussion about additional ways that the library can integrate into the Engineering Program. This individual is also a member of the University Accreditation Task Force and so a door is opened at the institutional level.

I also shared my findings with our instructional librarian and library administration so they could make use of them in lobbying at the top for greater emphasis on information literacy and clear acknowledgment of the library's role in the education process. We plan to include some of these results on our library's Information Literacy Web pages this summer to help illustrate why faculty need to address this issue. I am hoping it may be possible to present some of this information (perhaps as a poster session) at new faculty orientation in the Fall.

Communicating Effectively

In communicating with faculty and administration about information literacy, I have found the following helpful:

- Documenting the situation at your own institution speaks more clearly than pointing to other published studies. Use them together when you have administrators' attention.
- Figures and charts speak to most administrators more clearly than anecdote and supposition, even if based on years of experience.
- Go through departments' accreditation standards to identify areas where the library can

contribute. Mock up prototype suggestions for discussion purposes.
- Simplify and translate and the ACRL Information Literary standards into the department's terminology. Don't expect non-librarians to work through the ACRL document.
- Don't undervalue what you do and the skills you can teach, nor assume that your role in the educational process is obvious. Instead spell this out in terms of standards and outcomes.

NOTES

1. Gloria J. Leckie and Anne Fullerton, "Information Literacy in Science & Engineering Undergraduate Education: Faculty Attitudes and Pedagogical Practices at the University of Waterloo and the University of Western Ontario," *College & Research Libraries* 60, no. 1 (January 1999): 9-29; Gloria J. Leckie, "Desperately Seeking Citations: Uncovering Faculty Assumptions about the Undergraduate Research Process," *Journal of Academic Librarianship* 22 (May 1996): 201-208.

2. Association of College and Research Libraries, *Information Literacy Competency Standards for Higher Education* (Chicago: American Library Assn., 2000). Available: http://www.ala.org/acrl/ilintro.html. Accessed 15 April 2002.

3. Julie L. Rabine and Catherine Cardwell, "Start Making Sense: Practical Approaches to Outcomes Assessment for libraries," *Research Strategies* 17, no. 4 (2000): 319-335; Kenneth R. Smith, "New Roles and Responsibilities for the University Library: Advancing Student Learning through Outcomes Assessment," *Measurements of Research Libraries*, 213 (December 2000). Available:http://www.arl.org/newsltr/meas.html. Accessed 15 April 2002; also other articles at that site; ACRL *Task Force on Academic Library Outcomes Assessment Report* (Chicago: American Library Association., 27 June 1998). Available: http://www.ala.org/acrl/outcome.html. Accessed 15 April 2002.

4. The IME 102 Technical Communications Online Class Guide is at: http://www.wmich.edu/library/handouts/ime102.html.

5. Constance A Mellon, "Library Anxiety: A Grounded Theory and Its Development," *College & Research Libraries* 47 (March 1986): 160-165. Also Anthony John Onwuegbuzie, "I'll Go to the Library Later: the Relationship between Academic Procrastination and Library Anxiety," *College & Research Libraries* 61, no. 1 (Jan.2000): 45-54.

6. Philip M.Davis, "The Effect of the Web on Undergraduate Citation Behavior: A 2000 update," *College & Research Libraries* 63, no. 1 (Jan 2002): 53-60. Also Deborah J. Grimes and Carl H. Boening, "Worries with the Web: A Look at Student Use of Web Resources," *College & Research Libraries* 62, no. 1 (Jan 2001): 11-23. Additional background in *The Internet and Education: Findings of the Pew Internet & American Life Project* (Washington: Pew research Center). Available: http://www.pewinternet. org/reports/index.asp. Accessed 15 April 2002.

7. Peter Hernon & Robert E. Dugan, *An Action Plan for Outcomes Assessment in Your Library* (Chicago: American Library Assn., 2002); See also note 3 above.

8. Gloria J. Leckie, Karen E. Pettigrew & Christian Sylvain, "Modeling the Information Seeking of Professionals: A General Model Derived from Research on Engineers, Health Care Professionals, and Lawyers", *The Library Quarterly* 66 (Apr. 1996): 161-93; Maurita P. Holland & Christina K. Powell, "A Longitudinal Survey of the Information Seeking and Use Habits of Some Engineers," *College & Research Libraries* 56 (Jan. 1995): 7-15.

APPENDIX 1: LEARNING OBJECTIVES FOR THE B.I. COMPONENT OF IME 102 TECHNICAL COMMUNICATIONS

1. Increased understanding of and expertise in information retrieval and research for this field.

2. Increased confidence and expertise in utilizing WMU libraries for research needs.

3. Awareness of the kinds of information sources that are available (web sites, books, popular and scholarly articles etc.) and their relative appropriateness for different kinds of information needs.

4. Awareness of WMU libraries' resources (both print and online) and their value in answering particular research needs.

5. Familiarity with the physical organization of WMU's libraries (particularly Library of Congress call numbering, Science Reference desk, current periodicals, general stacks).

6. Orientation to pages on the libraries' web site where information relevant to Engineers and IME 102 has been consolidated.

7. Understanding the role of WestCat and the basics of using it to locate books and journals.

8. Appreciating the role and array of article indexes to locate various types of articles.

9. Knowing the rudiments about how an article index database operates and recognizing that how a search is constructed will influence the quality of what is retrieved.

10. Familiarity with using one or more of the First Search indexes relevant to Engineering, including using symbols and combining terms to refine searches, printing and e-mailing output and making Interlibrary loan requests

—BARBARA J. COCKRELL—

Appendix 2: The Pre-B.I. Questionnaire. Two forms of this questionnaire were made. Each form either had Question 10A or had Question 10B

IME 102 Library Questionnaire – *For questions 1-9* **_circle all answers that apply_**

1) Which year are you?   **Freshman   Sophomore   Junior   Senior   Non-traditional student**

2) What is your Major?   **Engineering (specify which) _____   Other (Specify) _____**

3) Are you: **From Michigan   Out of state   From another country**

4) Are you taking IME 102:   **For the First Time   Repeat**

5) Which of the following best describes how you feel about finding information for writing a paper for this class?
Very confident   OK   Somewhat apprehensive/concerned   Overwhelmed/worried

6) Have you used WMU libraries before?   **No   Yes**

7) Where have you had instruction about finding information previously? (Circle all that apply)

WMU   Another college/university   High school   Middle school   Elementary school   Nowhere

8) If you had **_high school_** library instruction was it from? (circle all that apply)   **a librarian   a teacher**

9) How many library instruction sessions have you attended in high school and at the college level combined ?
    0   1   2   3–5   more than 5

Either
FORM A 10) Which of the following were you taught? (check all that apply)

The library's classification system (e.g. Dewey Decimal or Library of Congress)

To use a library card catalog

To use an online library catalog

To use a printed article index (e.g. Readers Guide)

To use a web-based article index (e.g. InfoTrac)

To search the Internet

To select appropriate materials after performing a search

To cite references/sources in a particular style

Use of Boolean operators (connectors) when searching electronically

Or
FORM B 10) How do **_you_** gather the information you need to write a class paper? If there are any particular sources, interfaces or strategies that you typically use please name them.

Thanks for your input.

PARTICIPANTS

Tiff Adkins
Walter E. Helmke Library
Indiana Univ. Purdue Univ.
Fort Wayne
2101 E. Coliseum Blvd.
Fort Wayne, IN 46805-1499

Laurie Alexander
Univ Lib/Administration
818 Hatcher Graduate Lib
920 North University
Ann Arbor, MI 48109-1205

Sara Anderson
Library
Northfield Mount Hermon
School
Box 4111, 206 Main Street
Northfield, MA 01360

Helene Androski
Memorial Library
University of Wisconsin
Madison
728 State St.
Madison, WI 53706

Judith Arnold
Drinko Library
Marshall University
1 John Marshall Drive
Huntington, WV 25755

Nicole Auer
University Libraries
Virginia Tech
PO Box 90001
Blacksburg, VA 24060

Randal Baier
Halle Library
Eastern Michigan University
Ypsilanti, MI 49187

Jenifer Baldwin
Library
Drexel University
33rd & Market Streets
Philadelphia, PA 19104

Mary Barbosa-Jerez
University of Louisville
2301 South Third Street
Ekstrom Library, Reference
Dept.
Louisville, KY 40292

Lisa Barnett
Bracken Library
Ball State University
Muncie, IN 47306

Mary Ann Barton
Calvin T. Ryan Library
University of Nebraska
Kearney
2508 11th Ave.
Kearney, NE 68849

Susan Beck
University Library
MSC 3475 Box 30006
Las Cruces, NM 88003

Goodie Bhullar
Ellis Library
University of Missouri
Columbia, MO 65201

Deb Biggs Thomas
WCC Library
Washtenaw Community
College
4800 E. Huron River Drive
Ann Arbor, MI 48106

Cheryl Blackwell
Stockwell-Mudd Libraries
Albion College
602 E. Cass
Albion, MI 49224

Colleen Boff
Jerome Library
152 Information Services
Bowling Green State
University
Bowling Green, OH 43403

Janet Bogenschultz
Science, Industry, and
Business Library
New York Public Research
Libraries
188 Madison Avenue
New York, NY 10016

Jennifer Boone
Library
Rochester Community and
Technical College
851 30th Ave SE
Rochester, MN 55904

Celia Bouchard
Forest Park Library
St. Louis Community
College
5600 Oakland Avenue
St. Louis, MO 63110

Susanna Boylston
Science & Engineering
Library
University of Virginia
Charlottesville, VA 22904

Doreen Bradley
Univ Lib/Health Sci Lib
1135 E Catherine
Ann Arbor, MI 48109-0726

Carla Brooks
Mardigian Library
University of Michigan
Dearborn
4901 Evergreen Rd.
Dearborn, MI 48128

Carol Brown
University Libraries
Wright State University
3640 Colonel Glenn
Highway
Dayton, OH 45435

Melinda Brown
Central Library
Vanderbilt University
Nashville, TN 37204

Melissa Browne
Bracken Library
Ball State University
Muncie, IN 47306

John Bruenger
Halle Library
Eastern Michigan University
Ypsilanti, MI 48197

Elizabeth Bucciarelli
Halle Library
Eastern Michigan University
Ypsilanti, MI 48197

Joe Buenker
ASU West Library
4701 W. Thunderbird
Phoenix, AZ 85069

Rita Bullard
Halle Library
Eastern Michigan University
Ypsilanti, MI 48197

Maira Bundza
Waldo Library
Western Michigan University
Kalamazoo, MI 49008

Joanna M. Burkhardt
URI-Providence Campus
Library
80 Washington St.
Providence, RI 02903

Sarah Burns
Mortola Library
Pace University
Pleasantville, NY 10570

Gale Burrow
Honnold/Mudd Library
800 N. Dartmouth Ave.
Claremont, CA 91711

Laura G. Burtle
Pullen Library
Georgia State University
100 Decatur St., SE
Atlanta, GA 30303

John Butler
180 Wilson Library
University of Minnesota
309 19th Ave., S
Minneapolis, MN 55455

Catherine Cardwell
Jerome Library
152 Information Services
Bowling Green State
University
Bowling Green, OH 43403

Jennifer Carmody
Campbell Learning
Resources Center
Monroe County Community
College
1555 S. Raisinville Road
Monroe, MI 48161-9746

A. Carolyn Carpan
Olin Library
Rollins College
1000 Holt Avenue
Winter Park, FL 32789

Deborah Carter Peoples
University Libraries
Ohio Wesleyan University
43 Rowland Avenue
Delaware, OH 43015

Patricia Clark
Trinity College Library
60 Summit Street
Hartford, CT 06106

Kathy Clarke
MSC 1704
Carrier Library
James Madison University
Harrisonburg, VA 22807

Barbara J. Cockrell
Western Michigan University
1903 West Michigan Ave.
Kalamazoo, MI 49008

Ron Colman
Halle Library
Eastern Michigan University
Ypsilanti, MI 48197

Cynthia Comer
Reference Department, Mudd
Library
148 West College Street
Oberlin, OH 44074

Katheryn Converse
Davenport University Library
3444 East Patrick Road
Midland, MI 48642

Suellen Cox
Paulina June & George
Pollak Library
California State University,
Fullerton
P.O. Box 4150, 800 North
State College Blvd.
Fullerton CA 92834-4150

Heather Cuningham
Gerstein Science Information
Centre
7&9 King's College Circle
Toronto, Ontario
CANADA   M5S 1A5

Margaret Cunningham
University of Maryland
Libraries
User Education Services
2113 McKeldin Library
College Park, MD 20742

Inger Curth
Melvil Dewey Library
Jefferson Community
College
Outer Coffeen Street
Watetown, NY 13601

Diane Dallis
Main Library W121
Indiana University
Bloomington
1320 E. 10th St.
Bloomington, IN 47401

Marian Delmore
LRC/Library
Northern Virginia
Community College
8333 Little River Turnpike
Annandale, VA 22003

Esme DeVault
Wheelock College Library
132 Riverway
Boston, MA 02806

Raeann Dossett
R-232 Library
Parkland College
2400 W. Bradley Ave
Champaign, IL 61821-1899

Sidney Dreese
Musselman Library
Gettysbug College
Campus Box 420
Gettysburg, PA 17325

Sally Driscoll
Robert E. Eiche Library
Penn State Altoona
3000 Ivyside Dr.
Altoona, PA 16601

Susan Drummond
109 Stapleton Library
Indiana University of
Pennsylvania
Indiana, PA 15705

Judy Druse
Library
Washburn University
1700 SW College Avenue
Topeka, KS 66621

Lori Dubois
Undergraduate Library
University of Illinois
1402 W. Gregory Drive
Urbana, IL 61801

Doris Ebbert
Courtright Memorial Library
Otterbein College
861 Bedford Road
Westerville, OH 43081

Jennifer Egan
LRC/Library
Northern Virginia
Community College
1000 H. F. Byrd Highway
Sterling, VA 20164-8699

Carrie Esch
Library
Southern Methodist
University
P.O. Box 750375
Dallas, TX 75275

Mark Ewing
Library
Delta College
1961 Delta Rd.
University Center, MI 48710

Margaret Fain
Kimbel Library
Coastal Carolina University
P.O. Box 261954
Conway, SC 29528

Kimberly Farley
LCC Library
Lansing Community College
Lansing, MI 48901-7210

Pat Farthing
Belk Library
Appalachian State University
Boone, NC 28608

Amy Faubl
Library
McHenry County College
8900 U.S. Highway 14
Crystal Lake, IL 60012

Rebecca Feind
MSC 1704
Carrier Library
James Madison University
Harrisonburg, VA 22807

Marissa Finkey
N Westfield Apt A15
Oshkosh, WI 54902

Stephen Ford
Library
Anne Arundel Community
College
101 College Parkway
Arnold, MD 21012-1895

Patricia Forester
Forest Park Library
St. Louis Community
College
5600 Oakland Ave.
St. Louis, MO 63110

Amanda Forrester
Shapiro Undergraduate
Library
University of Michigan
Ann Arbor, MI 48109-1185

Kimberly Franklin
Honnold/Mudd Library
800 N. Dartmouth Ave.
Claremont, CA 91711

Meg Frazier
Cullom-Davis Library
Bradley University
1501 W. Bradley Ave
Peoria, IL 61625

Carolyn Frenger, User
Education Librarian
Gelman Library, Rm. 104
The George Washington
University
2130 H Street, NW
Washington, DC 20016

Anne Fullerton
Library
Univertsity of Waterloo
Waterloo, ON
CANADA N2L 3G1

Kathy Gallagher
Wilson Library
University of Missouri Rolla
1870 Miner Circle
Rolla, MO 65409

Joy Gambill
Belk Library
Appalachian State University
325 College Street
Boone, NC 28608

Jodie Gardner
Library
Delta College
1961 Delta Rd.
University Center, MI 48710

Mary Beth Garriott
Library
Centre College
600 W. Walnut
Danville, KY 40422

Lora Gault
Library
Purdue University Calumet
2200 169th Street
Hammond, IN 46323

Cynthia Gibbon
Musselman Library
Gettysbug College
Campus Box 420
Gettysburg, PA 17325

Anne Giffey
Library
Knox College
2 E South St
Galesburg, IL 61401

Ann Glannon
Wheelock College Library
132 Riverway
Boston, MA 02806

Corene Glotfelty
Library
Clarion University of
Pennsylvania
PO Box 505
Shippenville, PA 16254

Amanda Gluibizzi
Wheelock College Library
132 Riverway
Boston, MA 02806

Maria Grant
San Diego State University
San Diego, CA 92182

Barbara Greil
Hinkle Library
Alfred State College
Alfred, NY 148022

Jessica Grim
Reference Department, Mudd
Library
148 West College Street
Oberlin, OH 44074

Julia Gustafson
The College of Wooster
Libraries
1140 Beall Avenue
Wooster, OH 44691-2364

Carla Gruen
Delta College Library
1961 Delta Rd.
University Center, MI 48710

Trudi Bellardo Hahn
University of Maryland
Libraries
User Education Services
2113 McKeldin Library
College Park, MD 20742

Sarah Hammill
Library
Florida International
University
BBC 3000 NE 151th St.
North Miami, FL 33181

Julia Hansen
Lovejoy Library
Southern Illinois University
Edwardsville
Box 1063
Edwardsville, IL 62026

Debby Harris
LCC Library
Lansing Community College
1200 Woodwind Trail
Haslett, MI 48840

Katherine Harris
Bracken Library
Ball State University
Muncie, IN 47306

Rosemary Henders
Oesterle Library
North Central College
320 E. School St.
Naperville, IL 60540

Patricia Herrling
Steenbock Agriculture
Library
University of Wisconsin
Madison
550 Babcock Drive
Madison, WI 53706

Lisa Janicke Hinchliffe
8900 Milner Library
Illinois State University
Normal, IL 61790-8900

Jill Hobgood
Library
Saint Mary's College
5821-3A Shawnee Ct.
Mishawaka, IN 46545

Abby Holt
Ottenheimer Library
University of Arkansas at
Little Rock
2801 South University
Little Rock, AR 72204-1099

Sharon Howard
Library
Scottsdale Community
College
9000 E. Chaparral Road
Scottsdale, AZ 85256

Linda Irmen
Roosevelt University Library
Roosevelt University
1400 N. Roosevelt Blvd
Schaumburg, IL 60173

Joe Jackson
103 Library
Winona State University
Winona, MN 55987

Lydia Jackson
Lovejoy Library
Southern Illinois University
Edwardsville
Edwardsville, IL 62026

Elaine Anderson Jayne
Waldo Library
Western Michigan University
Kalamazoo, MI 49008

Shellie Jeffries
Woodhouse Library
Aquinas College
1607 Robinson Rd. SE
Grand Rapids, MI 49506

Mary Lee Jensen
Lakeland Community
College Library
7700 Clocktower Dr.
Kirtland, OH 44094-5198

Anna Marie Johnson
117B Ekstrom Library
University of Louisville
Louisville, KY 40292

Mary K. Johnson
Miller Library
Cornerstone University
1001 East Beltline N.E.
Grand Rapids, MI 49525

Carolyn Johnson
ASU West Library
4701 W. Thunderbird
Phoeniz, AZ   85069

Mary Lou Baker Jones
University Libraries
Wright State University
3640 Colonel Glenn
Highway
Dayton, OH 45435

Ellen N. Junn, PhD.
California State University,
Fullerton
Associate Dean, Col. Of
Human Dev. & Com. Servic.
800 N., State College Blvd.
Fullerton, Calif. 92834-6868

Jennean Kabat
Library
Delta College
1961 Delta Rd.
University Center, MI 48710

Joni Kanzler
Hesburgh Library
University of Notre Dame
Notre Dame, IN 46556

Laura Karas
Library
University of South Carolina
Spartanburg
800 University Way
Spartanburg, SC 29303

Marcia King-Blandford
Carlson Librarym, M.C. 509
The University of Toledo
Toledo, OH 43606-3390

Daniel Kipnis
Hekman Library
Thomas Jefferson University
1020 Walnut St
Philadelphia, PA 19107

Sonya Kirkwood
Library
Sinclair Community College
444 West Third Street
Dayton, OH 45402

Kristin Kroger
Meinhardt Memorial Library
Art Institute of Fort
Lauderdale
1799 SE 17 Street
Fort Lauderdale, FL 33316

Carrie Kruse
College Library, Helen C.
White Hall
University of Wisconsin
Madison
600 N. Park St.
Madison, WI 53704

Christine Kubiak
8900 Milner Library
Illinois State University
Normal, IL 61790-8900

Reid Larson
Skillman Library
Lafayette College
Easton, PA 18042

Paul Lee
Au Shue Hung Memorial
Library
Hong Kong Baptist
University
Kowloon Tong
Hong Kong

Sharon Legge
Library
Volunteer State Community
College
1480 Nashville Pike
Gallatin, TN 37066-3188

April Purcell Levy
Ludcke Library
Lesley University
30 Mellen Street
Cambridge, MA 02138

Julie Long
Library
Saint Mary's College
229 Marquette Ave.
South Bend, IN 46617

Abbie Loomis
Memorial Library
University of Wisconsin
Madison
728 State St.
Madison, WI 53706

Mary C. MacDonald
URI-Providence Campus
Library
80 Washington St.
Providence, RI 02903

Sara J. MacDonald
Library
University of the Arts
320 S. Broad St
Philadelphia, PA 19102

Gail MacKay
Library
Indiana University Kokomo
P.O. Box 9003
Kokomo, IN 46904-9003

Alexius Smith Macklin
Purdue University Libraries
1531 Stewart Center
West Lafayette, IN 47907-
1531

Kate Manuel
University Library
MSC 3475 Box 30006
Las Cruces, N.M. 88003

Carrie Marsh
Denison Library
800 N. Dartmouth Ave.
Claremont, CA 91711

Frances A. May
University of North Texas
Libraries
P.O. Box 305190
Denton, TX 76203-5190

Delores Nasom McBroome,
PhD.
Department of History
Humboldt State University
1 Harpst St.
Arcata, CA 95521-8299

Sara McDowell
Robarts Library
University of Toronto
Toronto, ON
Canada M5S 1A5

Sara Memmott
Mardigian Library
University of Michigan
Dearborn
4901 Evergreen
Dearborn, MI 48128

Heidi Mercado
Halle Library
Eastern Michigan University
Ypsilanti, MI 48197

Amber Meryman
Butler University Library
4600 Sunset Ave
Indianapolis, IN 46208

Trisha Mileham
Moellering Library
Valparaiso University
Valparaiso IN 46383

Marsha Miller
Library
Indiana State University
Terre Haute, IN 47809

Rebecca Miller
Donnelley Library
Lake Forest College
555 N. Sheridan
Lake Forest, IL 60045

Elizabeth Mulherrin
University of Maryland
University College
SFSC, Rm 2255F
3501 University Blvd. East
Adelphi, MD 2078

Sylvia Newman
Gerstein Science Information
Centre
University of Toronto
Toronto, ON
Canada M5S 1A5

Julia K. Nims
Halle Library
Eastern Michigan University
Ypsilanti, MI 48197

Rose Novil
Oakton Community College
Library
7701 N. Lincoln
Skokie, Ill 60077

Megan Oakleaf
Library
North Carolina State
University
2205 Hillsborough Street
Raleigh, NC 27695-7111

Karen Odato
Dana Biomedical Library
Dartmouth College
Hanover, NH 03755-3880

Emily Okada
Undergraduate Library
Indiana University
Bloomington
1320 E. 10th Street
Bloomington, IN 47401

Teague Orblych
Mardigian Library
University of Michigan
Dearborn
4901 Evergreen
Dearborn, MI 48128

Russell Palmer
Jack Tarver Library
Mercer University
1300 Edgewood Ave.
Macon, GA 31201-0001

Rory Patterson
Centennial Library
Cedarville University
251 N. Main St.
Cedarville, OH 45314

Maria Perez-Stable
Dwight B. Waldo Library
Western Michigan University
Kalamazoo, MI 49008

Michael Poma
Reinert Alumni Library
Creighton University
2500 California Plaza
Omaha, NE 68178

Teresa Prince
Library
Macomb Community College
44575 Garfield Road
Clinton Township, MI 48038

Twyla Racz
Halle Library
Eastern Michigan University
Ypsilanti, MI 48197

Robin Rank
Library
Kalamazoo College
1200 Academy Street
Kalamazoo, MI 49006

Dan Ream
James B. Cabell Library
VCU Libraries
P.O. Box 842033
Richmond, VA 23284-2033

Todd Reed
Library
Davenport University
643 S. Waverly Rd.
Holland, MI 49423

Jean Reese
Box 325 GPC Education
Library
Vanderbilt University
Nashville, TN 37204

Mary Reichel
Appalachian State University
Belk Library
P.O. Box 32026
Boone, NC 28608

Melanie Remy
Library
University of Southern
California
651 West 35th Street
Los Angeles, CA 90089-
0182

Patricia Renn-Scanlan
Library
Washburn University
1700 SW College Avenue
Topeka, KS 66621

Kelly Rhodes
Belk Library
Appalachian State University
325 College Street
Boone, NC 28608

Galen E. Rike
Room 101 Waldo Library
Western Michigan University
1903 West Michigan Ave.
Kalamazoo, MI 49008

Lisa Roberts
Marshall Brooks Library
Principia College
One Maybeck Place
Elsah, IL 62028

Ilene Rockman, PhD.
California State University
System
c/o CSU Hayward Library
25800 Carlos Bee Blvd.
Hayward, CA 94542

Claudia Ruediger
Kent Library
Southeast Missouri State
University
Box 1063
Cape Girardeau, MO 63701

Carol Rusinek
Library
Indiana University Northwest
3400 Broadway
Gary, IN 46408

Laurie Sabol
Tisch Library
Tufts University
35 Professors Row
Medford, MA 02155

Bruce Sajdak
Neilson Library
Smith College
Onc University Plaza
Northampton, MA 01063

Suzanne Sawyer
LCC Library
Lansing Community College
P.O. Box 40010
Lansing, MI 48901-7210

Barbara Schoenfield
Roosevelt University Library
Roosevelt University
1400 N. Roosevelt Blvd.
Schaumburg, IL 60173

Lynn Schott
Sidney Silverman Library
Bergen Community College
400 Paramus Road
Paramus, NJ 07652

Susan Scott
Denison University Libraries
Box L
Granville, OH 43023

Joel Seewald
Mardigian Library
University of Michigan
Dearborn
4901Evergreen Rd.
Dearborn, MI 48128

Juta Seibert
Library
Villanova University
800 Lancaster Ave.
Villanova, PA 19085

Greg Sennema
Calvin College Library
3201 Burton St., SE
Grand Rapids, Mich 49546

Barbara Shaffer
Penfield Library
SUNY Oswego
Oswego, NY 13126

Lynn Sheehan
Schoenbaum Library
University of Charleston
2300 MacCorkle Ave. SE
Charleston, WV 25304

Deborah F. Sheesley
101 Brookline Rd.
Ivyland, PA 18974

Linda Shirato
Halle Library
Eastern Michigan University
Ypsilanti, MI 48197

Karen Shockey
Penfield Library
SUNY Oswego
Oswego, NY 13126

Ruth Shoge
Miller Library
Washington College
300 Washington Avenue
Chestertown, MD 21620

Jennifer Sias
Drinko Library
Marshall University
One John Marshall Drive
Huntington, WV 25755

Samantha Skutnik
Library
Butler University
4600 Sunset Ave
Indianapolis, IN 46208

Trixi B. Smith
LCC Library
Lansing Community College
Lansing, MI 48901-7210

Keith Stanger
Halle Library
Eastern Michigan University
Ypsilanti, MI 48197

Rebecca Starkey
The Joseph Regenstein
Library
University of Chicago
1100 East 57th Street
Chicago, IL 60637

Bob Stevens
Kimbel Library
Coastal Carolina University
P.O. Box 261954
Conway, SC 29528

Glenn Ellen Starr Stilling
Appalachian State University
Belk Library
P.O. Box 32026
Boone, NC 28608

Carol Stookey
Marshall Brooks Library
Principia College
One Maybeck Place
Elsah, IL 62028

Andrew Stuart
Alden Library
Ohio University Libraries
Athens, OH 45701

Tammy S. Sugarman
Pullen Library
Georgia State University
100 Decatur St., SE
Atlanta, GA 30303

Naomi Sutherland
Lupton Library, Dept. 6456
University of Tennessee
Chattanooga
615 McCallie Avenue
Chattanooga, TN 37403-2598

Laurie Swartwout
Library
Cardinal Stritch University
6801 N. Yates Rd.
Milwaukee, WI 52317

Patricia A. Szeszulski, PhD.
Child and Adolescent Studies
California State University,
Fullerton
P.O. Box 4150
800 North State College
Blvd.
Fullerton CA 92834-4150

Peggy Tyler
R.M. Cooper Library
Clemson University
Box 343001
Clemson, SC 29634-3001

Diane Vander Pol
Hekman Library
Calvin College and Calvin
Theological Seminary
3207 Burton SE
Grand Rapids, MI 49546

Jasmine Vaughan
Library
Kenyon College
Gambier, OH 43022-9624

Jerilyn Veldof
180 Wilson Library
University of Minnesota
309 19th Ave., S
Minneapolis, MN 55455

Beth Walker
Library
Southern Methodist
University
P.O. Box 750135
Dallas, TX 75275

Dane Ward
8900 Milner Library
Illinois State University
Normal, IL 61790-8900

Signia Warner
Westfield State College
Library
623 Station Road
Amherst, MA 01086-1630

Gary Wasdin
Science, Industry, and
Business Library
New York Public Research
Libraries
P. O. Box 2880
New York, NY 10163-2880

Emily Werrell
Perkins Library
Duke University
Box 90175
Durham, NC 27708

Patricia Willingham
Kent Library
Southeast Missouri State
University
One University Plaza
Cape Girardeau, MO 63701

J. Robert Willingham
Kent Library
Southeast Missouri State
University
Box 1063
Cape Girardeau, MO 63701

Deborah Wills
Wilfrid Laurier University
Library
Waterloo, ON
Canada N2L 3C5

Song Yu
Mellon Library of
Chemistry
Purdue University
West Lafayette, IN 47907

Patricia Yocum
Shapiro Science Library
919 S. University
Ann Arbor, MI 48109-1185

James B. Young
New Century College
George Mason University
Fairfax, VA 22030-4444

Christy Zimmerman
Missouri Western State
College
Library
4525 Downs Drive
St. Joseph, MO 64507